MANAGERS OF THEIR HOMES

MANAGERS OF THEIR HOMES

A Practical Guide to Daily Scheduling for Christian Homeschool Families

By Steven and Teri Maxwell

 Communication Concepts, Inc.

MANAGERS OF THEIR HOMES

For information, address: Managers of Their Homes, 2416 South 15th Street, Leavenworth, Kansas, 66048. Phone: (913) 772-0392

Copyright © 1998–2002 by Communication Concepts, Inc.

Published by Communication Concepts, Inc., Leavenworth, Kansas 66048

ACKNOWLEDGEMENTS

Scripture taken from the HOLY BIBLE, KING JAMES VERSION.

ISBN 0-9669107-4-5

Printed in the United States of America

1   2   3   4   5   6

A supplemental resource to this book, which includes additional scheduling information, is located at:

www.Titus2.com

Communication Concepts, Inc. maintains a website at the address: www.we-communicate.com

This book was created in Microsoft's Word for Windows. Layout and design was performed using Quark Inc.'s QuarkXPress. All computers were Windows based systems running Windows 98/NT.

A Helpful Resource: Titus2.com

For the last few years the Maxwells have maintained a website for the purpose of encouraging and building up homeschool families. The website, with helpful information, fun facts and photos, is a perfect addition to the book.

http://www.titus2.com

There are also Question and Answer forums. Pictured below is our MOTHBoard (Managers of Their Homes Board) forum, where moms can interact with others interested in scheduling. The messageboards are 100% moderated: users don't have to worry about being flamed, having the board overrun with advertising, or bad language! The boards are a wonderful place to seek encouragement and counsel from other godly women.

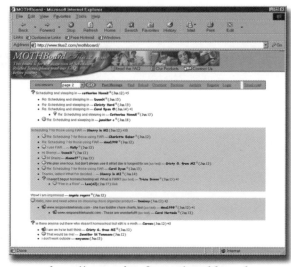

http://www.titus2.com/mothboard

Contents at a Glance

Preface

There is a saying I have heard recently, "If Mama is happy, everybody's happy. If Mama ain't happy, nobody's happy." How often this is true! God has placed a desire in each mother's heart to have a smooth-running, peaceful household.

Through the years, I have observed many homeschooling mothers and families. The moms who seem the most content can manage their families and homes. On the other hand, some of the most unhappy mothers I have known are the ones who can never keep up with their workload. A mother who is unorganized with her time is often burdened and discouraged.

There are things that discourage me. And, I occasionally feel overwhelmed by what I have to do. But, in general, I am able to keep up with the priorities and tasks I believe God has given to me. This is due to the fact that as my family began to grow, I saw the necessity of scheduling our time.

It began with baby naps. They had to be at the right time and length so the baby would go back to sleep at night. Next, we moved into scheduling schooltime. Why did three children choose to use the computer at the same time? Who wanted to have to deal with conflicts over the computer's usage each day? The solution was simple: schedule who could be on the computer at what time! This eventually led to the whole school day being scheduled. Mom no longer had to run through a check-list when one of the children said, "I'm finished with school," to make sure they had completed each assignment. They had scheduled times for every school subject, and when the school day was over, they were free—providing they had done their work during that assigned time.

With more years and more children, it became evident that we needed schedules to help us get up at a consistent time and to have dinner ready when Daddy was available to eat. Not only did Mom need the schedule for herself, but the children needed theirs too. They did not come to me and say, "Mom, I'm ready to do my chores now." It had to be a part of their routine, a habit which would not require constant prodding.

Several times over the past few years I have been asked how my day runs. Instead of trying to explain, I found it easier to give a copy of my schedule to these friends. They are not asking this question just because they are interested in what happens at my house. They want to see if there is anything in how I set up my day which will help them with theirs. The truth is that each family will function differently. We do not all have to fit into the same mold concerning how our time is spent. It is also true that seeing how another arranges her day can help us with ideas on how to plan ours. Even seeing a written schedule can be beneficial if scheduling is new to us.

I have seen many books on organization and time management. But, I have never seen one that addresses the unique needs of scheduling that a homeschool family generates or one that guides you through simple steps and worksheets to help you actually set up your own personalized schedule.

When we were nearly finished with the rough draft of this book, Steve and I discussed how benefi-cial it would be to have a family read *Managers of Their Homes* and "test" it. Through "Mothers of Many Young Siblings" (MOMYS), an e-mail list of which I was a member, I briefly explained

Managers of Their Homes and Scheduling Kit, putting out our request for a volunteer test family. Within the next few days, we had not one volunteer family but twenty-four!

Seeking the Lord, as to whether we should try to select one family or take all who had volunteered, we decided the book could only benefit by a larger test group. Before accepting a family, we asked them to commit to reading the book, making a schedule, and implementing it. We asked that each husband read our information and agree to his wife's participation. We still had twenty-four test families.

From this group have come almost all the comments you will find in the sidebars throughout the book. The biographical sketches, with personal scheduling testimonials, at the beginning of each chapter, are from these test families. The questions and answers chapter developed out of questions individual moms would write me and my responses to them. We shared these questions and answers with the whole test group in those early weeks. The group appreciated this so much that it was decided to turn them into a chapter of the book.

All the real-life sample schedules found in the Appendix come from homeschooling moms who have used *Managers of Their Homes* as a basis to make and implement their schedules. Most of them are large families; some have only young children. I think when you see what these women have been able to accomplish with their schedules, you too, will feel that it is possible for you. You will gain valuable ideas by looking over their schedules.

We believe you will be encouraged, as we have been, when you see how *Managers of Their Homes* has been used and implemented by real mothers in real homes. We are very grateful to each of these families for their participation in our test.

Managers of Their Homes is a joint effort of the Steven Maxwell family, who began homeschooling in 1985. Our family is comprised of Dad (Steve), Mom (Teri) and eight children: Nathan (1976), Christopher (1979), Sarah (1982), Joseph (1989), John (1991), Anna (1992), Jesse (1994), and Mary (1996). Nathan helped with initial style layout; Christopher designed the cover, did the layout and design, along with copy editing; and Sarah was proofreader.

Our appreciation also goes to Teri's sister, Tami Jassey, for her editing help; and Teri's father, Rex Frazer, for his editing and proofreading.

The Maxwell family delights in serving Jesus Christ. We love to help others toward this same goal. Therefore, our desire in writing this book has been to help free mothers from any burden of discouragement they carry when they cannot keep up with the demands on their time and to help them be better managers of their homes, for the glory of God.

Teri

MANAGERS OF THEIR HOMES

Dear Friends,

October 24th

My name is Cindy, and my husband is David. The Lord has blessed us with six little ones at this time: Mitchell (8), Joshua (7), Caleb (6), Amanda (4), Josiah (2), and little Abigail (3 months). Often I would jot down a schedule the night before or early in the morning of things I would like to accomplish the following day. The problem was that my children had no idea what my schedule for them was. And it would change every day.

At the same time, I was struggling, daily, to keep up with housework and schooling. I could be cleaning one room or schooling the older three boys according to my schedule, but my two and four-year-olds would be in the other rooms destroying what I had done earlier. UGH! I would want them to keep busy, but it was too hard to sit down every day and plan a day of activities for the whole family. It was also very frustrating to give an account of the day to my husband and to feel that I didn't really accomplish anything. Everything was half done for the day. It seemed I was busy all day but had no idea where the time went.

Well . . . I saw that Teri was looking for some volunteer families to test run their book for them. I read through the book and began putting a schedule together. I was amazed to sit down and write out not only what I had to accomplish during a day but also the children. We did have a lot to do!

I soon had the schedule completed, and we were off and running. After a couple of weeks, I had to change the schedule, but finally came up with a workable schedule for the family. I even gave a copy to my husband. I thought he might enjoy seeing what we were working on at a given time during the day and being able to pray accordingly. He could now tell where my time was used.

The reason this works so much better than my previous attempts is that I have something for everyone in the family to do, even the four and two-year-olds. The house is much neater when they aren't roaming free to get into whatever their little hands can find.

Scheduling a block of time for the older boys to help keep an eye on the little ones is a GREAT idea. They like to "teach" them different things, or they play something special with them. This has been the key to getting things to work. I had balked at letting one of the boys go to spend time with their little brother and sister. They had schooling to do! But I found that everyone got much more accomplished if they took a half-hour break from their work to do this. It cuts down on the discipline issues immensely.

Honestly, it has been almost two months since we began the first schedule, and we have not finished it exactly one day. BUT I am accomplishing more than I ever did before! I trust you will enjoy the rewards of being an efficient manager of your home. It certainly adds peace to our family.

From Cindy

Why Schedule?

Have you ever wished you could look at another mother's schedule? Have you felt that if you could just see how someone else organizes her day it might help you with yours? Perhaps you have asked a friend to assist you in making up a daily schedule.

One of the greatest challenges we face, as homeschool moms, is keeping up with the work a household entails plus homeschooling. How do we get it all done? Do we feel it is impossible? It is not! We can do all things through Christ Jesus our Lord. He can teach us to manage the ministry He has called us to in our home. The key to this home management is scheduling.

WHAT IS SCHEDULING?

What, exactly, is scheduling? Scheduling is a written plan for ordering your day and your children's day. It divides the day into increments filled with an activity for that particular time. Scheduling requires a faithfulness to following the written plan with flexibility allowed for unusual circumstances and emergencies.

God has given us a powerful example and analogy of scheduling in the natural world. Everything that He has created, from atoms to the universe, has a periodic cycle. There is a timetable God has applied to each part of His creation. This is easily seen in the weather. Year by year, each season comes at its "scheduled" time bringing with it predictable changes. Here we have a picture of our daily-life schedules. These change, too, as the "seasons" in our families change.

God has planned for interruptions to this seasonal pattern of creation. They come in the form of storms—winter snow storms, spring showers, tornados, summer thunderstorms—that blow in unplanned and unscheduled. They are often fierce, demanding attention, but sometimes they are gentle and refreshing. So, too, into our schedules, God pushes storms of interruptions. They can be as fierce and demanding as a medical emergency, or they can be as gentle and refreshing as an unexpected lunch date with your husband. If God felt it was important to place His creation on a schedule, perhaps we should seriously consider the need to schedule our own lives. Observing God's dealing with His universe can give us the pattern and motivation for our choice to plan and put a schedule into use in our homes.

It takes a conscious decision to be in charge of our homes and children rather than letting them be in charge of us. That decision is "bringing into captivity every thought to the obedience of Christ" (II Cor. 10:5b). When our thoughts are God's thoughts they go like this: "I can do all things through Christ which strengtheneth me" (Phil. 4:13); "My grace is sufficient for thee: for my strength is made perfect in weakness" (II Cor. 12:9); "For God hath not given us the spirit of fear; but of power, and of love, and of a sound mind" (II Tim. 1:7); "To every thing there is a season, and a time to

A Personal Word

My schedule has given me back my sanity!! I can't believe the way my life has changed since implementing a schedule. It's so great. Finally, my home is the place of ministry that I wanted it to be for so long! I can actually have people over, and things are straight. Even better than that, I don't feel like the drill sergeant to my children that I was beginning to become, because now they all have a place throughout the day, and they don't get bored to the point that they begin to misbehave. Tracy L.

Having a schedule has helped us in so many ways. I don't know where to begin. It helps me to see that I DO have time to do the things God has called me to do. It helps me to remember just exactly WHAT God has called me to do, because I tend to get so easily distracted by other "fun" things!

If for some reason, I don't get my scheduled time in an area today, I will get it in tomorrow. So the undone things are not so overwhelming. Things undone with no

every purpose under the heaven" (Ecclesiastes 3:1). These kinds of Biblical thoughts will encourage us as we undertake the discipline of scheduling our God-given responsibilities.

Please do not think scheduling will be the power or energy in your successful home management. This is not true. Any success in our homes comes from Jesus Christ, around Whom everything must revolve. He is the wisdom behind our schedules. He hears and answers the prayers we pray when preparing to plan a schedule. He gives the creativity for designing a schedule. We go to Him if there are rough areas in the schedule when we put it into use. It is His energy and strength which will allow us to maintain a schedule. He is the driving force behind the schedule. He is the One Who brings interruptions to our day, the One Who teaches us to be flexible with a servant's heart. We do not rely on the strength of our schedule but on the strength of our Lord Jesus Christ. "Some trust in chariots, and some in horses: but we will remember the name of the LORD our God" (Psalm 20:7). A schedule must not become an idol in our lives. We never want you to think that anything which is said in this book is separate from your dependence upon Jesus to work in your heart and your home.

A BIBLICAL MANDATE FOR SCHEDULING

Paul tells the young widows in I Timothy 5:14, "I will therefore that the younger women marry, bear children, guide the house, give none occasion to the adversary to speak reproachfully." This is powerful direction for us, as mothers, to determine to manage our homes. Paul is giving these instructions to women who have been widowed, but are still young enough to bear children. Not managing our homes is one reason the enemy would have opportunity to slander us and our ministry. It is a poor testimony to always be sinking under the burden of our home workload. Have you known mothers who looked tired and worn whenever you saw them? Their faces did not indicate they were joyful mothers of children or tell of a Jesus who says, "Take my yoke upon you, and learn of me; for I am meek and lowly in heart: and ye shall find rest unto your souls. For my yoke is easy, and my burden is light" (Matt. 11:29, 30). Scheduling is a key to gaining victory over our circumstances and time usage. It is within the ability and grasp of every woman who would decide to follow this path.

As mothers, we want to learn to be home managers versus victims of circumstances. We can, by choice, be managers of our homes and our children in much the same way as a manager in the work force. Picture an office manager who comes to work at a different time every day. He arrives at his desk trying to decide what to do. Immediately, each of his four employees runs to him asking what project they should begin. That office would be chaos, just as our home will be if we do not have a plan in place for its operation. Many homeschool moms feel they can never keep up with the demands on their time. They are pressured, stressed, and discouraged. The joy and delight of staying home with their children is being robbed from their hearts. Scheduling helps us to manage these time demands. It allows us to keep up with them. Scheduling is a powerful tool in the hands of a home manager, just as it is for an office manager.

SCHEDULING BENEFITS

Scheduling enables you to focus on your God-given priorities. You will not reach the end of the day wishing you had spent your time differently. It will have been used as you have chosen. The urgent does not push out the important. Your quiet time with the Lord is part of the schedule. Exercise and personal hygiene are there too. Meal preparation, cleanup, housecleaning, and schooling—whatever you need to do is planned into the schedule. You know you are spending individual time with your children because it is scheduled. There is a set time to accomplish each priority. At the end of a day, you can look back and know exactly what you have done with every hour.

In many ways, a schedule can relieve stress from your life. When tasks become routine, they require much less physical and emotional energy. A normal day is easier to get through without having to: make numerous draining decisions, answer questions from other family members concerning their direction, or feel the day has come to an end without getting anything done. You start your day with a plan already in place for what comes next. You know you will accomplish what you need to throughout each day unless the Lord brings unexpected circumstances. You don't have to feel discouraged with being overloaded and overworked because you have scheduled time to keep up with your tasks. You can have the emotional resources you need to be pleasant with the children since your day is not in upheaval. A schedule brings ordered direction to a day that in turn lowers stress levels for those involved.

A schedule lets you plan activities into the day that are important to you, ones there are never enough available hours for. What would you like to have time to do? Maybe it is your personal devotion or reading to your children. Perhaps it is sewing, a craft project, reading, ministry, exercise, or writing. A schedule will give you a specific time for each desire of your heart.

Scheduling gives direction to your children. They need to know what to do and when to do it. Throughout the day, this will save you from having to tell them what they should be doing. Even young children quickly learn the rou-

prospect of getting done are discouraging to me.

We are truly, truly excited. The book was excellent and written for me! Kristi

I cannot tell you how great having a schedule is!!!! It has cut down on a lot of the bickering that used to happen (very common with five boys between the ages of six and four), and I have enjoyed having things scheduled for myself (quilting and reading). My house is much neater now, and I am able to get extra projects done (like refinishing the coffee tables) that I wasn't sure how I was going to fit in. My day starts earlier, but I actually enjoy that early morning time all to myself. I have thanked God many times, in my prayers, that you sent me the information. Amy

It is so nice having a plan for the day! Things just seem to run more smoothly, in general. Everyone has some direction to be going in without constant instruction from me. We also get lots of schoolwork done each day, which wasn't always the case "pre-schedule" or with a looser schedule. I feel like I spent more time with my

preschoolers. That was nice! I have a tendency to be chatty on the phone or "waste" time in other ways and the schedule wouldn't allow that. So it really helped me to be more diligent. Ricki

Our schedule helps the children to know what is expected of them. They are not always asking, "Can we play yet?" And they accept chore time better when they can count on it at the same time every day. I am not interrupting their play with a list of chores. The older children are also enjoying their time with the baby. Even the times the children play together are less stressful because they don't drag on and on. The children know the time is limited so they don't waste it fighting (well, usually). Also, I am less frustrated, which means I am kinder and more patient with them, which, of course, makes them happy. Kathy

Since implementing my schedule, I have become more spiritually, emotionally, physically, and organizationally disciplined. Our family is running much more smoothly, and we are accomplishing so much more now that we have a schedule! I

tine and sequence of a schedule. You do not have to answer constant questions from them as to what they are to do next. They have chores, schoolwork, music practicing, room upkeep, personal hygiene, devotions, and more. Without a schedule, the day can fade away with them accomplishing little. This leads to frustration on Mom's part because what needed to be done was not. It is also difficult for the child. He is in trouble with Mom; he has to catch up; he likely faces additional disciplinary consequences. A schedule becomes your child's helpful taskmaster, leading him through his days.

Using a schedule allows normal routine to continue in your absence. This creates stability when you are gone or ill. It sees that the family's needs are being met. Having a schedule allows others to take over managing your home with ease. Your children maintain their routine, and everything can function smoothly. Whether it is Dad, one of the older children, a baby-sitter, or grandparents, they will know what to do at the proper time. The children are more comfortable with Mom's absence and so is Mom. It also ensures that the children will continue to keep up with what they are to be doing. With the routine in place, the caretaker in Mom's absence should have an easier time focusing on the children. Scheduling is a great blessing at these times.

Your desire for children and delight in them could be greatly facilitated by the use of scheduling. Many couples have made the decision to let God control the size of their family. For some of these families, there isn't great joy at the discovery of a pregnancy. They wonder how they will manage their household, chaotic as it is, when they add yet another baby. On the other hand, it is possible to be pleased and excited by the news of Mom's pregnancy. Part of this is because there is no fear of fitting a baby into your lives or the extra work he will entail. You know that God will enable you to put a schedule in place which will easily meet the baby's needs. It will also meet the other children's needs, get school done, and keep up with the house and meals.

Scheduling can even provide the framework supporting gracious flexibility when the Lord brings unforeseen events into the day. Having used a schedule to keep up with her life, a mother can feel the freedom to meet unusual needs knowing her home and family have been properly cared for. Because she is current on her tasks, she should not feel unhappy with the interruption. If a call comes from a friend desperately wanting counsel, it can be taken while the rest of the family continues on the schedule which they know how to follow. When the call is finished, Mom can step back into the schedule knowing that her faithfulness to her duties has allowed this need to not cause a major disruption to the family. A schedule provides a mother with the availability of spiritual resources to meet these needs because she has daily time with the Lord. She has the emotional energy necessary to deal with unexpected circumstances, since she is not using this energy up in daily decision making. Lastly, she will have physical energy because she is receiving essential rest while still keeping up with her workload.

In addition to the present advantages of scheduling, we want to emphasize the long-term ones. Efficiency in your home, allowing you to accomplish much more, nets a significant return over the years. This will impact the amount of school you are able to do with your children, your ministry within and without your home, and your own level of personal growth.

Think of the advantages your children will reap from having lived with a role model who has chosen to implement the discipline of scheduling which yields an organized and planned life. As teens, they should have the skills to be able to schedule their discretionary time. When they outgrow your management of their schedules, they will be able to manage their own. Surely, these are advantages each of us would like to experience.

In Conclusion

We encourage you to prayerfully consider the information presented in this book. It may be in line with what you are already doing. If so, it will strengthen your resolve. Perhaps it will give you helpful new ideas or insights. On the other hand, it may be completely foreign to your lifestyle right now. In that case, you will gain greatly from reading this information and implementing it in your home. You will see for yourself whether these benefits are true. Read with an open mind and heart to see if God has anything from these pages that might cause you to be a better manager of the family and home He has given you.

don't even feel frazzled or guilty if we don't get to everything, because even if something comes up in the afternoon, we have already done so much more in the morning than we used to do (before schedule) all day long! I am looking forward to what we will continue to accomplish because we finally have a workable schedule! Corrie

My schedule is working quite well! Even if I don't do everything on my schedule, it pulls me back to where I want to be and helps me accomplish more than if I didn't have one at all. Kathleen

I am glad God sent your ideas my way before my life was so out of control it would seem impossible. Before I read your book, it seemed like a huge mountain, and now I feel it is manageable. Renée

Dear Friends,   October 24th

Our family is in its fifth year of homeschooling. We have six children: a thirteen-year-old boy, eight-year-old girl, six-year-old girl, four-year-old girl, two-year-old girl, and a one-year-old boy. My husband is gone from 6 a.m. to 6 p.m. daily, so morning family devotions are not a possibility at this time in our lives. We have them at night, and I do a time of Bible, hymn singing, and Bible memory in the morning.

I am usually very diligent and organized except that, in the last couple of years, I have not been successful in getting what I wanted done in school. I needed a plan and was frustrated at the lack of knowing how to go about creating one. I would try, but it would then fall apart because of all the little ones and the interruptions of the day.

When I saw Teri calling for people to be test pilots, I just knew that this was an answer to prayer. I was at the point of being desperate and despondent because of my frazzled school days. I wanted to be victorious and a joyful mother of children, but I knew if I went on anymore in the way I was going, I would be cast for the role of the Wicked Witch of the West.

So I went to work on my schedule, and it revolutionized my life! I was now feeling as if I really could do all I wanted to do and keep my sanity at the same time. There is a time slot for every-thing (devotions, exercise, computer, etc.).

I wasn't able to do my whole schedule all at once, but, little by little, I added to it until we were accomplishing much more than I ever dreamed we could! In those first weeks, where we only did half of my schedule, we accomplished much more than when we floundered around for a whole day without a schedule. Even on the days when we experienced blessed interruptions, I could keep calm and then quietly resume the next day . . . not worrying that we were going to be far behind, but knowing that because I had been on a steady path it wouldn't take much to catch up.

I encourage all moms who have much to accomplish to consider this way of scheduling. I had looked at almost every organizational book there was, and I still couldn't get to where I wanted to be until I applied this method! It REALLY works, and it makes sense. It is a lot of fun; you won't be sorry you tried! Your children will rise up and call you blessed. Your husband will think that you are just the most wonderful woman that ever walked on the face of the earth . . . well, he will be pleased!

From Corrie

The Key to Successful Scheduling

There IS a starting point for success in daily scheduling . . . schedule our own personal time with the Lord each day. When we can schedule and remain faithful to this time, the foundation and corner-stone of our day, we can succeed in scheduling. For us to have time alone with the Lord, we are going to find we must plan for those particularly important moments. If we simply try to have our devotion during our first free, quiet moment, we will probably come to the end of the day and real-ize it has not happened. We will resolve to try harder tomorrow, but the cycle will be repeated the next day and the next.

We are not wise women if we are trying to accomplish the Lord's agenda in our own energy and strength. Where does our dependence on the Lord come from? Where do we gather our daily manna? Is it not from our private time alone in the Word, in prayer, in memorizing Scripture, and meditating on it? This is an absolutely crucial time for us. Is your life busy and full? Absolutely! Could you spend this time doing something else? Absolutely! Is there any other way for you to use this time that would produce more lasting or greater benefits for you or your family? NO!

HOW TO SCHEDULE A QUIET TIME

How, practically speaking, do you schedule a personal quiet time despite all the responsibilities and demands you experience as a homeschool mom? You pray, look at your day, and be creative. You make your quiet time a planned part of your day and remain faithful to it. Does it have to be early in the morning? No, but that often is the best time. You start the day with your focus on the Lord, your heart seeking Him. If you have little children, it is easier to be undisturbed if your devotion is while they are still sleeping.

Will it be hard to get up earlier? Probably. But why make up your mind that you are too tired to get up? Just try it! For years, I felt I needed eight hours of sleep to function well. But, I also regularly struggled with long, sleepless nights. Then, I changed to seven hours of sleep with a short rest in the afternoon. It has been wonderful, because now I sleep great at night. Had you told me several years ago that I would have to survive on seven hours of sleep, my fear of being tired all day, every day, would have been overwhelming.

My husband and I go to bed at 10:30 p.m., and the alarm clock goes off at 5:25 a.m. I go in to nurse the baby and then have a half-hour devotion before family morning Bible time at 6:25 a.m. I spend ten minutes reading a chapter in the Bible, picking a verse which is meaningful to me, copying it in

CHAPTER TWO

A Personal Word

Oh! The best benefit of all is I am consistently spending time with my Saviour. Sheri

It is so exciting to be meditating on His Word again. I look back at the time my household was the most content. The boys were most obedient and delightful when I was spending time memorizing large portions of Scripture.

I have spent the last year wondering why we were struggling more with their attitudes. I have to confess that I kept looking for a system of discipline to kick in and solve all these heart issues. Somehow I didn't connect my lack of time spent in His Word with the daily struggles we were having. How humbling! I think I figured things were a little too chaotic to devote much time to His Word. If I could just get my house in order, then I would have more time to spend doing those "spiritual" things. But who has time when things are crazy?

Somehow I forgot to connect that I need to straighten out my priorities. Seek Him first. Seems so silly because I

a notebook, and writing a short prayer concerning it. Then I have the next ten minutes for memorizing Scripture. The final minutes are for prayer. Could I easily spend more time? Without a doubt! But I am grateful to spend the time I have and offer it to the Lord for Him to use.

There may be times when early morning devotions do not work out for you. Does that mean you stop having devotions? No! You plan for that time with the Lord to be during an hour that better accommodates your needs. Perhaps it will be while the little ones nap in the afternoon or at night before bedtime. Whenever you choose to schedule your time with the Lord, it should be a part of your day, as fundamental as making dinner.

HOW MUCH TIME? MORE THAN ONE?

Another common hesitation about time with the Lord is, "I barely get started with fifteen minutes or a half-hour, so, why bother? Why not wait until I can find the large amount of time I really want?" The reason is that day after day will go by when you never find an hour to spend with the Lord. How much better to consistently, each day, spend a half-hour with the Lord, finding it adds up to three and one-half hours a week, than to always look for the hour or two that never happen.

There may be seasons in your life when you will need to schedule either more than one time each day with the Lord or a longer time. These are times when you need extra encouragement from the Lord in the middle of the day even though you already had a time in the morning.

One recent summer, I was battling discouragement over some issues with the children. By early afternoon, I felt like my hands were dragging on the ground I would be so worn out from dealing with these issues. As I was sewing one day, bemoaning my discouragement, the Lord showed me that I needed to spend extra time with Him. My unhappiness with the situations and stewing over them produced no benefit, only negative consequences for me and my family as I moped around. But, by turning those needs to Jesus Christ—the One Who carries our burdens, provides peace and rest through trials, and gives direction—He could lift my spirit. So I began getting out my spiritual notebook and getting on my knees at 2:00 p.m. each afternoon for another half-hour. For my heart, that extra time with the Lord was like a banquet to a starving person.

MARY OR MARTHA?

Here is a story you may relate to. "Now it came to pass, as they went, that he entered into a certain village: and a certain woman named Martha received him into her house. And she had a sister called Mary, which also sat at Jesus' feet, and heard his word. But Martha was cumbered about much serving, and came to him, and said, Lord, dost thou not care that my sister hath left me to serve alone? bid her therefore that she help me. And Jesus answered and said unto her, Martha, Martha, thou art careful and troubled about many things: But one thing is needful: and Mary hath chosen that good part, which shall not be taken away from her" (Luke 10:38-42).

In Conclusion

Your life as a wife, mother, and teacher is filled with Martha activities. Do not give up what Jesus Himself says is better. The foundation for everything you do, in and out of your home, grows from your relationship with Jesus. Plan that time with Him every day. Make it the beginning point of your commitment to scheduling. Be faithful to it. Remember, if you cannot schedule this quiet time with the Lord and keep it daily, you will not be able to schedule the rest of the day. This time is absolutely crucial to the success of scheduling. It puts your focus on your strength, Jesus Christ. He is the One Who will enable you to use scheduling as a tool in your home. Do not try to begin or carry out this process on your own.

have known that since I was very young. Cindy

⁓

So far, the schedule has been working great! My children are constantly talking about how much they like it, and hubby loves hearing about how our day went, when he gets home. You know, I also want to say that this is CHANGING my life. For once, I feel like I'm getting something done! Your book has truly been an answer to my prayers. Tracy L.

Dear Friends,

October 29th

We are Dave and Debbie Klein, and we have eight children: Zak (9), Abi (8), Ben (6), Sarah-Beth (5), Solomon John (4), Hannah (3), Joanna (1), and Rebekah (1 month). We have home-schooled for about 5 years now.

We have seen the need to have order in our lives since the birth of our first child, and with each new baby, have implemented certain changes to make things more orderly. Initially, this was just motivated by "survival."

Scheduling is a tool, but you have to know what you want to accomplish. So, its been very helpful for us to take a look at what we are doing and why. Time is a gift from God, just like anything else, and we have to be good stewards of it. With a schedule, it's easier to quantify, appreciate, and be thankful for our time. So, this book has really helped us to have a simple way of doing these things.

I didn't think I could stick to a schedule. I didn't want to be rigid about everything; it seemed too stressful. But, this reaction was mostly motivated by a desire to NOT be totally accountable for my time. Or not wanting to set myself up for failure. I have big expectations, because I know God will enable us to do more than just survive. And we strongly feel that God did not give us these children so we would be frazzled, disorganized, and confused all the time. So, we know God has given us the time we need to do what He wants us to do. We must be sure we are doing what He wants us to do.

After Rebekah's arrival, we benefited from having a good schedule in place to keep the household running while I was resting. Dave found it very helpful, because he didn't have to try to figure out our routine, and the children were already used to it. Now, we are back at school and are excited. We can see some areas that need work and realize that certain interruptions are inevitable. I'd like to say I have arrived and am very self-disciplined, but I think my weak areas have been magnified even more through this change. But, when I am weak, He is strong! We are very encouraged in the Lord and want to share that with others, who feel they are in over their heads.

Our family schedule is really a big help for me in being a manager of my home. It doesn't replace walking in the Spirit, and relying on God, but it does help me to remember what I am to be doing and why.

Thanks for your encouragement to seek the Lord as we take on the awesome task of serving Him through the ministry of parenting!

From Debbie

Scheduling Children's Days

Children function better with a routine and schedule to govern their days. Have you noticed what happens to children left to themselves for too long? They quarrel and bicker. They become bored. They get into mischief. Although some might say children are happiest when they are free to do whatever they please with their time, this is not the case. Little ones are more peaceful, content, and obedient when their days are planned and routine, including regular changes of activity.

PLANNED CHANGE OF ACTIVITY

The key to making a child's schedule is planned activity change. One-half hour increments work well. You will want to pray, discuss with your husband, and be creative to figure out what half-hour activities will best fill your child's day. Some of these periods will be structured, some will not. Some will involve you, some will not. Some will include others, some will not.

Plan the routine and then stick to it. Make it work by regularity. Before long the child will know the schedule; you will no longer need to tell him what will happen next. You must have a daily routine, and then, keep it every day. This is so important to proper scheduling!

For school age children, school will occupy a great part of the day. There is enough information we want to present on this subject that we have devoted another chapter to it. You will find a detailed discussion of scheduling schooltime in Chapter Four, "Scheduling School."

ASSIGNED PLAYTIME

You might try having assigned playtimes for one sibling with one other sibling as part of your schedule. Around the age of four, a child should be able to handle a playtime with a baby who is crawling age or older. Your discernment of your child's maturity and responsibility level will govern who can oversee a little one and what age the little one should be. This playtime must take place in a safe play area with an adult in earshot to help, if needed. Safety rules about not carrying the baby, watching that nothing small goes into the baby's mouth, training on how to play kindly with a baby, and other instruction will be necessary.

This playtime is a good occupation for the baby. In addition, being able to care for a baby is a valuable skill for a child to have. And it is a marvelous way for these two children to build and cement their relationship.

A Personal Word

We did have some attitude problems, today, but most of them were short-lived due to switching activities every half-hour. The babies didn't have time to get bored. Ellen

One very successful point in the morning has been the girls' individual time with the baby. They have really enjoyed taking him to themselves alone and doing something with him. He has learned to ride the rocking horse and a few other things since they have taken the time to play with him. He really enjoys the time with them too. Rebecca

Here is Jacob's play schedule:

Monday - Legos

Tuesday - Dinosaurs or Army men

Wednesday - Colored blocks

Thursday - Hot Wheels cars

Friday - Train set

Tracy L.

Older children will often not have an opportunity to play with only one of their siblings at a time if there are many children in the family. Not only do you want them to be able to all play together, but you want them to enjoy individual one-on-one relationships. They will often look forward to their playtime with a specific brother or sister. Our children jealously guarded their playtime with three-year-old Jesse. It was not unusual for one to call out to me, "Mom, it is my playtime with Jesse, and Anna is in here trying to play too."

If you have several young children in a family, trading the playmates around half-hour by half-hour can take up a good portion of a morning. Three-year-old Jesse's morning looked like this after his breakfast.

Jesse's (Age 3) Morning Schedule	
8:30 a.m.	Preschool/Bible time with Mom
9:15 a.m.	Play with John (7)
9:45 a.m.	Computer time
10:00 a.m.	Family school Bible time
10:30 a.m.	Play with Anna (5)
10:45 a.m.	Play with Sarah (16) and other little ones
11:15 a.m.	Play alone
11:45 a.m.	Play with Joseph (9)
12:15 p.m.	Lunch

You will be amazed at how much these scheduled playtimes and changes of activities will help to minimize the difficulties of a home. The difficulties are not eliminated but are much more manageable.

SCHEDULED PLAY PLACES AND TOYS

When children have scheduled playtimes, they can be assigned a specific place to play or items to play with. Weather permitting, one playtime could be outside, another in the child's bedroom, and another in the family room.

You can have sets of toys which only come out on certain days and can then be looked forward to when that day arrives. The toys would be taken out for the half-hour playtime and then returned afterwards. The play sets remain exciting and fun since they are only being played with for a short while each week. Here is an example.

Play Set Rotation	
Monday	Match box cars/Wooden blocks
Tuesday	Play tools
Wednesday	Duplo blocks
Thursday	Preschool PlayMobiles
Friday	Fischer Techniques

Usually during these half-hour playtimes, everything will be going smoothly when the time is up. The temptation is to leave things alone rather than making the activity change. This undermines the success of your plan and schedule. One of the keys to the success of this method—regular changes of activity, despite the lack of apparent problems. The changes prevent discontent and help eliminate discipline problems. Be faithful to sticking with the schedule and making those changes every half-hour.

If your children are allowed to play with neighborhood children, you would be wise to have this playtime scheduled for your sake and the children's. It is always best for you to directly supervise their play. This can only be accomplished if the time is planned into your day. It will be a great sacrifice for a busy mother, but a most necessary one. If you find the playmates unacceptable influences on your children, you can easily end the playtime. This will be based on your direct observation rather than after a major problem surfaces as a result of unsupervised play with other children. A half-hour scheduled each afternoon or a couple of afternoons a week, at the same time, would allow playtime if you feel it necessary. It will also eliminate queries to play other times, since the neighbor children will soon know your children's available playtime.

Scheduling a half-hour with the art supplies is another beneficial use of a child's time. Often a school age child will not have time for this, but it can fill part of a preschooler's day. The art supplies, which are age appropriate for the child, can be put in an area he can access. He can get them out, work with them, and cleanup after himself. His creations could be displayed on the refrigerator door until the next one is made. This is a creative use of a child's time and develops his interest in drawing, coloring, pasting, cutting, and gluing.

It will be so good to have it on paper so I can see that I do do things, and I will have a lot less days where I wonder what I did. So often I forget all the little things that do get done and feel so behind at the end of the day. It will also help those in our family to see what they can help with and how much they are needed. But the biggest help will be to me to keep my focus and not get sidetracked. I have already put some things into practice and feel it was well needed, especially the shorter playtimes. I tended to leave things until a problem arose. I am now avoiding the problems by changing the activity before boredom sets in. Terri

Yesterday, I didn't stay on my schedule, and I regretted it all day. My house was such a mess, and the children were irritating each other—I felt like I wanted to run away. Today has been a world of difference. We got started on time, and aside from the "little" problems that have come from having so many young children, my day has been great. I've even been able to start back on my prayer list. Tracy L.

Benefits I've gained from scheduling:

* lots of schoolwork done

* a sense of order in the house, even when Mommy is busy

* everyone gets attention at some point, not just the "high maintenance" children

* dinner on time!!!!

* Mom is no longer the drill sergeant, everyone knows what they are supposed to be doing

* discourages idleness

* helps me keep my priorities in line. Ricki

Things are going great. I bought the children alarm clocks, and after three to four days of alarms blaring with no response, they now jump from their beds to shut them off, and then wake little brothers and sisters to help them get ready. This is so exciting. Kristi

I'm telling you, my life is completely different with my schedule. So much so that a lady in my school support group just dropped by, and

If you have any good children's shows on a local Christian radio station, these can be scheduled into a child's day. This is particularly handy if they are during the afternoon. An older child could listen to the shows as part of his afternoon quiet time. If the child naps and the children's radio show's timing coordinates, setting a radio alarm for the child's wake up is possible. Be wary even of Christian children's radio shows as some may not have the same values that you have for your children. Even if they do, they may present so much bad and evil, despite the eventual good outcome, that you would not want your children exposed to them.

SCHEDULING FOR GOOD WORK HABITS

Children also need to have blocks of time throughout the day for developing work habits. There are many household chores that they can accomplish. They should become completely responsible for their own bedrooms. They can also: clean sinks; empty trash; take recycling out; pick up and put away items; sweep; and set, clear, and wash the table. The list is limitless.

These chore times will fall naturally: early morning upon rising, mealtimes, bedtime, and perhaps late afternoon. One family had a half-hour break in the middle of the school morning from 10 to 10:30 for household cleaning chores. Each person, including Mom, had assigned cleaning tasks. If these jobs were finished in a timely, well-done fashion, there was a waiting snack.

You have to start by investing the time to train your child for the task you want him to learn. This will need to be a scheduled time in your day as you begin the process. For example, if you are training a child to set the table for a meal, the time you use may come at dinner time when you normally set the table. But, you could also have a half-hour block of time set aside each day for chore training. You would use this time to work with a child in the learning process. Of course, the desire is that the child will soon become proficient enough to perform the task alone. Work with the child until the skill is learned. Help him understand that when the learning process is finished he will be responsible for taking over the job and doing it without your constant help and companionship.

To maintain quality control over the work of your children, you will want to inspect the work frequently. Consequences must be in place for not doing the job or for doing a poor job. One consequence which is always reasonable is to have the child return to do the job better. Sometimes this may require several returns. Often this is enough discipline, since the child will lose free time having to redo the inadequate work. For Mother, it can be hard to remain firm during this time of a child learning to be diligent and thorough in his work. A mother's heart will not like seeing her child having to use his playtime to return to a job. However, the end benefits will be worth the difficulty the moment requires. If you cannot, or will not, enforce what you are asking or teaching, the child's bad habits will not become better with time, but rather become more entrenched.

Even preschoolers can learn to do some chores on their own. They can learn to put a napkin on each plate. They can pull clothes out of the dryer, placing them in the laundry basket beneath. Picking up toys and putting them away is a high priority. With little ones, it is often best if Mother works next to them. It would be much easier for her to do the work herself. The advantages of letting young children help are two fold: they love to be helpers so they are developing the right attitudes toward work, and they are learning to do the actual work.

Another scheduled use of a preschooler's time is with Mother when she is working. For example, if Mother has a half-hour scheduled each day to fold and put away laundry, she could include her preschoolers in this time. Her little ones would learn some simple folding. They could carry folded laundry to the appropriate rooms. Children this age love being useful, especially when they can work with Mother and are praised for their efforts. This time can be multiplied by spending it singing together too.

INDIVIDUAL PLAYTIME

From infancy up, children can have a half-hour playtime alone. We instituted this practice in our home after reading *Creative Family Times* (see Resources section in the Appendix). Children can play individually for one-half hour or more at a specified time each day. This gives them the opportunity to have some quiet time to themselves. With the busy, active lives of most families these days, there is benefit in a child having a small part of the day when there is no noise or activity. This is also a good chance for them to learn that they do not have to have someone else with them to entertain them every moment of the day. They need to have the ability to find creative ways to spend time all by themselves.

This time offers benefits not only to the child but to the mother. Playtime alone will take a child away from the other siblings in the family. Immediately, many of the situations that will require a mother's attention will be gone. This frees Mother to do tasks that she does better without distraction.

Playtime alone should be scheduled at the same time each day. It should also be held in the same place. This time, if you choose to have it, must have your child's safety first and foremost in mind. Little ones can have their playtime in their crib, stocked with many fun toys, until they are at an age to be trustworthy in a bedroom or playroom by themselves.

my house was CLEAN!!!!!!! You wouldn't believe how many times my house was a wreck, and I couldn't open my door because of humiliation. I was so thrilled. I've always thought that my home was supposed to be part of my ministry, and only now am I able to follow through with that. I feel like my life has completely changed. Tracy L.

Now that I am using a schedule, I don't get discouraged from household tasks not being done. It would be nice if my house was always clean, but at least now that it is under control, I feel more peaceful knowing things are slated to be accomplished. With school, I have a plan to get things done, whereas before, it was always a real trick to get tasks completed. There were MANY contingencies. Of course, there are always other factors to consider, and sometimes things don't go as planned, but I used to not really have any plan at all. Debbie

Anyway, your system is wonderful and can work for anyone. I fully believe it will even work for me. Sheri

We are still loving our weekly schedule so much so that my husband suggested that we put one together for Sundays, so we did! This week was our first Sunday on it, and, boy, what a difference it made. We were on time, but, most importantly, we had been able to spend time praying and worshipping together to prepare for church. It was great!!! Tracy L.

Today we were talking at dinner about our schedule when I asked the children how they felt about it. The seven-year-old said he likes having a schedule because it helps him to behave better.

Wanting to know more, I asked him why he would behave better on a schedule. He said, "Because everything has an order, and we know what to do. Also Mom is calmer, and I don't fight with my brother so much."

The four-year-old said, "I like the schedule because there is a time for my brother to play with me, so I don't have to beg! And Mommy plays with me more." Kathy

The room they play in alone must contain only toys and an environment which is safe for a child of their age. Even if a child is trustworthy when you are around, do not have anything that could be dangerous for the child in their play alone room. They will become very creative in their playtime and may venture into things they would not if they were being watched.

You could have one playtime alone per child in the morning and another one in the afternoon if it is successful. When children outgrow naps, this playtime alone can be done quietly in their bedroom during the afternoon, allowing Mother to have a time to rest if she needs it.

DADDY TAPES

A most worthwhile use of this playtime alone is to have a cassette tape that Daddy has made to be played during this time. This idea also came from *Creative Family Times* (listed in the Resources section of the Appendix). It is precious time for Daddy to be investing in the life and heart of his child. He can talk about and teach anything he wants his child to know. This could include spiritual goals and truths for his child, Bible verses or basic Bible information, songs, character traits or attitudes he wants the child to develop, and academic information. His voice and thoughts become very familiar to the child.

Our three-year-old listened to his Daddy tape twice a day. The first time was when he had his playtime alone in the morning. When the tape ended, his playtime was over; he knew to come upstairs. The second time was when he went down for his nap. The tape was turned on when he was tucked into bed and kissed. It played as he went to sleep and automatically turned off when the side was finished. We have copied Daddy's tape onto both sides of the cassette tape so it doesn't have to be rewound. Daddy has greatly appreciated being able to have this daily teaching time.

SCHEDULING NAP TIME

Afternoon naps will be another scheduled time for your children. Nap length will, of course, vary depending on the age and needs of the child. Many mothers let their children stop taking naps much earlier than is wise. This creates problems since tired children cry, whine, bicker, and are generally more difficult. Think about how we, as adults, can struggle at times to be kind and loving. It is all the worse for children, especially tired ones.

In our family, we have our children up until 9:30 p.m. so that they can have time with Daddy in the evening. Because of the short nighttime sleep our children receive, they continue to take afternoon naps as long as needed. The need is based on the behavior we observe in them. Our seven-year-old, who awakened at 7:30 a.m. and went to bed at 9:30 p.m., napped for one hour five days a week. This seemed to give him an adequate amount of sleep. You can probably detect by your children's behavior when they are experiencing a sleep deficit. Be careful to take this into consideration when planning a schedule.

For quiet time or nap time in our home, we try to have only one child per room. This has meant, as the children got older, they move out of their bedroom for their rest since there are several children sharing a bedroom. The littlest one is left to use the bedroom for napping while the older ones find other places. They take their pillows from their bed and have blankets, if needed, that are usually stored under their beds.

John slept on a couch in the playroom for his nap when he was six and seven years old. He had a clock radio set to wake him at the proper time so I could continue what I was doing without having to get him up.

Even if a child does not sleep in the afternoon, you will want to have a scheduled time of rest and quiet activities. At age eight for rest time, Joseph made a nest on the floor in Dad and Mom's bedroom. This nest was next to the book shelves where our children's and school resource books are kept. He loved to browse through these books. No other time during the day did he choose to come in to do this, but when the books were next to him, he was using them.

Again, these older children's rest times vary with their need for sleep according to age, evening bedtime, morning rising time, and attitudes.

In Conclusion

Scheduling your child's days will make a pleasant framework for his time. Your child will learn the disciplines of balancing his time, being efficient, getting along with others, being diligent, and more. You will be free from the constant pressure of children asking what they can do or need to do next. Your day will have direction and foresight to meet the needs and demands it presents. At the end of the day you can look back and easily see what has been accomplished by and with your children.

I really enjoyed your rest time suggestions. That is working wonderfully—all the children are agreeable to it, and even Katie the oldest is getting a consistent nap or rest that she hasn't gotten since she was four. Now she lays down and reads using your alarm clock idea. A few times I've gone down to get her up and found her sleeping with the alarm clock ringing next to her head for over an hour. I guess she really needed that rest since it's so difficult for her to wake up! Renée

My five-year-old has wanted reading lessons for quite awhile, and I kept putting her off. Now she knows that every day at 4 p.m. she gets them, and she is so excited to be reading her first words already!

It is on the schedule to bake every Friday with my girls. They love to bake, but we rarely did it. Now it is on the schedule, and we have a great time. Kathleen

Dear Friends,   *November 7th*

We are Steve and Ellen Blinn from Indianapolis, Indiana. God has blessed our home with five lively sons: Ryan (8), Brandon (6), William (4) and twins, Austin and Evan (18 months). We are committed homeschoolers and are involved in a local homeschool group. We are also very active in our church. Steve is a deacon and teen Sunday School teacher. Both of us sing in our church choir and help sponsor the youth group. I serve as an AWANA Guards director, president of the Ladies' Fellowship, sing in a ladies' ensemble, and am involved with handchime choir. Our lives are further complicated by Steve's ever-shifting work schedule, varying quantities of overtime, and his two classes per week at a local Bible college.

For us, life without a schedule was madness! My dear husband had been encouraging me for years to settle on a workable routine for myself and the children, but I couldn't come up with anything truly suitable. I had read several time-management books, but always got bogged down when it came to actually making the suggested scheduling techniques work for us. Principles that had sounded great in theory spawned a logistical disaster when applied to our larger-than-average family! So, whether I was following a "schedule" or not, I was worn to a frazzle trying to keep everyone on task during schooltime, which "always" took much longer than the time I had allotted. And because we had no dependable plan, the house was seldom fit for company, we were losing the laundry battle, dishes were frequently piled in the sink, and meals were often late.

Teri's plea for families to test her book was an answer to prayer. This is a plan that will work for ANY size family. I've raved about this method so much in our home, Steve is even planning to cut and paste his own "individual" schedule! It's so simple to change the schedule when the need arises too! Just as the children and I had become accustomed to our new schedule, my husband's work hours shifted. It was a relatively simple operation to go back and move the colored "squares" around and come up with an "alternate" schedule! We can now shift back and forth between schedules as necessary and not miss a beat!

Of course, change doesn't come overnight, and juggling school, housework, and "extra" activities is still a daunting challenge, but praise God, we now have a plan that works in real life! I had been so reluctant to commit to a schedule this structured, but it is so freeing! Once you become accustomed to the rhythm of the schedule you've prayed about; planned for; created; culled the flaws from; and tweaked until it "just fits"; why, it doesn't "feel" strict at all! There is so much "more" time available for our use now! Our schedule has even made it possible for me to host (with my husband's enthusiastic blessing!) a ladies' Bible study in our home once a week. God is truly blessing our more orderly family life!

From Ellen

Scheduling School

A homeschool mother fills much of her day with school. Knowing how best to plan, schedule, and manage this time is a major hurdle to overcome. Her ability in this will greatly affect not only school hours but the rest of her day.

It is very effective to break the school day into time increments—quarter-hour, half-hour, three-fourths of an hour, or hour blocks depending on the age of the child and his needs. Each child's units may be the same length, or they may vary depending on the time necessary for each subject or activity.

Much of a child's schoolwork can be completed on his own with only a small amount of your one-on-one tutoring time. Many mothers are frustrated with their school schedule being too full. My experience talking to these mothers leads me to believe they are spending too long with each individual child. Children should be tutored, by Mom, in several subjects, and then taught to complete the follow-up work or assignments alone. A homeschool mother with several school age children will not be able to spend two or three hours with each one individually. If she says her child does not complete his work unless she is with him, then there are character issues that need to be focused on and addressed. For some children, this will be a long term task requiring great faithfulness in character training on the parents' part. I cannot overstress the importance of this area. If a child always needs Mother beside him to get through his schoolwork, what kind of employee will he be as an adult?

HIGH SCHOOL

For a high schooler, you will want to have three-fourths to one hour classes. This allows longer amounts of concentrated time for the more intense study which high school subjects require. Tutoring with Mom should run from one-half to one hour a day. For our tenth grader, we scheduled a forty-five minute tutoring with Mom, but found after the first few weeks of school, we usually finished in one-half of an hour. At that point, we revised our schedule to allow both of us to use that extra fifteen minutes in a different way. During our thirty minutes together, we read math lessons and work practice problems. Other subjects she is able to read, digest, and work through on her own. We also spend our one-on-one meetings going over missed items from any of her assignments. This assures us that we are applying our efforts in the most profitable way, where her needs are.

ELEMENTARY

In elementary grades, many subjects, such as math, English, and reading, will generally take a child one-half hour of independent work each. Other subjects, like handwriting and spelling, will only use

A Personal Word

So many things I read were like a light bulb going on in my head!! So you really can "let the children go," so to speak, in their schoolwork for a time, and check them later! And here I was feeling guilty all this time for not guiding them through every minute of their learning! Ellen

I switched the schedule and decided to do some schooling in the afternoon when the youngest are sleeping. I think if I do phonics and reading with my oldest, it will help him concentrate on what he is doing. He won't be as distracted by the younger ones. This has also allowed me a half hour time slot for my two-year-old. Cindy

I'm working on finishing my schedule this week too. Your suggestion about having a meeting time with the older children, and giving them their day's assignments, is really excellent, so that's what I will do. I'm certain it will make a big difference, and also keep them

fifteen minutes. Two shorter subjects could be scheduled back-to-back to fill a one half-hour time block. Here again, plan into the schedule time for one-on-one tutoring, but allow your child to learn to work diligently on his own to complete his assignments.

Alternating workbook type of school with other school segments is effective for elementary age children. For example, a half-hour of seat work might be followed by a half-hour of piano practice, another half-hour of seat work, and then family Bible study, more seat work, and finally a tutoring time with Mom. If a child finishes his assignment before the allotted time is up, he could be rewarded by being allowed to choose how to spend the rest of that time segment. This is often a motivation to work diligently, and the break helps burn off always present energy.

Mom's tutoring of an elementary age student, from second grade on up, should fit into a one-half to one hour segment. These may need to be revised after the first few weeks of using a new school year schedule. At that point, you will have determined how long your meeting with your child actually should be. If you are pushing the child to hurry, and feeling pressured during this tutoring time, it needs to be lengthened. If you are finishing early each day, it could be shortened or left as it is for a bonus break for both of you.

Working with a kindergartner or first grader will require your greatest investment of time and will need to be broken up more. Their attention span is shorter, and they can get frustrated with the intensity of learning, if the time span is too long. Often several fifteen or thirty minute sessions for phonics and math will be best. We have found an hour and a half a day to be plenty of actual schooltime for a kindergartner. Most of this will need to be scheduled with you or an older sibling, but he can do some handwriting practice and simple seat work independently. His learning sessions can be interspersed with other activities that require more physical energy.

Maximize your tutoring by concentrating on the weak areas of the child, and letting him work in the strong ones on his own. With our third grade son, we go over math, English, and reading during our meeting. He works on science, social studies, spelling, and handwriting independently. For math, we cover any new material, do drill work, oral exercises, and timed tests together, but he completes his math lesson during an assigned math time of one-half hour. He reads his reading lesson out loud but does his workbook in the afternoon. English we work on together, and he completes his lesson orally, except for what can only be done by writing it out. That he does with me, using the white board, which is a treat for him.

Our third grader's school morning looked like this.

Joseph's (3rd Grade) Morning Schedule	
8:30 a.m.	Handwriting, spelling, help John (6) with phonics workbook as needed
9:00 a.m.	Piano practice
9:30 a.m.	History
10:00 a.m.	Family school Bible study
10:30 a.m.	Tutoring time with Mom (Math, English, Reading)
11:15 a.m.	Science
11:45 a.m.	Play with Mary (1) and Jesse (3)
12:15 p.m.	Lunch

The afternoon had another hour and one-half scheduled for this third grader to complete his reading and math assignments.

SCHEDULING WORKS WITH ANY HOMESCHOOLING METHOD

One marvelous aspect of scheduling is that it lends itself to all of the various homeschooling methods. It simply adapts to the needs of each particular style and ensures the necessary time is set aside daily to complete the chosen studies.

You may opt not to break the scheduled school time down into half-hour or hour increments but rather leave it as a whole block. If you need a chunk of time for unit studies or read alouds, schedule that time. Make your school schedule work for you, taking into consideration the specific aspects of your particular homeschooling method.

The key for success of a schedule with any style of homeschooling is the willingness to stop what you are doing – at the scheduled time – even if it doesn't feel like a good stopping place. Allowing yourself to continue until a seemingly convenient ending point throws off the rest of the schedule. On those days when a part of the school schedule doesn't go as you had planned, resist the temptation to delay what comes next in order to finish what didn't fit in the allotted time frame. This is a difficult discipline and generally does not come naturally!

motivated to get their work done more quickly. Debbie

I sense that these regular activity shifts will be just the ticket to help the second eldest, "dig in and do it, cause it won't last that long anyway." He has often been SOOOO reluctant to start math, phonics, you name it, because I have always doggedly kept at it until we finish the number of pages listed on the lesson plan I made a week in advance. It never works, I give up, and within a few weeks we always get far behind where I'd like to be.

But with a "time limit," my son could actually see light at the end of the tunnel. He finished his work this morning with flying colors. I wrote down what we had accomplished in my plan book, and it's wonderful to have actually "done" everything I have written there! Ellen

What a great idea to have the older children have playtimes with the younger ones. My older children are looking forward to the times they will be sharing with the younger ones. My oldest, who is an eight-year-old boy,

has always wanted to do crafts. He thinks of different drawing, pasting, and general craft projects. I don't generally feel like doing crafts. I decided today to let him be in charge of putting together a craft time for the younger children while I do dinner preparations. He is so excited. I should have thought of it earlier. Cindy

I wish we were on schedule, because it seems to keep the children out of trouble. Pauline

Here's the funny part. Just to let you know how consuming this process has been and what a change it has made, my husband has actually stayed home for awhile this morning just to see what I've been doing. He's really impressed at the changes last week brought, and he wants to see first hand!! Tracy L.

It's a new concept for me to work on something for a set period of time and then put it away until tomorrow. Of course, I can see the benefit and sense in doing things this way, but my gut instinct is to stick with each job until the bitter end, no matter how long that takes. Ellen

Changing scheduled school activities at the assigned time will assure steady daily progress in each one. Long term you will be amazed at all you have done through the year even though there were days you had to quit a school section before you felt ready. If you don't discipline yourself in this area, you will soon experience frustration over what is being missed!

When you set up a schedule, allow an adequate amount of time so that you will complete each of your scheduled school activities at or before the schedule says to end. If you find you never accomplish what is desired during a particular schedule block, then you need to revise the schedule so that you have an amount of time assuring the progress you want to make each day.

Disciplining yourself to quit when the scheduled time is over and picking up there, again, the next day really does work! This is very much in tune with the Biblical principle of "precept upon precept, line upon line." Pray, discuss with your husband, and revise your schedule if necessary, but don't habitually push one scheduled school activity into the following one's time block.

USING OLDER STUDENTS WITH YOUNGER STUDENTS

Great benefits often result when school age children are scheduled to work with a younger brother or sister. For instance, in our home, six-year-old John drilled his four-year-old sister, Anna, on her basic ABC phonics sounds. He went through the phonics cards which showed the letter, a word representing the letter's sound, and a picture illustration. These were the phonics cards he had learned with me the previous year. Not only did Anna learn her sounds without me spending time drilling her, but John was being reinforced in what he had already learned. This did require my regular supervision, though, as one day I discovered they had abandoned using the cards since John had them memorized. Anna was repeating after him while she sat at the computer playing on a drawing program. This practice would teach her the sounds, but she needed to learn the association of the letter with its name by viewing the cards.

Eight-year-old Joseph had a half-hour scheduled to help six-year-old John with his phonics workbook. Much in this workbook John could do independently, but have you ever looked at the pictures in a phonics book and tried to discern what the picture actually was? Joseph had the teacher's book, so, when John needed to know a picture, Joseph would look it up. Joseph would also help John read each page's directions and listen to him read the required words out loud. During this half-hour, Joseph worked on his own spelling workbook and handwriting, since all of his time and attention were not needed with John.

An older child can also be scheduled to read books to little brothers and sisters. This valuable use of schooltime will educationally occupy younger children, while providing the reader excellent reading practice.

WHAT TO DO WITH YOUNGER CHILDREN

Please schedule a preschool time into your school day if you have children under school age. Thirty minutes to an hour a day is reasonable. Your little ones will look forward to this time each day. They will even hold you accountable to it! Not only is it fun for them, but it prepares them to want to do real school in a few years. It is also a "balm" for your heart's desire to spend time with your little children. Often moms with school age children and younger children feel they are neglecting their little ones in favor of schooltime with the older ones. It is possible to manage your time so that all of your children receive a budgeted amount of Mom!

There are many possibilities for how to spend your preschool time. We have purchased a Sunday School preschool curriculum (see Resources in Appendix) that we use for our home preschool. We also go through the months of the year, days of the week, and identify the current date on a calendar. Then my preschoolers alternate days of choosing the activity from a list of educational activities I read to them. The current list includes: water color painting, preschool workbooks, Hammer Game, ABC Game, Bug Game, In the Forest Game, puzzles, preschool activity box, cutting and gluing, magnets, rubber stamping, playdough, sponge painting, and looking at photo albums. There are several preschool curriculums available through various homeschool catalogs that you could use in your preschool time.

Another invaluable help for your homeschooling will be the scheduling of a half-hour playtime with an older child to oversee the younger preschool age children. Toddlers need constant supervision, which is difficult to do while you are concentrating on one-on-one schooltime with one of your children. If an older child has oversight of the little ones, including keeping them constructively entertained, this frees you to work with another child. This time can be beneficial not only for you, the child you are working with, and the little ones, but also for the supervising child.

You can instruct this older child in: how he is to go about playing with the little ones; what kind of attitudes you expect on his part; how he is to deal with disputes; and when he is to come to you. Then you will need to check up with the child on how he is doing with his responsibility. Depending on how you structure this time, and how much training and accountability you maintain, the sibling playtime could be counted as school hours for the older child.

I just thought of why this schedule will work for me. It will work because I will be accountable to it. If I have something that says "do this," it will get done. If it is left floating in my over-crowded mind, it seems to stay there floating. Your system simplifies it down to those little increments of time that fly by if we are not paying attention and holds us accountable to itself. Our minds need that, I think. Terri

I have been hard at work on my schedule, with lots of praying intermixed. I have read the book twice and love all the Scripture and reminders to pray. I am about to sit and piece together my final schedule. I love the worksheets; I feel as though I am forgetting nothing, and I know this is going to work! What an answer to prayer. Sheri

I like having a framework set up for the day, even if I chose to deviate from it. It just helps to have it down in writing. Robyn

My mornings are going GREAT!!!! Everyone knows what to do and is actually doing it. So much is accomplished. Kathy

The schedule is pretty much in full force and has been from Day One, which was Monday. It is working WONDERFULLY. Rebecca

Here are two hindrances I had to the idea of scheduling. First, I felt if I was a "good" mom, then I would already be doing all this naturally. So to develop a schedule felt like I was showing that I wasn't a "good" mom. It was validating for me to realize the tremendous amount of work that is involved for a mom to successfully accomplish the goals she has for her family. I don't have to be magic, I just have to decide what I want to do and when I should do it.

Secondly, I felt that developing a schedule would make me compulsively rigid. I worried that I would be a "mean" mom "ordering" my children around all day long like a drill sergeant. I like the idea that my schedule is a tool, not a task master. Tracy W.

How much older does the supervising child have to be? You will need to be the judge of your child's maturity. Our eight-year-old can handle a playtime for the one, three, and four-year-old. Our six-year-old had a playtime with the three and four-year-old, but did not have the one-year-old during that time. Our almost five-year-old had an assigned playtime with the three-year-old and another one with only the one-year-old. Age four or five is the earliest you would want to give a child responsibility for playtime with a younger one.

Schedule preschool children for their playtime together during school hours. When our three and four-year-old have assigned playtime together, they are expected to play nicely with each other. If this expectation is not met, the discipline is for both of them to sit on dining room chairs during the remainder of the playtime. Although the administration of the discipline creates a short interruption to your teaching time, it is an appropriate discipline, and maintains the quiet you need for finishing your one-on-one time with your other child.

In Conclusion

Whether it is a three-year-old cooperating with a sibling, or an eight-year-old "teaching" phonics, there are many ways, even a young child can be a contributing member of the family schoolhouse. Certainly the schoolhouse function of a home requires a great amount of time each day and is filled with significant challenges for scheduling. This is particularly true the more children involved, since meshing the various schedules, without making conflicts, is truly a logic exercise. When you have completed your school schedule, you will be pleased with the efficiency and peace your school room experiences. The resulting benefits through the next nine months will make the initial investment of time worthwhile.

Ellen's Activity Worksheet	
Quiet time	1/2 hr
Family devotions	1/2 hr
Exercise	1/2 hr
Shower	1/2 hr
Prepare breakfast and lunch/Eat	1/2 hr
Feed children breakfast/Cleanup	1/2 hr
School	4 hrs
Ryan 1 hr	
Brandon 1 hr	
William 1 hr	
Family Bible 1/2 hr	
Music/Art 1/2 hr	
Teaching time with twins	1/2 hr
Reading to older children	1/2 hr
Reading to little children	1/2 hr
Project time (Gifts, sewing, scrapbooks, etc.)	1 hr
Lunch	1/2 hr
Rest	1/2 hr
Ministry (Missionary letters, AWANA, Ladies Fellowship)	1/2 hr
Cleaning/Chores	1/2 hr
Supper prep	1/2 hr
Supper	1 hr
Family events (AWANA, Family nights, Hospitality)	1 1/2 hr
Bath and Cleanup	1 hr
Laundry	1/2 hr
Computer time	1/2 hr
Sleep	7 1/2 hrs
Total	24 hrs

Dear Friends,   October 24th

I am J'Aimée (35) married to Alex (36) for 11 years. We have eight children: Benjamin (10), Zachary (9), Rebekah (8), Elisabeth (6), Abigail (5), Jonathan (3), Nathanael (2), and Susanna (7 months). We are now in our seventh year of homeschooling. My husband has a 7:30 a.m. - 4:30 p.m. job, but is also going back to college. He is the Military Ministry Director at our church, so our family is involved working with military personnel. We also are working to encourage homeschoolers in our church, as well as participating in various other ministries as we are able.

I have had a desire to homeschool and have a large family, from the beginning of our marriage, but sometimes felt that the two desires were opposing each other. I knew that the Lord would not design that conflict into my life, so I wanted to rearrange my life in order to make them both compatible again. My children are all about 1½ years apart, so that meant I was adding a new student every year or every other year, as well as welcoming new babies into the family. I have never seen myself as a super-disciplined person and basically "winged" it for the first few years.

My husband, on the other hand, had developed into a super-disciplined person and was accomplishing much with the use of a schedule. He seemed to balance all the necessary things in his life so well, and spent a lot of time teaching and playing with the children. Of course, he had been encouraging me to develop a schedule as well, but I had never gotten around to it. After the birth of our eighth child, I felt like something had to change, because we were not accomplishing what we needed to be doing, both in housework and schoolwork. I began to gather sample schedules and organizing resources, but didn't know where to begin.

I really felt like MANAGERS OF THEIR HOMES was sent by the Lord at just the right time for our family. It gave me the step-by-step encouragement to try out a daily schedule. By having a set time for everything, we seem to be able to do more things that, previously, we never got around to doing. The basic housework is being completed, schoolwork is better, and I have spent more focused time one-on-one with each individual child, something I have desired for a long time.

We don't always follow the schedule to the tee. I make adjustments as necessary throughout the day. It has become a framework and a tool, not the master! But if there are interruptions that can't be avoided, the children can keep going on, until I can get back to them, because they know what to do. A daily schedule ties into many other areas mentioned in the book like chore charts and cleaning routines. We are refining and adjusting these areas, as well, as each child grows and matures.

Working with a schedule has not only helped our family to accomplish much more than before, it has given me more confidence that, trusting in the Lord's help and wisdom, I will be able to meet the blessings and challenges of the future!

From J'Aimée

Scheduling and Babies

Learning how to manage a family schedule when it includes a baby has provided many benefits for our babies, in addition to our whole family. As a result, the enjoyment of babyhood has been far greater with our last five babies than it was with the first three. These first babies were raised determining their own schedules for eating, sleeping, and waking. They were more difficult and less content babies, not sleeping through the night until six months of age or later. Because planning a baby into our family's schedule has worked so well for us, we desire to pass the information on to others who might benefit from it too.

Please keep in mind what we share with you in this chapter is completely optional in the scheduling arena. We have had many moms be successful family schedulers who do not want to schedule their babies. That is fine, and it works well. These moms just include their babies in whatever they are doing. If you are a mom who doesn't choose to schedule her babies and one who even finds that idea offensive, we suggest you skip this section altogether!

This chapter is simply a compilation of our family's experience with scheduling our own babies. It is not medical advice. We have been told that many medical professionals will recommend nursing a baby on demand. That is why we were so surprised with the vastly different results we found in our demand fed babies versus our scheduled babies. All babies are different, and we encourage each one reading this chapter to make researched, informed decisions with regards to caring for their infants. The baby's best is always the goal - a healthy, happy, weight-gaining child.

BENEFITS OF SCHEDULING A BABY'S DAY

When a baby is part of the family schedule, we are able to plan the rest of our lives around the baby's needs. We know when he will sleep and when he will eat. We can make sure our meals are not during the baby's nursing time, and we can schedule appointments between nursings. Dad and Mom may go out, knowing the baby will not be home crying because of hunger. The most intense schooltime is scheduled for when the baby is asleep. If the baby determines his own schedule, each of these could cause conflict between the family activity and the baby's needs. This produces anxiety for the mother and discomfort for the baby. On the other hand, with a schedule, the baby's needs are being met along with the requirements of the rest of the family.

When a baby is fed according to a schedule, he learns other ways to find comfort in addition to nursing. If it is fifteen minutes until nursing time and the baby starts fussing, the family members will seek to

A Personal Word

What a blessing this is becoming for me and my family. I am actually putting my three-week-old on a schedule! First time for me with any baby! I was able to fix dinner and eat it with my family while the baby napped! Tracy W.

Well, there is good news on the home front. This is the second day of complete implementation!!!! I actually did it! The whole day!!! I even managed to take a sick child to the doctor, and run errands, and STILL get all the school and housework done. I even had dinner ready on time! It was amazing!!! Everything else seems to fall into place when there is structure. I managed to spend time with the Lord. I was relaxed and patient with the children, so the discipline was more consistent, and the problems didn't seem to escalate. AND THE BABY IS SLEEPING THROUGH THE NIGHT!!! Praise the Lord! He has helped me stay committed and faithful, to reap the rewards of discipline. WHEW!!! What a relief!!! Kathy

pacify him. This may mean Mom or others, spend extra time talking to the baby or playing with him. Often when a baby is fussy, he is tired. If he has recently nursed and begins to cry, it is nap time. He is learning to find contentment in more than simply food.

Plan the baby's schedule to allow him to be nursed just before sleeping and also to go to bed independently. It is advantageous for a baby to be able to sometimes go to sleep without nursing. This way others can put him to bed when necessary. It will also teach good habits for going to sleep when not nursing as frequently or when weaning.

In our experience, babies who begin life with regular habits are better sleepers. They will often sleep through the night by two to three months of age. They take good naps, developing sleeping patterns that are beneficial to them and those who live with them.

What is shared here is based on personal experience. We encourage you to adapt the information to your particular situation and your baby's needs.

CONSIDERATIONS FOR A NEWBORN'S SCHEDULE

After the milk comes in, I begin a three hour schedule except during the night and the afternoon. This schedule is set from the time I want to get up in the morning. For us this has been 5:30 a.m. That means the nursings are at 6 a.m., 9 a.m., 12 noon, 4 p.m., 7 p.m., and 10 p.m. The afternoon nursing is stretched, if the baby will sleep that long, since I want to develop the longest nap then.

To facilitate napping at a time that works with other children's afternoon naps, I keep a baby awake as long as I can before I want him to start the afternoon nap. For us that is 1:30 p.m. I keep the baby awake from the noon nursing until he can no longer stay awake, usually an hour and fifteen minutes to an hour and a half. I won't wake the baby until 4:00 p.m. when it is time to nurse again.

One important aspect of making a schedule work is being willing to wake a baby. In order for the baby to be ready to go down for an afternoon nap, he must be awakened for his noon feeding, if he is sleeping. Since a sleeping baby is easy to care for, waking him will be hard to do until you learn the benefits of scheduling! I have found that, in the long run, learning to wake the baby and keep him on a schedule, has given me greater efficiency. The baby's sleep needs are being met, and I know how to schedule my day around the baby's naps.

A newborn will normally only stay awake an hour, or an hour and a half, between naps. It is important to keep this in mind when planning a schedule for your newborn. He should be allowed to get the amount of sleep he needs. We can tell when our baby is getting tired by the onset of fussing, a signal that he is ready for bed. We try keeping him awake a bit longer, but then it is time for his nap. Our baby is awakened early enough, from his nap, to be ready to go back to sleep for the next nap or bedtime.

Another consideration in setting up a newborn's schedule should be the time Dad is available to spend with the baby. We have read other baby scheduling materials where the baby is put to bed for the night at six or seven in the evening. For our family and most other families, that is the only time Dad has to spend with the baby. We want our baby awake and with the family then. Keeping him up during the evening, when Dad is home, works well with getting him to sleep at the other children's bedtime.

Sample Baby's Schedule From Two Weeks to Three Months	
6:00 a.m.	Nurse and back down
9:00 a.m.	Nurse and stay up
10:30 a.m.	Nap
12:00 p.m.	Nurse and stay up
1:30 p.m.	Nap
4:00 p.m.	Nurse and stay up
5:30 p.m.	Nap
7:00 p.m.	Nurse and stay up
9:00 p.m.	Nurse and put down for the night

SLEEPING THROUGH THE NIGHT

One of our main goals for each baby is that he sleeps through the night. There are several things we do to start this process. Simply putting the baby on a schedule has allowed this to happen by two months of age with little, if any, encouragement.

We make sure the baby is ready to go to bed at the other children's bedtime. This means the baby needs to be awake long enough before bedtime so he is ready to go to sleep. If he is allowed to sleep too long during the evening, he will be wide awake late at night.

One way we wake a sleepy baby is with an evening bath. It makes for a bright-eyed, alert baby. Since a nightly bath is not needed for cleanliness, as our infant gets older and more able to stay awake on his own, we will space out his baths.

As for my baby, he is now seven weeks, and I have continued to schedule his feedings which look like this: 6:00 a.m., 9:00 a.m., 12:00 p.m., 4:00 p.m., and 8:00 p.m. It could be earlier on this last one, if he doesn't last four hours. I'm trying to get this nursing to coincide with our family story-time. It was difficult to schedule nursing around mealtimes (11:30 lunch and 6:00 dinner), but this seems to work well, so far. It finally dawned on me that I didn't have to make the last nursing necessarily coincide with his bedtime. If I nurse him a little earlier at 7:00 p.m., I can still put him down at 8:00 p.m. for bedtime. As for the early mornings, I tried what you said and just waited to see how long he would last, and he did make it until 9:00 a.m., so it has not really been a problem like I thought it might be. Tracy W.

I see I need to set the nursing time to begin at the same time every day and keep it consistent. Cindy

I have never scheduled a baby before and always thought it was crazy. But

while reading that chapter, I can't wait to try. It would make things a lot easier to know when the baby will be doing what. Pauline

As for baby's schedule, last night she actually slept from 12:30 a.m. to 6:00 a.m.! HOORAY! Mama feels like a new person. I woke her at 6 a.m. then put her back down at 6:20 a.m. BUT she woke up again at 6:40 a.m., and I nursed her until 7. Then she went back down. I am very glad she slept through the night, except for waking at 12:00 a.m. Kathy

I even caught my husband looking at our beautifully colored Master Schedule, "sticky-tacked" to our dining room wall, when the baby started to fuss to see if it was time for him to nurse or just be picked up because he was getting lonely! Tracy W.

Scheduling the baby was really challenging! He's four months old. It goes against every fiber of my being to wake a sleeping baby!!! Anyway, I wasn't really rigid with him but tried to keep him fairly close to the schedule. Ricki

We also do not put our baby to sleep in a quiet place for his evening nap. We keep him out with the noise and activity of the family for this nap. Our babies love to curl up on Daddy's chest. And, once again, we choose to wake our baby from an evening nap early enough so he will be ready to go to sleep for the night at the time we have planned.

Our babies are nursed just before they are put down for the night. When they awake in the night, they are nursed and put back to bed. We do not stay up with them in the night even if they would like to be awake. We do not change diapers or turn on bright lights, unless it is necessary. Our goal is to give them as much opportunity to be able to go back to sleep as possible. Even if they fuss, we have felt it is better to leave them alone. It doesn't take long for them to learn to go back to sleep. But if I begin sitting up with them, it won't take long for them to learn that if they complain I will spend time with them. Their bodies are beginning to adjust to their sleeping and nursing patterns. When I allow them to be "night owls," I am helping set sleep patterns that are not good for them or for me.

CONSIDERATIONS FOR A BABY'S SCHEDULE

Setting up a baby's schedule is a matter of prayer and planning. As we look at our family, its daily activities, and our baby's need for food and sleep, we have to formulate a unique schedule that will work for each individual baby. Even within our family, we have found this will vary from baby to baby. The most important goal of our schedule is that our baby is content, healthy, and gaining weight. This goal comes before any other. If our baby was not gaining weight on a three hour schedule, we would move the nursings closer together until we found the timing that did produce a weight gain. This hasn't yet been necessary with our babies, but we would make the adjustments to the schedule if it was.

When Mary was about four months old, on a three hour nursing schedule, she began refusing to nurse or would only take in a tiny bit. It seemed she just wasn't hungry at feeding time. After a few days of this, we changed her to a 3½ to 4 hour feeding schedule and she settled into nursing well again.

When our baby is sick, we again make adjustments to the schedule for a few days. A sick baby needs more liquids and will be likely to wake up during sleep times. This calls for flexibility in our baby's schedule, with additional nursing to meet the added needs. We will usually try to nurse a sick baby before he goes down for a nap and when he gets up. A sick baby will sometimes wake up in the night crying, so I will go in to nurse him. We have found that when he returns to good health he will also return to sleeping through the night.

We do not introduce solid foods to our babies until they are six months old and sometimes not until eight months. It depends on their ability to sit up and their interest in solid foods. Despite late introduction of solids, having a baby on a nursing schedule has still allowed my milk supply to keep up with the growing baby's demands. I haven't found it necessary to make adjustments to the schedule unless the baby suddenly becomes fussy, which has seldom happened. Then, I treat the fussy baby as I do a sick baby for a couple of days. When we go back to the normal schedule, it has been fine.

MAKING A BABY'S SCHEDULE

Once we have the considerations for our baby's schedule in mind, it is helpful to write it out so that we can see a layout of the day. This also allows us to fine-tune the schedule, since there may be parts of it that are not workable. We can use our written schedule to make adjustments as the baby grows. When I start working out a baby's schedule, I begin with:

1) the time I need to be finished nursing so I can start the morning,

2) the time I want all the little ones down for a nap,

3) the time my husband and I need to go to bed.

Starting Factors for Baby's Schedule	
Time	Activity
6:25 a.m.	Family devotion
1:30 p.m.	Naps
9:30 p.m.	Bedtime

My next step is to fill in the nursing times. In working out the schedule, I am more concerned about the baby's needs and the family's needs, than I am about having a rigid "three hour" schedule. For me, this has often meant a baby gets up from his afternoon nap at 4:00 p.m. and goes to bed for the

I found that I got a little bogged down trying to figure out a nursing AND nap schedule for my four-week-old baby. I finally decided just to schedule the nursing and worry about the nap part later, since he sleeps all the time and is awake whenever. This helped me get started on a schedule for him which was my main goal. Tracy W.

We have also started family devotions in the evening with my husband leading. Not only are the children thrilled to have such a special time with Daddy, but he's also excited about getting to teach them every day. I wanted to mention that we video-tape some of our more exciting school activities. On Friday evenings, we have "show and tell" where the children are able to show Daddy their tape and their papers and let him see a glimpse of what they've learned that week.

This week we've built a volcano, and the children are so excited about letting Daddy see their tape tonight. They had so much fun making it. Tracy L.

My schedule keeps me on track with homeschooling, plus I have seen SLLL-LOOOOOWWWW progress in other areas (other than homeschooling). I must confess I have not completely stuck to the schedule for a single day, but I have come close and accomplished more than if I did no scheduling at all.

I am better at keeping promises to my children because we get it on the schedule. They are enjoying a wider variety of activities. My house is consistently cleaner. Kathleen

Your book is great and I am rereading it just for the encouragement. I have always been an organizing junkie, but I never seem to get off the starting line. This time, I am off of the starting line and smoothly sailing towards the finish line. Corrie

Even trying to follow a schedule produces better results and then, when we ACTUALLY achieve it all in one day, wow, that's been a good day! I would encourage other schedule-phobic moms to give it a try, because even

night at 9:00 p.m. There are only five hours from 4 to 9, so I nurse half way between those two times.

Sample Baby's Schedule With Nursing Times Filled In	
Time	Activity
6:00 a.m.	Nurse
6:25	Family devotion
9:00	Nurse
12:00 p.m.	Nurse
4:00	Nurse
6:30	Nurse
9:00	Nurse
9:30 p.m.	Bedtime

The rest of the schedule can now be filled in. I schedule meals, school, and other activities, working around baby's nursing and sleep times. (See Chapter 13, "Putting the Schedule Together," for complete scheduling techniques.)

As Baby Grows

A well planned and executed schedule for a two-month-old baby will be different from that of a four-month-old. We regularly revise the schedule to meet the changing needs of our growing baby. This involves adjusting the starting time and length of the naps. Often our babies stay on a three hour nursing schedule until they are well established on solid food. It is only their sleeping and awake times that vary as they grow. (See Mary's Nursing and Sleeping Schedule in the Appendix.)

We gauge when the baby is ready for a nap by the onset of fussy behavior. As he gets older, the time between being awakened and the onset of crankiness lengthens. Though we put the baby to bed later because he is staying happy longer, we must still get him up at the set time. If we don't do this, our baby will not be ready for his next feeding and nap.

Another signal that indicates a need for a rearrangement of the napping schedule is a baby who does not go to sleep when put down for his nap. Normally within a short time after being laid in bed, the baby should be falling asleep. When the baby is not tired at nap time, it is usually an

Complete Sample Baby's Schedule	
Time	Activity
5:30 a.m.	Mom rises and has her devotion
6:00	Baby nurses and goes back to sleep
6:25	Family devotion
7:00	Mom walks and showers
8:00	Family breakfast
9:00	Baby nurses and has playtime alone
9:30	School for Mom and older children
10:30	Baby naps/School continues
12:00 p.m.	Baby nurses and stays up
12:30	Family lunch preparation and lunch
1:30	Little ones down for naps
4:00	Baby nurses and stays up
4:30	Mom prepares dinner
5:45	Family eats dinner/Baby naps
6:30	Baby nurses and stays up
7:30	Baby naps
8:00	Baby up, bathed, and stays up
9:00	Nurse baby and put down for the night
9:30 p.m.	Dad and Mom to bed

the process of making and trying to follow a schedule is very enlightening and stretching (causes growth!). J'Aimée

Thanks for giving me the inspiration to be successful in my personal life. This was our first week of school, and although we didn't accomplish everything I would like to accomplish, we accomplished a great deal more than usual. Corrie

There have been so many benefits for us from our schedule! The children are more organized, actually getting schoolwork completed without hassles. Discipline is more consistent, because I am calmer and more even keeled, knowing what to expect at any given moment. I can really tell when we stray from the schedule. My whole personality swings as does the children. I can see just how tremendously helpful this will be if the Lord blesses us with more children. It has been a God-send. Kristi

What makes MANAGERS OF THEIR HOMES so unique is the practical application of the wisdom provided in its

pages. If I had never cut out those little slips of colored paper and painstakingly fit them on the charts, then I would probably never really complete my schedule. I would have had good intentions, but ended up with a thumbnail sketch of what I wanted to do and become discouraged and confused before I ever had a chance to use what I'd learned. Ellen

You don't know how "unscheduled" I have been! It is very hard for me to stick to this all the time, but as I have seen the benefits it keeps calling me back. The children like it, we accomplish more, and my husband is happy. What more could I want? The little ones always ask, "Who is my teacher now? Can older brother or sister be my teacher?" They really like having more focused attention. And I have gotten a lot of reading lessons done with my six-year-old daughter. Even my almost five-year-old daughter is doing a LOT of Kindergarten, something I found impossible last year! J'Aimée

The children were very excited and motivated by the schedule (me too!) the

indication that his previous nap was too long. The previous nap must be shortened by getting the baby up earlier. For example, if the afternoon nap is to start at 1:30 p.m. but our baby is playing or crying until 2:00 p.m. in his bed, we look at the ending time of the earlier nap. If that nap has ended at 12 noon, we begin getting the baby up at 11:30 a.m. for several days. We are soon able to tell if this has made the necessary adjustment so that the baby is now ready to go to sleep near 1:30 p.m. again.

During those first eighteen months, the length of time that our baby sleeps will continually become shorter and shorter. But still, we want to maintain a good afternoon nap throughout our baby's early childhood—even up to five or six years of age.

If a child, during his second or third year, begins to struggle with taking naps, we do not allow him to stop napping. This is usually a passing phase, and we will be rewarded if we persist in continuing the nap habit. There are several benefits to this. First, many behavior problems in young children stem from being tired. An afternoon nap helps alleviate the tiredness. Second, it develops a good self-discipline for the child by being required to stay in bed and be still. Third, it gives the mother needed rest and regeneration for the remainder of her day.

Even if our little children do not immediately fall asleep when put to bed at night, we do not stop their nap. The quiet time, waiting for sleep in the evening, is a good opportunity to wind down from the day.

Another tip for your baby is to always nurse the baby in the same place. We began this practice several years ago when we felt Mom's modesty was important with boys who were almost teens. Mom began going to the baby's room to nurse, in the rocking chair. From this, the baby learned that he nursed in his room. As he became older, he did not ask to nurse other places. We have been able to continue this through the past five babies. It also allows Mom to have a quiet, relaxing time with her baby. It is disturbing to baby and Mom, if Mom has to try to handle problems between other children while she is nursing. If there is no one to watch young children while Mom nurses, you could put each little one in a separate play or reading place.

As you can see, a baby's schedule is regularly changing, but the adjustments are minor. They can easily be accommodated in the family's schedule. For your convenience and consideration, we have included Mary's baby schedules from birth to eighteen months in the Appendix.

Scheduling Baby Activities

Whatever daily activities you want your baby to have will need to be planned into his schedule. It is very easy for moms to get busy with their work and life, more or less letting the baby get along on his own without the attention she would truly like him to have. By choosing to make a baby part of the schedule, you will be assuring his needs are being met: physical needs, emotional needs, mental needs, and spiritual needs. If you want to sing hymns to your baby, you will make that a part of your schedule. It may not be a separate time, but could be included in another activity so that you are able to receive double benefits. Your schedule might have: Mom - 5:30 p.m. Prepare dinner, sing, and talk to Mary; Mary - 5:30 p.m. With Mom. If you desire to read Scripture to your baby, you will put that on your schedule, perhaps at one of your nursing times. A playtime can be planned into your baby's day with each of your children who are old enough and responsible enough to oversee a baby.

Individual Playtime

A baby will greatly benefit if he learns to play alone. This individual playtime will have several advantages not only for the baby but also for Mother and the rest of the family. A few minutes of play alone each day teaches the baby to be able to be by himself. In a growing family, babies will seldom find themselves without companionship or entertainment. He will become a very demanding child if he is never taught that he can play alone. Note that Jesus went away for times alone with the Father. Even as a baby, it is not too early to begin training for a time of quiet that will lay a foundation for future personal devotions. This time alone must be planned into a baby's day and the schedule adhered to.

A baby's playtime alone is also helpful to mother. During this time, mother can accomplish tasks that are difficult with baby around. These might include showering, vacuuming, baking with frequent oven checks, or school with another child. Mother knows baby is safe and content while she is accomplishing these things.

A playtime alone for baby works best if we are careful when we schedule it into the baby's day. It should occur when the baby is neither tired nor hungry, soon after a nap and feeding. Mother wants to have an activity scheduled for her that will maximize the use of the time when baby does not need her attention or supervision.

Facilitating Individual Playtime

How do we go about helping baby to learn to have a playtime alone? We start with short periods of ten to fifteen minutes a day. We make this a part

first two days. By ‸ day they were star‸ wander from it, but ‸stead of me having to play "drill sergeant," I was able to refer them to the schedule! It was great! Ricki

The book is a treasure chest of "golden" ideas. The ideas are inspiring and encouraging. Even if you don't find all of them ones that will fit your family, they will get your mind going off in new directions, and you will come up with new ones of your own.

If you haven't already been convicted and convinced about your family's need for a schedule, the first chapter will really speak to you. If, on the other hand, you are just having trouble working your schedule out, the chapter on "Challenges" will be a tremendous boost. This chapter reminds me of the charts that come with appliances. "If your schedule is . . . try this."

Jesus says that His yoke is easy, and His burden is light. He desires for us to give to Him what is burdensome. By careful planning of my mornings and evenings, all blanketed in prayer, my burden is light. Our afternoons are free for creative pursuits. It is like having the best of both worlds, scheduling and free time. Things are running so smoothly this way. With no schedule, chaos reins, and obviously something or some things will not be accomplished. Lorrie

It's ten o'clock in the morning at my house! I did stay on my schedule until 9:30 this morning, and I can't believe the difference! By this time in the morning, I'm usually lucky to be out of my p.j.'s, but beds are made, teeth brushed, lots of school is finished, we've had outside time, etc. I can't believe how much has been done. I feel like I've really accomplished something today, and I've still not even gotten through half of the day!! I'm so excited, I think that I might go until 11:00 a.m. tomorrow! Tracy L.

School has been much easier with the time increments of a half-hour for each subject. Although, as I said, it's not being done at the specifically scheduled times every day, I do try to work on different subjects for that period of time. It's good not to get bogged down. We say, "Let's do it; we don't have much time." So Katie works

of our schedule so it happens each day at the same time. We place the baby in a crib or playpen, preferably not one in which they sleep. We are very careful, as they get older, that it is steady so when they are pulling up there is no chance of them tipping the crib or playpen over. The crib is filled with toys that are only played with during this special time. For a young infant, we use a Fisher Price musical mobile that plays and turns for fifteen minutes.

As we put our baby in the crib for playtime, we talk about how he is going to play alone for a few minutes. We tell him we will be back soon to get him, and we want him to be good. There are ages when the baby may cry or fuss when we leave him. If we persevere, he will soon learn to play nicely during this time. When the playtime is up, we go back into the room praising our baby for the great job he did playing by himself.

After a few weeks of the ten to fifteen minute a day playtime, we add another five minutes for several days, then a little more until we reach our goal. A half-hour at a time is plenty, and a reasonable amount of time for a baby or young child, to play alone. They will reach an age, sometimes not until almost three years old, when the crib is no longer the safest place for them. At that point, the playtime switches to a bedroom or playroom. We make sure it is a child-proof room. We would never test a young child's obedience with dangerous, unsupervised play.

Our youngest child began having a playtime alone when she was four months old. At that time, we put her on her back to watch her musical mobile. She loved it and would squeal with delight. I talked to her about enjoying her playtime by herself. I told her that Mommy would be back soon. We only left her for fifteen minutes. I would set a kitchen timer to remind me to go back and get her out.

One day I forgot to set the timer. Suddenly, in the middle of making dinner, I wondered where Mary was. Then I remembered she was playing in her bed. I rushed in to find a happy little girl, who had enjoyed a twenty-five minute playtime, instead of her normal fifteen minutes!

By fourteen months of age, her playtime alone had lengthened to thirty minutes a day. She had a crib filled with toys and books. She was also allowed to take her favorite blanket with her. Though she didn't have a very big vocabulary yet, when we finished her morning nursing, I was convinced she would say, "Bed, bed," as she crawled toward the crib. I would tell her each day that it was time to play in her bed, and that I would see her in a little bit. I told her to have fun and to say, "bye, bye," to Mommy. She is a secure, happy child. She does not cry when I leave her for her playtime or when I have to leave her other times.

This playtime alone can also be used as a valuable teaching time for baby, just as it is with older children. Mother or Father can make a cassette tape that can be played for the baby when the baby has playtime alone. Some possibilities for including on it are: character traits we want our children to develop and stories to reinforce them, songs, Scripture, poems, ABC's, counting, name, address, phone number, prayers, expressions of love, and our expectations for the baby. The tape gives you an opportunity to teach and instruct your child in character and Godliness at times when you are unavailable to teach him directly.

BASIC BABY EQUIPMENT THAT FACILITATES THE FAMILY SCHEDULE

We have found some basic baby equipment helpful for making life with a baby smoother. A baby swing is good for the first three or four months. We use ours during schooltime and mealtime when others, who would normally hold the baby, have their hands occupied. There have been occasions when a fussy baby was soothed by rocking in the swing.

A bouncy infant seat has also worked well. The one we have has a cloth seat mounted on a metal tubular frame. The baby, belted in the seat, can be gently bounced up and down. Our kitchen counters are large enough to safely place the baby in the bouncy seat, on the counter, when Mother is making a meal. It is a good time for Mother to talk to Baby, and Baby usually enjoys watching Mother working. He might hold a toy in his hand or play with the attached bouncy seat toys.

We mentioned the long-playing mobile earlier in this chapter. Our babies love watching a mobile, but one that plays for quite a while is a must. This can be used for Baby's playtime alone. We also sometimes put Baby in his crib, with his mobile on, at mealtime before the baby is old enough to join us in a highchair.

A baby gym placed over where the baby lies is great. The attached toys are within eyesight and reach. This will often occupy much time for a baby.

The last piece of baby equipment we love is the stationary exerciser. It is similar to a baby walker but is immovable, fastened to a large plastic saucer. From about four months until crawling stage the exerciser is useful. Ours has enough support to allow a four-month-old baby to sit in it. They like to be upright where they can watch what is happening around them. The attached toys occupy them, and the exerciser can be kept where the family activity is. Again, we have frequently used this at mealtime for a baby who cannot yet sit in a highchair.

better when she knows we need to get it done, and it will be over with.

I could go on and on with affirmations of your ideas. They seemed to make sense. I just hadn't thought of them in the way that you spelled out so clearly. I know I have a long way to go to be on a real, complete schedule, but even the progress I've made so far has made me feel much better about the day. It's wonderful to know that everything CAN fit into a day and a week. It is manageable after all! Renée

I do not feel that overwhelming sense of oppression; it is now all scheduled, and bit by bit it will get caught up! Lisa

The children are excited about starting our schedule. I left two hours per night unscheduled because every night would be different (Church on Sunday and Thursday, hospitality some Wednesdays, and other projects or meetings). I will try to get into a routine on that as well. Maybe, Monday nights - sewing, Tuesday - Homemaking club with girls, etc. J'Aimée

I was thinking of developing a training schedule for two or three weeks. I had thought that I might need to work more individually with each of my children on learning chores and going over rules of this house. After we get some basics down, then we can start school. Sheri

Each of these items has increased our ability to enjoy and care for our babies. None of them are necessary, but are nice if you have them available. With our first babies we did not have the finances for these baby accessories. Then, as these last five babies began arriving and our parents would buy us one nice piece of baby equipment as a baby gift, we were able to expand beyond the basics. As we shopped, we would question what items might be beneficial and which ones would end up stuck away, unused, in a corner. Perhaps our experience as to items we have found useful will help you determine what extra baby equipment you would like for your baby to help his schedule run more smoothly.

In Conclusion

God gives babies as blessings. "Lo, children are an heritage of the LORD: and the fruit of the womb is his reward" (Psalm 127:3). Yet many people have come to view them as burdens. Could this be because of the frustrations they cause when their needs are constantly creating interruptions to the family's life? We have found such delight with our babies as we have included them in our family's schedule, working our needs around theirs and their needs around ours.

J'Aimée's Activity Worksheet	
Quiet time/Dress/Straighten bedroom/Nurse	1 hr
Exercise/Shower	1 hr
Breakfast	1/2 hr
Family Bible devotion	1/2 hr
School	3 1/2 hrs
Preschool 1 hr	
Abigail (K) 1/2 hr	
Elisabeth (K/1) 1/2 hr	
Rebekah (3rd) 1/2 hr	
Zachary (5th) 1/2 hr	
Benjamin (6th) 1/2 hr	
Lunch	1/2 hr
Cleanup/Nap prep	1/2 hr
Reading out loud	1/2 hr
Dinner prep	1 hr
Dinner	1 hr
Laundry fold/Put away	1/2 hr
Computer time/Phone calls	1/2 hr
Time with Alex	1/2 hr
Sewing/Reading/Letter writing	1 hr
Evening devotions	1/2 hr
Sleep	7 hrs
Teach/Supervise/Inspect chores/Corrections	1/2 hr
Unit study/Projects/Art and Music	1 hr
Evening activity	2 hr
Total	23 1/2

Friday:
   Paper work
   Cleaning
   Menu/Shopping List

Saturday:
   Organizing
   Shopping
   Church prep/Ironing

Dear Friends,   October 20th

We are a farming family with four young children, ages 3-9. I am a 40-year-old homemaker and the business manager of our organic farm. We are in our first year of homeschooling, plus we are expecting our first "reversal baby," having recently put our family planning in the Lord's hands. Being new to homeschooling and expecting a baby, along with all the work that goes into farming, plus already feeling a bit overwhelmed to begin with, I was very grateful to be accepted as a test family for this book.

I have always loved being organized and neat. But, I found that the more children I had the less organized I was, because I had never really developed good habits. Most days were chaotic, and I dreaded anyone ever dropping by!

I found immediate benefits from having a schedule. The first thing I did was to schedule chore time and begin training the three older children to do a majority of the cleaning plus help cleanup after mealtime. This lifted such a big weight from my shoulders that the thought of homeschooling was no longer overwhelming. Our house is still chaotic on some days, especially when Mom oversleeps after a bad night of being very pregnant, but we usually get back on track within a day or so.

A schedule gave me a skeleton upon which to build our homeschooling day. I am more of a relaxed homeschooler, so I don't set timers or anything. If we end up doing science for most of the morning, I don't worry about cutting math short that day, but having a schedule helps me make sure we are at least hitting the basics most days.

My schedule is more open than some. We live in the country and want the children to have time outside in undirected play. You can do this and still have a schedule; it is a great guideline.

The specific idea I have liked the best in the book was to have everyone take a rest in a different room. I always had a breaktime every day, but the children would get so noisy playing in their rooms that I never got much rest. Now they all go to different rooms for "Rest and Read Time." The older two have improved their reading skills already, and their love of reading has increased because of this, plus Mom actually gets to relax a bit! The only problem is that we are out of rooms, so I don't know where the baby will rest and read!

The other idea I liked was the "half-hour a day" concept. I find that, indeed, I am beginning to take some bites out of projects that seemed insurmountable before.

The thing I personally want to say is that you can have about any type of personality or parenting style and still benefit from scheduling. I am a semi-relaxed homeschooler. I don't direct or schedule my children's free play. I plan to demand feed our new baby as I did all the rest. This appears quite different from some of the sample schedules I viewed in the book, and I wondered if scheduling would work for us. But it has, and I would recommend it to ANYBODY!

From Kathleen

Chapter 6

Scheduling Chores

Scheduling facilitates the completion of daily and weekly chores for both a mother and her children. Having an assigned time to do chores helps insure nothing is left "undone." One of the greatest areas of need and conflict a mother can have with her children is trying to get them to be responsible for their portion of the home upkeep. It is important that children learn the disciplines that come from being given the responsibility of chores. They need to become dependable, diligent, thorough, attentive to detail, and efficient. They also need to share the load of maintaining the home they live in, since they are contributing to the messes in it. When a chore time is specified in a family's schedule, the children will be directed to their jobs. Mother, too, will do better if there is a planned time in her day and week for housecleaning and laundry.

Your schedule will likely include daily chore times. You will probably have a time early in the morning upon rising when the children will be expected to get dressed, make their beds, and straighten up the room. They may also have other tasks to do during this time, such as bringing laundry to the laundry area, emptying trash, cleaning sinks, or helping a younger brother or sister.

Meal preparation is another designated chore time. If one child is mother's helper for making the meal, other children may be assigned additional tasks. In our home, twice a week, one of the children vacuums the front part of the house, while another child is Mom's dinner helper.

Before bedtime is another logical place for chores to fall into the schedule. Here you will allow for toy pick up, teeth brushing, changing into pajamas, and putting away clothes. Remember these tasks will more likely be accomplished when they are planned into your schedule and become part of your daily routine. Children are not prone to choosing to do these things of their own volition!

There will also be weekly chores that need a place on the schedule. These are the major jobs that do not have to be done every day. Here again, if you reserve a specific time, you will not face the frustration of finding them left undone or of having to constantly push for their completion. You will know that you have a specific time to tackle the weekly cleaning jobs that are your responsibility too.

TEACHING CHILDREN CHORE RESPONSIBILITY

Mothers need to start planning and thinking about what chores they can give to their children throughout the years of growth and development. Even as young as two years old, a child can be taught basic chores, such as putting his dirty clothes in the hamper, picking up his toys, and even setting the table. There will be chores that will be appropriate for a child to learn at each age. It takes work and planning to figure out what to have a child do, teach him, and then follow-up to see that it is being done well.

A Personal Word

We are heading into the weekend with a tidy house, and my husband is thrilled. He has plans for us all; it will be nice to do something enjoyable tomorrow, and then, come home to a clean house! Sheri

We have been partially implementing the schedule, and it has been going very well. We will start full-force next week. I would like to share one benefit which was such a wonderful blessing to me. I have a home business which takes me out of the house for two to three full days every three months. I leave very early in the morning and often don't return until early evening. In the past, the house has usually been in utter chaos by the end of those two days, and it was so discouraging. This time I told the children that they were to keep their regular schedule of chores even though I wasn't there. While things were not done to the standards they would have been had I been home, it was so much better I couldn't believe it!!!! They really did their best for being trained such a short time. In the future, I will expect it to

Once the chores have been planned for a child, Mother will need to schedule time into her day, for a short while, to teach the child his chores. She will start with instructing and demonstrating. Then she needs to work alongside the child, and finally, supervise the child while he works. Since this process does take time, it is prudent for Mother to make sure she puts the training time into her schedule so that she is not frustrated with conflicting demands. Usually fifteen minutes a day will go a long way in training a child for new chores, and this can be dropped as soon as he is able to handle the chore himself.

A child is facilitated in his accomplishment of daily chores if he has a scheduled time to work on them. To rely on the child to take time out of his playtime to do chores is to set the child up for failure. If, on the other hand, everyone who has daily responsibilities is assigned specific chore times, the chores will more likely be completed.

WHAT ABOUT LAUNDRY?

Laundry is a necessary part of each mother's responsibility. How do you schedule laundry? This will partly depend on the quantity of laundry generated in your home each week.

If your amount of laundry is small, you may want to have laundry scheduled for one day per week. This will mean you put loads of laundry in the washer, move them to the dryer, and finally take them to the folding area throughout the day. You need to schedule an adequate block of time, after the laundry has been through the washer and dryer, for folding and putting it away. Children can be involved in this process too. Your laundry folding time will need to be one of those variable time blocks, since you will only be doing this chore once a week. This time could be used for grocery shopping, cleaning, ironing, or other needed activities on the days that are not laundry days.

My preference for scheduling laundry is to have it divided up through the weekdays. This allows me to keep my schedule stable each day. In our home, we need to wash at least two loads of laundry every weekday. I start a load as we change a morning activity. Then I will go back to the laundry at another activity change, to move the load from the washer to the dryer, and start another load. In the early evening, I have a scheduled half-hour for folding and dispersing the clean clothes. This is time that I can sit and talk with my husband or children, in addition to accomplishing one of my daily chores.

Even in the area of laundry, you will discover, when you have a scheduled time each day for this task, it will easily be completed. No longer will you wake to the daunting sight of clean laundry lying in heaps throughout the house, wrinkled clothes packed in the dryer, or wet, smelly towels left in the washer. You will be pleased to find that laundry is a "conquerable mountain."

MASTER CHORE LIST

Develop a Master Chore List, in writing! This is much easier than trying to remember which child is responsible for which job, especially when you find a job left undone and must determine who shirked his duty. We find it works well to have the children keep the same daily and weekly chores rather than rotate them. This helps the child learn the chores better and become more efficient at his particular chores. The routine is easier for Mother and Child to keep up with since it is consistent, not varying every day and week. The Appendix has some sample chore charts which might give you ideas for generating your own unique charts.

Our daily and weekly chores are divided between the older children and Mom (see Appendix). From the list of chores that must be done every day and week, we can assign each person, old enough to assist, a fair share of the work. List the person responsible for the chore next to it on the master list.

In addition to the basic weekly chores, we suggest having one or two "extra chores" which the child does once a month (see Maxwell's Extra Chore Chart in the Appendix). These are jobs that need to be done periodically but not every week. You develop this chore list by observing needs in the house when you see them. Some of these might include washing the dining room light globes, washing the tops of the washing machine and dryer, waxing the linoleum floors, dusting baseboards, dusting picture frames, and others. Most of these jobs are not difficult and can be handled by a child age ten or older.

Week 1, 2, 3, and 4 have "extra chores" assigned to them and week 5, when it occurs, is a free bonus. You can keep track of what week it is by the day you clean house. If you clean on Fridays, then the first Friday of the month "Week 1" extra chores are tackled, and the second Friday of the month "Week 2" extra chores are to be done. This list of "extra chores" grows as other areas of need are discovered.

As the disciplines of learning and establishing daily and weekly chores are being practiced, much of the eventual success will depend on Mother checking the work. Consequences should be established for either failing to do the job or doing a poor job. If necessary, these consequences begin to be administered immediately after the job details have been mastered. If you allow

be even better and will have consequences for jobs left undone, but for this time I was utterly thrilled at the efforts they made. Kathleen

You should have seen Josiah sweetly sort the laundry that was his chore to do this a.m., and dear Miss Abigail cleaning up the kitchen. I was sitting down to nurse Matthias at 7:15 a.m. or so, and there she was, wiping off the table as Samuel was sweeping! "What blessings you are, dears," I said, and they really were!! Lisa

One thing I thought of that you might want to consider mentioning more of is scheduling housework. It is easier to schedule school because we know exactly which subjects need to be done and about how much time it will take to complete. Dinner prep and eating time is pretty easy too, but there are many who do not really know where to begin with general housework.

When I was first married and even up until a few years ago, I would let most jobs accumulate until they were BIG jobs and HAD to be done. I wouldn't fold the laundry until the pile was so big on the couch that I had to do it, and even then it might not get put away for quite a few days. We always had laundry of some sort in our living room. Now I put it on the table, and it has to be folded and put away by dinner time if not before.

Simple things like, take the clothes out right away and they won't wrinkle . . . saves on ironing.

I would wait to clean the bathroom until it also got bad. One day when we were at my sister-in-law's house, she had just finished getting ready for the morning. Before leaving the bathroom, she grabbed some toilet paper and quickly wiped down the toilet. She damp mopped the floor and rinsed out the sink. The bathroom took maybe five minutes at the most, and it looked really good. She said she does this at least once, if not more, each day, and so, the bathroom is always presentable.

Now this may seem obvious to some, but I had never thought of it. I would wait until it was unbearable.

I would also do this with our kitchen stove, and then, realized that appliances and counters are best kept clean if I washed them every time I did the dishes, not just

children to get by with poor workmanship, it is unlikely to improve on its own and quite likely will actually deteriorate as the children realize what they can get by with.

To facilitate your development of a Master Chore List, we have included a chores worksheet titled, **Diligence Worksheet**, and another titled, **Diligence Assignments Worksheet**, in the **Scheduling Kit**. We used the word "diligence" rather than "chores" on these worksheets to remind us that raising diligent, responsible children—who will become diligent, responsible adults—is one of our primary goals as parents. Keeping focused on the benefit of chores, in the achievement of this goal, is a helpful mindset. When we choose to give children chores, not only will the work needed to maintain a home be accomplished, but life training will take place as well.

The worksheets will allow you to write down the chores that need to be done, determine their frequency, and then assign a person to complete the chore. Our family's Master Chore List is included in the Appendix plus two other families' real life chore charts. These should help get you started with your family's chore list.

STEPS TO DEVELOPING YOUR MASTER CHORE LIST

Step One: Start a list of the chores you feel need to be done daily, weekly, monthly, and infrequently. On the **Diligence Worksheet** (located in the **Scheduling Kit**), you can write the chore description, how frequently it needs to be done, the age at which you feel a child would be capable of accomplishing the chore, and the amount of time the chore should take. This basic information will be an aid when you begin the task of dividing up the chores.

To help you with your **Diligence Worksheet**, we have collected many chore charts—ones families are actually using! These charts will give you additional ideas based on what chores other families are having their children do. The sample chore charts are found at www.Titus2.com.

I worked on our list over the course of several days. It was easy to come up with some chores on my list, but I knew I was missing others. Each day I would be reminded of chores I wanted to add to the list. If I was out emptying trash, I might notice the garage step, that the trash can sits on, gets pretty messy. I would add to my list, "Garage step to be swept and straightened." It didn't need to be done every week so I wrote the frequency as "Monthly." I felt it would require the skills of at least a seven-year-old and take about fifteen minutes.

I also became aware that the inside of our van was looking quite junky, since the children loaded many items in to take somewhere, but never remembered to take them out. So I added, "Clean out the inside of the van," to the list as a weekly chore that would take about ten minutes and could be done by a six-year-old or older child.

There are many more chores that are being accomplished in our home, now that I have several helpers, than were tackled when I only had little children. These chores were okay with me to leave undone. It was more important to spend time with my children than to undertake these tasks. As the children have grown and are able to receive more responsibility, we now have ceiling fans dusted each week, computer screens wiped off, and hot air registers dusted.

Step Two: Assign the chores to a specific family member and a specific day to do them. You can designate the person to do the chore on the **Diligence Worksheet**. Sometimes looking at the column for capable age will easily determine who needs to do the job. If the capable age is 13 years and all of your children are ages ten and under, you will obviously be the person for that chore. Other times there will be several in the family who could be responsible for the task. You can, then, look at the "approximate times needed" to help you evenly divide the workload.

You need to decide if you want to spread weekly and monthly chores throughout the week or do them in one larger cleaning session. Monthly chores can be assigned on a weekly rotating basis. How many chore helpers there are will determine how many weekly and monthly chores each one will have. If Mom is doing most of the housework herself, there may be monthly chores that are not worth investing her time in, but will be worth assigning a child to do when he is old enough.

I suggest leaving infrequent chores to be done on Saturdays or during the summer, when school is out or slowed down. During the summer my kitchen cabinets get a thorough cleaning inside and out, the closets are cleaned, the storage shelves reorganized, and the refrigerator and stove cleaned. I keep a list of chores that are too big to take on during normal cleaning time so that, when I have a Saturday morning to devote to cleaning or need direction for summer cleaning, I know what I want to do. I have to make a list of these chores, because I forget too easily.

Once the chores have been assigned, you can transfer them to the **Diligence Assignments Worksheet** with Daily Chores, Weekly Chores, and Rotating Chores. I place our names across the top row and then fill in the chores underneath. If a weekly chore has a specific day it needs to be done, you can indicate that in the appropriate box.

when the gunk was really embarrassing.

And speaking of dishes it is best if they are done at least once a day. Getting the dish water ready before dinner, and washing up the dinner prep things is a really good idea too. You might be one who does the dishes three or more times a day but this was an adjustment for me.

Also, clean the frig right before you get groceries. Have the children do general cleanup in rooms throughout the day. Previously, I would be extremely happy if I saw the floor in my boys' bedroom once a week . . . now, it better be clean most of the day.

Actually, my room is usually the worst. I am going to try to commit to picking up every morning, right after I get dressed. Usually, I am out the door, never to return until I am ready for bed, and then I do not feel like cleaning it. Debbie

The children do so like the schedule, and it seems I can already sense less resistance to chores, since they are scheduled, along with the really fun stuff, like being read to and played with. Lisa

Well, this is the second day of our schedule, and to be honest it is overwhelming for me; I have never had a schedule before. It is flushing out discipline problems and motivational problems. And my children don't even know how to complete a task on their own!!! I did not realize what a mess we were in until now. I have not given up on the schedule, and IT IS GOING TO WORK one way or another. Sheri

You could also make up a chore chart for each child, but the advantage of our **Diligence Assignments Worksheet** is that you can quickly see exactly who is doing which chore, at what time.

Step Three: Once you have completed the **Diligence Assignments Worksheet**, post it in a place where you can refer to it easily. Ours is taped inside a cabinet in our laundry area that also holds the cleaning supplies. Within a few weeks of using your **Diligence Assignments Worksheet**, you and your children will probably have the chores memorized for each day and week, no longer needing to refer to your worksheet.

IN CONCLUSION

Chores are an important part of daily life. Children need to learn the skills involved in the chores since this is a normal responsibility. Learning to work is needful. The workload for one person, Mother, is usually greater than her time or physical energy will allow, especially if she is homeschooling. Dividing and balancing these jobs among family members frees her for other priorities that God has called her to have. The family members are learning and developing life skills and attitudes that will be useful to them. Make this important area of chores a part of your schedule. Your children's future employers and spouses will thank you.

Tracy W.'s Activity Worksheet	
Bible study	1/2 hr
Dress/Get ready	1/2 hr
Shower	1/2 hr
Breakfast	1/2 hr
Lunch	1/2 hr
Dinner/Cleanup/Morning prep	1 hr
Storytime/Naptime	1/2 hr
Sleep	7 hrs
Dinner prep	1/2 hr
Phone calls	1/2 hr
Laundry/Morning chores	1/2 hr
Cleanup toys	1/2 hr
Schooltime	4 hrs
Preschool time	1/2 hr
Rest	1/2 hr
Play outside with children/P.E.	1/2 hr
Bathe children	1/2 hr
Hymn time/Verse	1/2 hr
Goodnite to children	1/4 hr
Training time	1/2 hr
Photo albums	1/2 hr
Mending	1/2 hr
Mailbox (Time alone with each child)	1/4 hr
SSA work time	1 1/2 hr
E-mail/Learn computer skills	1/2 hr
Total	23 1/2
Weekly or Monthly Activities	
Grocery shopping (Weekly) - 1 hr	
Weekly planning (School, meals, etc.) - 1/2 hr	
Bake bread (Twice weekly) - 1 hr	
Date night (Weekly)	
Sports in park/Bike trail with Dad (Weekly)	
Go to park (Weekly)	
Invite families over for dinner (Weekly)	
Target/Costco shopping (Monthly) - 3 hours	

Dear Friends,   *October 8th*

Our family began back in the fall of 1989. For me it was love at first sight, but my husband felt I was too old and mature to even look his way. However, God brought us together about a month later, two very different people from very different backgrounds. But our Creator knows what is best and truly knows how to make two into one flesh! Our first daughter was born in March of 1991, and we named her Kati. Joshua followed in July of 1992. With three years of nurturing and growth, God saw fit to bless us with Sarah in June of 1995. And finally, for now, July of 1996 brought Braden. Our precious arrows are just that, precious. We knew we had a great responsibility before us, to raise them in the fear and admonition of the Lord.

I am desirous of an organized and scheduled type of life. It is because of this that I wanted to be a part of this program. So we prayerfully entered into the principles found in MANAGERS OF THEIR HOMES. What a God-send this book and its materials have been.

I loved the scheduling worksheets, and my husband even decided to schedule his day. Then, when we began to put everything into our master schedule, I was so amazed. The colors were wonderful, and I now knew what everyone was doing, when. More importantly to my husband, he knew what was going on daily, at home, so he could pray for us while we were doing school and call us at times that would not interfere with the schedule. He loves it. He feels in order for him to truly be in charge of our home, the Principal, so to speak, he must know the daily "ins" and "outs" of the schooling process. This system has allowed him to know exactly that.

We needed a schedule. I have never been a big supporter of just letting things happen on their own. Things simply do not get done, and I do not feel that I am being a good steward of the time God has provided to me.

We are rather busy folks, to say the least, and this schedule has greatly helped us to keep our priorities in line. Often there are days when someone will invite me to go somewhere; I look at my schedule and realize that I simply must say, "no." It is hard, but it really helps to hold me accountable to the principles God has established for me as a mommy. My husband's evening Bible Institute classes are included in our schedule, as well as the two monthly Bible studies I lead, plus my Crisis Pregnancy work.

We love this material and this program! We feel that to be organized is following directly in line with the character of God, Who Himself said that He was a God of order, not disorder and confusion. We need to follow His example. He most definitely had a plan in creation, in life, and in everything He has done. Shouldn't we, too, have a plan and some order in everything we do? This book provides the basics for doing just that. Praise the Lord for these principles and practical helps.

From Kristi

Scheduling in the Kitchen

Time in the kitchen will be a substantial part of every mother's schedule. Each of us is interested in minimizing this time and becoming more efficient with the hours we spend in the kitchen. Part of your daily schedule will include meal preparation, eating, and cleanup.

MEAL HELPERS

One of the benefits of time in the kitchen is that it can be used for dual purposes. Having a child with you will give one-on-one time with that child while they start learning valuable skills. In the beginning, having a kitchen helper will slow down your work, but by the time a child is four or five years of age they can help enough to be able to assist on their own. Working with you will teach them how to work in the kitchen without an actual "lesson" sort of situation. Your children will soon be able to do many things independently, even at four years old. Some jobs you will still do together, but when time is pressing, the child can be counted on to set the table, make tossed salads, fill the glasses with ice, and wash the preparation dishes.

As your children grow, spend some time thinking about what kitchen chores are age appropriate for each child. During the summer you will often have some extra time for teaching kitchen chores that have not already been learned by working together. At the age of three, a child can be taught to set the table. The learning process is usually fun for them, if Mom is willing to work with them patiently, meal after meal. It is a mighty proud three-year-old who announces to everyone at the dinner table, "I set the table all by myself!" And then receives the praise of his family. Six-year-olds and up can help clear the table, wash it, and sweep the floor after a meal. All of these tasks are more pleasant for the child if they are working along side, or at least at the same time as, someone else in the same room.

You can assign one child as a dinner helper for each weekday evening. I start with the oldest and work down to the youngest, so I can remember whose day it is to help. Some may find it more useful to write it on a chart. Your children will be anxious for it to be their day as the helper. They will ask, during the day, whose day it is to be the dinner helper. The praise Daddy gives them, when he learns who made his salad, lights up their faces with pleasure. You will enjoy the time you spend with your child, plus you know he is learning valuable kitchen skills under your supervision.

Have your children keep the same kitchen chores for at least a year. This is a time saver in a couple of ways. First the children become efficient at their assigned chores. They have practiced enough to

A Personal Word

I also have a half-hour block at 8:00 a.m. called "Training Time," and so far I have taught the four older children (ages seven and younger) how to wash their hands with soap in the bathroom without making a mess or pumping out half the bottle of soap; how to quickly get down from the table, put their dishes on the counter, wash their hands and face and go into the toy room; and how to do the morning routine properly (get up, dressed, make bed, tidy room, look at a book on their bed). They actually enjoy the practice time, since I am calm and not stressed. And, it's fun to have everyone else watching them as they do a task right. I have seen how just this little bit of practice has gone a long way!! I think I will keep a list of things I want to teach them (like where to stand when someone rings the doorbell, how to quickly get their seat belts on, answering the phone correctly, etc.) posted on my fridge. Tracy W.

You asked before about chores and how I worked it out. Well, that is easy; I used your method! I started a list

know them well. Second, they can accomplish their work without supervision. Then, if you want to rotate chores so they progress on to more difficult tasks and become proficient in all of them, make the changes during the summer. This is the time you would most likely be able to invest in the teaching and training of new jobs.

You may also want to have a daily, extra-kitchen-cleanup chore. These are done during the dinner-cleanup time. They are listed on a chart posted inside a cabinet door. There is a different chore for each day, Monday through Saturday. These jobs are ones that are hard to fit in at other cleaning times, but need to be done regularly. The list might include: cleaning the microwave inside and out; wiping the counters under the microwave, canisters, and mixer; damp wiping the kitchen cabinets (one-half of them on two different days); wiping the counter ledges and wallpaper; and washing the dish drainer. This system works quite well, and if there are nights when time is limited, missing the extra chore isn't of great concern.

MASTER KITCHEN LISTS

To make meal planning easier you should have a Master Meals List. This list will include all the evening dinner meals you have prepared for your family. It can be kept in your recipe box or taped inside the cupboard door. When it comes time to write out your weekly menu and you cannot think of anything to put on it, your Master Meals List is at your fingertips. It will also bring back to mind meals you have drifted away from but which might be a big hit if reintroduced. You may even choose to organize them according to low, medium, and high cost meals. This could help manage a grocery budget.

You will also want to have a Master Grocery Shopping List. This list will have items you purchase every week at the grocery store in addition to your weekly meal plan. On the right hand side of your Master Grocery Shopping List, jot the days of the week with a space beside each for writing in the meal for that evening. Staples like flour, sugar, eggs, and margarine should be on the left side of the page. Put the items you buy almost every week on this grocery shopping list. We have even arranged our list by aisles in our grocery store. This shortens the shopping time. You can generate your Master Grocery Shopping List on the computer or by hand. If you make this list by hand, photocopy a supply to last six months or a year.

When you plan the meals for the week, write them directly on the Master Grocery Shopping List, along with any needed ingredients. The master list is a tremendous help in reducing the number of trips back to the store for forgotten items. When you are filling in your shopping list for the week, the list of staples will remind you to check to see if you need any of these items. Look in your kitchen, with list in hand, as you mark down the items. You can cross off what you don't need and number or checkmark, those you do. Write in additional items, that are not on the Master Grocery Shopping List, between columns.

If this list is stored in a known place, other family members can add to it. For instance, in our home, when a staple hits half empty, it is to be written on the grocery list. Sometimes the baby is ready for a new bib or the kitchen sponge requires a replacement. These can be added to the Master Grocery Shopping List whenever the need comes to our attention.

Be sure to save the portion of your list with the weekly meal plan so that you can remember what to prepare each evening. It may sound like a big project to develop a Master Grocery Shopping List, but I assure you it will save so much time, in the long run, that you'll be pleased you decided to do it.

We have included our Master Grocery Shopping List as a sample for you to glean ideas. Since this Master Grocery Shopping List is kept in a file on the computer, I print a supply. I can pull one out of my "in-box" to keep handy on my desk, through the week, and complete before grocery shopping night.

MASTER GROCERY SHOPPING LIST

A	-	Carrots	8a	-	Frozen Corn
A	-	Lettuce	8b	-	Frozen French Fries
A	-	Broccoli	10	-	Baby Food
A	-	Apples	11	-	Toilet Paper
A	-	Bananas	16	-	Crackers
A	-	Margarine	16	-	Crackers
A	-	Milk			Pizza Sauce
1	-	Eggs			Rice Krispies (Nathan)
1	-	Tortillas			
3	-	Tomato Soup			
4	-	Macaroni and Cheese			
5	-	Frozen Pizza (end)			
5	-	Chimichangas (end)			
7	-	Sugar			
7	-	Powdered Sugar			
7	-	Flour			

Dinner Meals

Friday - Pizza
Saturday - Frozen Pizza
Sunday - Burritos
Monday -
Tuesday -
Wednesday -
Thursday -

If you shop at a bulk discount store, like SAMS Club or Costco, you will want to have a separate Master Shopping List. I have everything we buy at SAMS on this list. The night before the monthly SAMS shopping trip, I get out a copy of my master SAMS list. I go through each item on it, checking the cupboards and shelves to see what the current stock of the item is and whether it needs to be purchased. If an item is needed, I write beside it how

of things that needed to be done daily and weekly, prayed over them, and spent the next day making sure I didn't forget anything. Then I separated them by rooms for weekly chores and assigned them to the family members. Each day we work on a different room or area (i.e. Monday - Living room). In the afternoon, we do our daily chores (trash, sweeping, etc). It is working! Sheri

My six-year-old, who hates to lift a finger without much prodding, is now preparing breakfast, serving it, and cleaning up!!! PTL!!! And he is enjoying it. My seven-year-old daughter is doing the same for lunch. It is great. I saw this as a time for me to have one-on-one with my children while we prepare and cleanup. It has really been neat. Kristi

A Master Grocery List is a great idea! I am going to do one for my food co-op too! Corrie

This system for scheduling was a breath of fresh air! Even though I have been a "scheduler" out of necessity for years, it has never been so easy. Your charts and

method of setting up a schedule was fun—kind of like one big puzzle. I REALLY enjoyed doing it this way and since I have done a fair number of schedules, I know your system makes it much easier. By breaking it up into easily digestible, bite-sized pieces, it is an enjoyable job to plan your hours. Lorrie

The schedule was a little "slippery" this morning in that I did not change activities on time every time, but it did, indeed, bless me many times over. I am starting to see the benefits of having as many decisions as possible already made. I began to feel as though not enough time had been allotted for each activity, but I realize part of that is just learning the schedule. Lisa

I think it helps to be aware of the value of time and the importance of making the most of it. I am encouraged that I will have lots of time with my children as they grow up, because I am home-schooling them. However, God holds me accountable for all that time, and I need to improve on my stewardship. And, God wants us to teach our children to be good stew-

many Steve should purchase. If we are not going to buy the item, it is crossed off the list. Having this master list helps avoid forgotten items. This is especially helpful in homes where the dad does the shopping, like ours. Since Mother is not in the store, she does not have the opportunity to be reminded to buy something while walking past it on the grocery shelf.

More Time Savers

Schedule your meal planning for once a week. Instead of making that decision each day, you only have to make it once a week. Your scheduled time for this might be half an hour in the afternoon that rotates day by day. Use that time for meal planning on grocery shopping day. On other days, you might schedule this time for correspondence, phone calls, cleaning, or reading.

Consider having two or three family-favorite meals that are the same every week. For instance, in our home, Friday night is home-made pizza night; Saturday is Steve's and my date night, so the children cook frozen pizza and french fries; and Sunday's dinner is burritos. Every one in our family likes those meals and looks forward to having them. This makes three meals for my weekly menu without any thought at all. That brings it down to four meals, for variety, during the week.

This idea helps for lunches, too, but with lunch you can take it even further. The goal is to eliminate as many decisions as possible—since decisions take up much of your time and emotional energy. Plan the same thing for lunch every Monday, and something different for Tuesday but have that same thing each Tuesday. If you do this for each day of the week, you have given

Master Lunch Menu	
Monday	Ramen
Tuesday	Tortillas and cheese
Wednesday	Soup
Thursday	Frozen burritos
Friday	Leftovers
Saturday	Macaroni and cheese

yourself some valuable extra time that you used to spend making lunch menu decisions.

Whenever possible, double your evening meal, freezing one batch. Some people do once-a-month cooking, but for others that is not a viable option. Making two meals at a time, and freezing one, is a worthwhile time saver. Making more than a double batch often means extra preparation time. This is not reasonable for a routine dinner meal and would cause greater time for packaging and cleanup. Use your frozen meals on nights when you know you will not have your normal meal preparation time.

Another time saving tip is to only plan meals that can be completed in an hour. Save more time-consuming meals for the weekend. Your evening dinner preparation will be scheduled, but if you plan meals with lengthy preparation time, you will be cutting into some other scheduled block. There are meals, particularly soups, which must be started in the morning. These will be harder because they require morning time that has already been designated for other things. When you do have a meal that needs to cook all day, you can sometimes put it together the night before. This only works, though, if there is room in the refrigerator for the pot or pan!

IN CONCLUSION

Kitchen time must be scheduled and can be streamlined. Always be on the lookout for ways to economize these hours in the kitchen. Be open to reevaluating how you do your kitchen work. Learning how to manage your kitchen responsibilities, and feeling in control of them, will go a long ways toward freeing up time in your schedule for other priorities.

ards of the time He gives them too. *Debbie*

I love the way you write!! The style is friendly and encouraging, and familiar Scriptures are used in an appropriate and very helpful manner. Ellen

Tonight the children were talking about their scheduled, evening, children's playtime with Mom. Josiah said, "I want to keep doing this schedule. Okay, Mommy?" Did I really ever think they would NOT like a schedule that would give them several blocks of time with their parents? Lisa

Dear Friends,   *November 14th*

My name is Lisa, and I am married to dear Kurt. We have been married for almost 7 years, and we have 5 blessings so far: the twins, Josiah and Abigail (6); Samuel (4); Jesse (2); and Matthias (5 months). This is our second year homeschooling.

I realized that this year held many more challenges for me: a new baby, first grade, and Samuel in K4. I am also learning to play the piano, and I want to acquire milk goats. How in the world to fit it all in?? I did not like promising the children something, and then not getting to it, like reading to them, doing crafts with them, and sewing things for them!

I desired very much to have my days under control enough that, when my husband came home, he would not feel as though he was starting his second job! I wanted coming home to be peaceful and relaxing. I did not want to "need" him so much he could not enjoy his children and wife.

When I saw that Teri was asking for volunteers, I jumped at the chance. However, the working out of the schedule was a special challenge to me. I had not learned to diligently work on a task, a little at a time, seeing it slowly and faithfully to its finish. I had become accustomed to the all-or-nothing strategy, which was not working at all. As I was encouraged to by Teri, I worked on my schedule-making for a half an hour a day, until it was done.

I was implementing parts of my schedule before I finished it, and more since. Each day I follow it, I am blessed in many ways. It is such a relief and a freedom to be able to do a certain thing for a period of time and then stop, knowing that it will come around again tomorrow. Feeling overwhelmed by a month's work that you want to accomplish in one day is no fun, but when you create a schedule for your family, the schedule controls such feelings. Isaiah 28:10, which says, "For precept must be upon precept, precept upon precept; line upon line, line upon line; here a little, and there a little," is borne out as you do the things in a day that your husband and the Lord would have you do. "To every thing there is a season, and a time to every purpose under the heaven . . ." This verse is truly lived out when you have a wise schedule for your family!

It has been especially blessed to do preschool time with my two-year-old. He has learned "Zaccheus" and "The Wise Man," and he LOVES having me spend time coloring with him, writing his name, and such. My children have also enjoyed knowing that there are certain times for work and certain times for play and fun with Mommy and Poppy. I find they don't mind the work so much when I remind them that we only have to fold laundry for a half an hour! Time for me to read to them happens twice in the day, and there is also a playtime when we can do puzzles together or play with their toys. I feel like more of the mommy God wants me to be when I make time for these things! I thank the Lord and the Maxwells for their sacrifice in writing this book!

From Lisa

Scheduling for Priorities

Four jumpers, two culotte jumpers, two vests, two baby outfits, one skirt, putting ruffles on ten baby outfits turning them from pant sets to dresses, plus keeping current on mending projects. That is the list I came up with as I thought back over my sewing accomplishments the past eight months. Is it really possible to run a home with eight children, homeschool them, lead a local homeschool support group, and sew? Absolutely! "Well, how do you ever find time?" you ask. I'd love to share the key to this treasure of mine because, for me, having time to sew is a treasure.

A Half-Hour a Day

This special key is "a half-hour a day." I have scheduled in my day a half-hour of sewing every afternoon during the week. It takes time to get the project out and to put it away so actual sewing is only 20 to 25 minutes. Over the course of a year, just a little bit each day adds up to—four jumpers, two culotte jumpers, two vests . . . You might think, "Why bother for such a few minutes to actually sew?" For me, the slow, steady progress and accomplishment is better than not sewing at all. If I did not have this half-hour set aside for sewing, I would not get around to it. Other urgent things would fill this time space. So at 1:30 p.m., I am busy. I do not plan other activities during this time. It is reserved for sewing.

Fifteen Minutes a Day

My schedule continues, even at 3:30 p.m. You might question, "What is she doing since school is over for the day?" Once more I will share the key to my treasure. I had a desire in my heart, for a couple of years, to have reading time with our little children. Between homeschooling, household chores, meals, babies, and toddlers there always seemed to be something to keep me from sitting down and reading to our precious children. This special key is "fifteen minutes a day." Beginning several years ago, I scheduled a fifteen minute reading period for Joseph and John at the end of their naps, while the littler ones were still sleeping. Then, the next year I added another reading session for John and Anna, since Anna was now old enough to enjoy being read to. Finally another year, I included a separate reading period for Jesse, then a toddler, right after his nap ended. Now Mary, our youngest, has joined Jesse's reading time.

Reading out loud to my children totals forty-five minutes of my afternoon. It started with only fifteen minutes a day. Reading time is planned and set aside in our schedule just like our morning school, therefore, it happens every day. These are cherished minutes, looked forward to by the chil-

CHAPTER EIGHT

A Personal Word

I am grateful for the schedule, because even though I am not yet doing everything planned, I have read to my children more then ever, and my two boys are taking Spanish, something I wanted to do for years but "never got around to it!" J'Aimée

We also have "individual time" with each child. The children go to bed by 9:00 p.m., and each child gets a turn to stay up for an extra fifteen to thirty minutes to spend with me. My daughter's time is Thursday evening. We have decided, that at least for now, that is going to be our "tea time." We fill the tea pot with concentrated juice and the creamer with water, so she can add the water to the juice in the cups to dilute it. Last Thursday was our first tea time. We both enjoyed it, and she is looking forward to this Thursday. I believe these children will keep me accountable on this aspect of the schedule. They each have different ideas as to how they would like to spend their time. I have wanted to do this for years but never set a specific time. Cindy

dren and me. It is a special, close, memory-building time. And, it is a portion of the day properly devoted to some of my highest priorities rather than being driven by the urgent.

Here is another "fifteen minute a day" example. John, as a kindergartner, came to me begging to learn to read so he could read his Bible. With a new baby, I had not planned to teach him to read until first grade, but how could a mommy turn down such a godly request? Though I wanted to fulfill his desire, I could not even come up with a half-hour block of time to work with him. I began praying and discussed it with Steve. Then the Lord showed me I had some fifteen minute time segments throughout the day that I could devote to phonics with John. As we got started, I found four of these times each day. I was able to work with him for a total of one hour a day, and the fifteen minute lessons were probably better for his attention span than a solid hour would have been.

A Half-Hour Twice a Week

I will give you one more key to my treasure. This key is a half-hour once or twice a week. Again, I had a yearning in my heart to have one-on-one time with our younger children. But, as usual, the weeks would fly by with the normal routine and no special individual time with a child. Then the Lord showed me that even if I could not spend individual playtime with each child each day, I could do it once or twice a week. So I started having an individual preschool time with each of our little ones twice a week. Were they unhappy that it didn't happen every day? No, they looked forward to their preschool time on their day. Presently with our new group of preschool children, we have a scheduled preschool half-hour four mornings a week.

As the children grow older, preschool time no longer fits the age so the title changes to fun school. This is a time I spend with one child when they get to pick the activity from a list of fun educational choices.

Scheduling Treasures Passed On

Even our older children are implementing some of these scheduling ideas they have seen me practice over the past few years. At age 16, Sarah still had playtime with the little ones each day, but she also began another special time with Anna, who was five, once a month. Steve and our two older boys had a church men's meeting once a month, so that meant Sarah and I were home with the little ones. Sarah had a dolly or paper doll playtime with Anna for half an hour that night. It is something she had wanted to do with Anna, but it never happened. This type of play didn't seem to work well when the little boys and baby were a part of the group. Now that it was planned and scheduled, there was no way to forget it; Anna made sure of that! Jesse, the next youngest one after Anna, soon began asking Sarah for a playtime with just him!

Nathan, when he was 21 years old, began to have a half-hour model making time with Joseph, who was eight. It was set for 7:30 p.m. each Saturday. They had a little "modeling" table in a corner of Steve's shop. Nathan produced a big bag of Starburst candy that he put on the table to be enjoyed as they worked together. The other children could "hang" around if they didn't become disruptive. They could have some candy too.

We appreciate our older children seeing the value of spending time with their younger siblings. It brings great joy to our hearts when they choose to use their discretionary time in this way. They have had assigned playtime that was required of them to spend with their younger brothers and sisters through the years. But now, they are continuing to do this when it is no longer mandatory.

You are laying the foundations in your family in these areas of relationships. By your example of scheduling your day, being careful to keep relationship priorities in focus, you are modeling this discipline for your children. By scheduling playtimes for just two children together, you are helping them develop relationships built to last a lifetime.

IN CONCLUSION

What is this treasure which I have been giving you my keys to? The treasure is time spent on the priorities God has led me to have. The Lord has given us each the same number of hours in our day and responsibilities, which we must fulfill during this time. We can always be driven by the urgent, or we can take control of our days. We can set aside time for not only the responsibilities but also those God-given "heart desires." Scheduling allows for all of these to happen. Our time is our most valuable asset, but we must take charge of how it is used.

These are examples from my life. What about you? What project have you put off because you never have time for it? What have you wanted to do with your children but are always too busy for? Seek the Lord to see if He would have you spend any of your time in these areas. If He directs, try scheduling fifteen or thirty minutes, each day at a set time, and make those things happen. See how even a little bit, day after day, can net satisfying results at the end of a month or year. Try the key to the treasure which the Lord has given to me. Perhaps it will be the key to unlocking treasure in your life too.

I am a very organized person, although I was not born this way; I've grown into it out of necessity with six children. I have always had a schedule for my family since we began homeschooling. For me the beauty of your system has been the ease of setting it up. I LOVE your worksheets and step by step approach. I know that someone who has never worked out a schedule before would find it so easy with your system that they would wonder what all the fuss over scheduling drudgery was about. You lead us through it so gently and in such small, easy to swallow steps (just the way we should train our children!!!) that it is no big deal. Lorrie

I believe this book was a gift from God. I know that it will be just the vehicle I need to accomplish His plans. I'm excited about it. Sheila

Dear Friends,   October 11th

We are Randy and Lorrie Flem of Maple Valley, Washington, and the proud parents of John (11), Levi (8), Drew (6), Dessaly (4), Kiley (2), and Haley (12 weeks old). Randy has an insurance brokerage, and I'm so glad that I get to be a stay-at-home mom and homeschooler! I love being home!

For our family of eight, a schedule is mandatory in order to accomplish anything! This is not a matter of personal preference but a necessity for my sanity! With no schedule to follow, the days just melt away with me simply trying to mop up the messes and have some semblance of dinner ready before Daddy gets home. I have been known to sauté garlic so that it at least SMELLS as if something has been done for dinner!

By following our own family's custom schedule, we have a vision for how it is possible to accomplish certain things that we need to do each day. More than that, with our schedule we are able to successfully finish MORE than ever before, so it is not just our basic needs that we finish. With a plan we are able to enjoy some of the before only dreamt of things, like quilting and writing a newsletter!

At first glance, the time required to juggle everything around may seem to be too much. Let me assure you that it is worth every minute. In fact, my initial investment of time has paid off with interest. Our schedule actually "gives" us more time because we don't use precious minutes with Mom trying to figure out what needs to be done. By having it all spelled out in advance we have the consistency we need to keep on track and enough flexibility to avoid too much backtracking.

I could say so much more, but I am afraid you will be wondering what button to push in order to turn me off! I love our schedule and the freedom that its structure provides us.

From Lorrie

Planning for the School Year

For homeschool families, time must be spent preparing for each new school year. Because home-schooling works best when both husband and wife are involved, planning for the school year should be done together. This will obviously need to occur in the spring or summer prior to each upcoming school year.

Ideally, it is great for the couple to go away for the planning day. If your husband works in an office building, this can be an excellent place. Often there is a conference room you could use on a Saturday. Take your music, snacks, and materials. The room will be quiet, without disturbances; the chairs comfortable. We have enjoyed the availability of a big white board in the conference room that we used. We make many notes on it. A church would be another possibility for finding an open room for a husband and wife school-planning day. If you cannot get away for the day, try to have activities planned to keep the children busy so you will have as few interruptions as possible.

PREPARATION AND PRAYER

We suggest Mom prepare an information sheet for her husband. She is the one more intimately involved in the schooling and will need to give her husband some background information to pray over, and upon which to base decisions. The information sheet will include:

What the school schedule was like the past year.

What subjects each child studied.

How much time was given to each subject.

What went well through the year.

What didn't go well.

What changes should be considered for the coming year.

What materials you are interested in using.

This sheet should be made up and given to the husband several weeks before the planning session. This will give him time to read it, pray over it, and ask any questions that would need to be addressed before the planning day.

CHAPTER NINE

A Personal Word

There is so much I want to do with the children but never seem to have time. I want to spend more time studying character traits but always seem to be just surviving. Those things that should be most important get pushed aside. Cindy

The schedule helps me see what we are actually doing (and not getting done). Time goes by so quickly with little ones that I don't want to waste anymore time. J'Aimée

You're right about the time it will take to make my schedule. I prayed, "Lord, I have my timeline, but please show me Yours. And please show me how to fit it all in." Well, that's why I believe your book is an answer to prayer. Sheila

When you arrive at the location you selected for your planning day, get everything set up. Then pray. You want to seek the wisdom and guidance of Jesus Christ as you begin making decisions that will affect the next nine months and your children's future.

GOALS AND PLANS

Spend some time listing strengths, weaknesses, and goals for each child. This will give you direction on making decisions for the school year. You can later take the goal sheet, which has two or three goals per child on it, type it, and post it on your bathroom mirror so you can be reminded of your focus for each child throughout the school year.

The final step of your planning day will be to make a school plan for each child. You can review possible school materials, if you have brought them with you, or you can read catalog descriptions. Make a list of what you want that child to study. Prioritize what is to be done. And then you can decide, bearing in mind the length of your school day, how much time per day or week to have the child spend on each subject. This is where the large white board can come in handy, by listing and working with these subjects and the times available. Your ideals and wants for what your children should do in a school year may be greater than the amount of time allotted for school!

Once these decisions are jointly made, it is up to the wife to work out the actual schedule of how the school day will function, unless she wants help. Generally each new school year will necessitate another schedule to accommodate the changes that come with it. Because this will be time consuming, you will not want to leave school-planning day until the last minute. The actual scheduling requires a great deal of prayer and time to put the pieces of the schedule together. Often there will be school books that need to be ordered. Looking through catalogs and preparing the order will also require time.

IN CONCLUSION

Apply every effort possible to make a school-planning day a yearly event. You will anticipate this day. It may be a highlight of your spring or summer; it is for us. Your hearts will be knit together as you pray about and discuss your children and their future. You will enjoy the talking and planning, and you will be pleased with the decisions you come to. Excitement is built for the new school year. Your school-planning day will be the foundation upon which your school year schedule rests.

Cindy's Activity Worksheet	
Dress/Bedroom	1/2 hr
Quiet time/Character quality focus/Nurse	1 hr
Exercise/Shower	1/2 hr
Breakfast/Cleanup	1 hr
School	4 hr
Amanda 1/2 hr	
Caleb and Mitchell 1 hr	
Listen to reading 1/2 hr	
Joshua 1/2 hr	
History 1/2 hr	
Math 1/2 hr	
Science 1/4 hr	
Greek/Latin 1/4 hr	
General cleanup (Kitchen)	1/2 hr
Lunch	1/2 hr
Get little ones down for nap/Read out loud/Nurse	1/2 hr
Paperwork (Bills, letters, filing, etc.) or Errands	1/2 hr
Rest or Errands	1/2 hr
Character quality focus	1/4 hr
Read to David	1/2 hr
Individual children's time	1/2 hr
Dinner prep	1 hr
Dinner and Cleanup	1 hr
Little ones baths/Play with Mom/Ready for bed	1 hr
Evening devotions and Scripture memorization	1/2 hr
Computer	1/2 hr
Time with David	1/2 hr
Sleep	7 1/2 hrs
Cello practice/Stamping or Errands	1/2 hr
Train dog	1/4 hr
Total	23 1/2 hrs

Dear Friends,   November 4th

My name is Pauline, and I am 32 years old with six children. Their ages are 12, 7, 6, 3, 2, and 4 months.

Organization has never been easy for me. I would much rather do whatever was fun at the moment. I knew I needed to improve in this area, especially with the number of our children increasing. I had prayed for years for the Lord to send someone to disciple me in this area, so when Teri mentioned she was looking for test families, I jumped at the chance.

I knew I needed some accountability in order to stick with this project. I had tried other planners and organizers, but they were just blank forms, and I could never get them filled out. As I read Teri's book, I was so excited that I couldn't wait to get started. She actually addressed issues I deal with, and explained how to handle them, fitting them into my schedule. I am a real visual, hands-on, tell-me-how-to-do-it type person, and that's exactly how Teri attacks this job of scheduling. Before the schedule, I had a routine; you know, bedtimes, meals, etc., but never a written schedule. There is a difference. Routine is subject to change at any given time, but when there is a written plan, you feel committed to it. You don't have to think about what you should do or what you need to do; it's all written down and is well thought out and prayed over.

At first when I started the process, I was a little overwhelmed and wanted to give up, but thank goodness I couldn't. Once I got to the cutting of the "squares" and the "sticky tac," I was somewhat irritated, thinking it was a waste of time. But as I dug in and got my hands on it, I realized how much fun it was and how the scheduling process came alive to me. It was an answer to prayer for this visual, hands-on mom! The children loved helping with the "sticky tac."

There are times when we don't follow our schedule totally or even at all. I really feel the effects of that. We don't accomplish nearly as much, and the children start "bouncing off the walls." At those times, my schedule keeps calling me back. When we are on our schedule, there is much more peace; we get much more done; and I don't feel stressed by making decisions all day. The children no longer say, "May I do this or that?" They just look at the schedule. When we are off the schedule, they sure let me know about it. They seem to feel more secure when they know what to expect.

From Pauline

Scheduling Summer

For many families, a summer schedule will vary from the schedule they use during the school year. Individual preferences for what you want to accomplish during the summer will determine what your schedule is like.

If the desire is for a break from routine, then summer may be left rather open with just the basics for life maintenance scheduled. The time between necessities can be left for relaxing, free play, fun directed activities—whatever happens to seem right. This could be a needed and refreshing change for a family. It can also be an opportunity to slow down the pace of life.

SCHOOL THROUGH THE SUMMER

It is common to find that freedom from routine brings more problems than blessings. All the reasons for scheduling that we have discussed will apply to summer months. At our August homeschool support group meeting, we ask the ladies to share what they are looking forward to about their school year. Usually there are several who say, "I am most excited about getting back onto our schedule."

We have used our summers to do light schoolwork—reading and math—so that we can have easy days on Fridays, throughout the school year. The children know, that for every day they do math and reading through the summer, they do not have to do those subjects on Fridays during the school year. Four days of school for ten weeks during the summer gives us forty days of completed work in those subjects, just about perfect for a 36 week school year. Having some schoolwork gives positive direction to the children's summer days. They love having their Fridays "light" during the school year, and they are motivated to keep up with math and reading through the summer.

SCHEDULED SUMMER ACTIVITIES

I use summer months for organizing and cleaning. Setting aside a specific hour each day, I can make fantastic progress on projects I wish to tackle. I work for the hour and quit no matter where I am in the project, then pick it up the next day. The older children play with and occupy little ones for me during this time. When this is not possible, I put summer cleaning and organizing in the evening, if my husband is available to watch the children. This is not my preference, though, because there is not the same energy level for cleaning, by evening, as in the morning.

I keep a running list through the school year of jobs I would like to get to, but cannot fit into the schedule. These include: cleaning the refrigerator, kitchen and bathroom cupboards; organizing closets, storage shelves, and school boxes; packing winter clothes away; putting photos in albums; making a school schedule; and more.

A Personal Word

We stayed on the schedule until 5 p.m. yesterday. My six-year-old daughter made a comment about how great our day was. There was no fussing and complaining; everyone knew that they had direction to their day, and it went very smoothly. I think the best thing was not having to rush madly around the house in the evening preparing for my hubby to come home. Everything was completed with time to run and refresh myself before he arrived!! I think the best thing for my children was getting to play with things like playdough. We don't usually have time for that! It's amazing how much time my schedule gives me for special things like that!! Tracy L.

I am so grateful for this help. You have made my family very happy! We have been needing something like this for a long time (and will need it already in place when more children come along). We have tried so many other things and given up after a few days of frustration. Thank you so much. I know we will not give this one up. We will just keep

I plan time to spend with the children in activities we do not have time for during the school year. Usually I will manage to schedule a half an hour a day with each child. Science experiments go well, with this time, for the school age children. We discovered science experiments proceed more smoothly when it is only Mother and one child. If we attempt a science experiment with all the children, it often turns into chaos. I come away frustrated, rather than feeling good about our time together. During my individual time with each younger child, we work puzzles, play games, do an art project, or perhaps read.

We also have a scheduled time for a morning walk and an evening playtime with Mom, in the backyard. Having these "fun" times planned and written into the schedule gives me accountability. I do not continue cleaning for longer than my hour because a child knows it is his time with Mommy. I don't have to review back over the summer and feel that I didn't take time to play with the children in the backyard. It is part of the schedule; the children know it; I know it; and we play.

You can look over your upcoming school year, what your plans are for how much school you will do, and organize your summer around that. It will allow you to know how many weeks you can fully take off, how many for a light school schedule, and where to fit these weeks. I always plan for some leeway to cover school days lost to unforeseen circumstances such as illness.

SUMMER CHARACTER TRAINING

A very beneficial use of summer time is to work diligently with your children in discipline and child training areas. Schedule this character training into your summer days.

Do you have a child who is struggling with making his bed neatly? Use part of character training time each morning, for a week, to go over the basics of making a bed with him. Demonstrate the process, talking through the steps. Then watch as your child tries on his own. You will be amazed at how much this helps those weak areas.

What about accountability? Are you frustrated when you walk through the dining room to find the floor sweeper has done a poor job? Use your summer time to target these needs and prompt yourself to check up on your children's proficiency. If they are not completing their jobs according to the standards you have set, go back to the training time and reteach the tasks.

Character issues can also be addressed with the slower pace of summer. One summer we were teaching our children to answer with, "Yes, Ma'am. No, Ma'am. Yes, Sir. No, Sir." This was accomplished by dropping one M&M

candy into a mug with their name on it each time they responded in the desired fashion. Then periodically they were allowed to eat their candy. We made this into a game during character training time, several days, when there was a major cleanup to be done.

"Jesse."

"Yes, Ma'am."

"Please pick up the Legos."

"Yes, Ma'am." Two M&M's are popped into his mouth and another one when he returns after finishing his pick up.

"Anna."

"Yes, Ma'am."

"Mommy wants you to take these dirty socks and put them in the dirty clothes hamper."

"Yes, Ma'am." Again, two M&M's are immediately eaten and a third one given when she returns. We continue until all the little tasks are completed, and would you believe they don't want to stop, even when we can't find anything else to do?

SUMMER CHARACTER GOALS

Targeting two or three character goals for the summer will give a positive focus to this time. Remind your children frequently through the day of these goals. Find Scriptures you can memorize that reinforce the goals. Learn a hymn or Christian children's song as part of the theme. Bring up these goals when situations occur that have positively demonstrated fulfillment. On the other hand, there will certainly be examples of missing the goal—discuss these too. Make a game of play-acting positive situations involving your goals.

Make up little books about the character focus. The children will love to write, illustrate, and read these books. If a child is too young to write, he can dictate the story to you, but do the drawing himself. We have some books made by our children when they were three and four-year-olds, which we treasure. The people are heads with arms and legs, and the stories they thought up to illustrate the character trait are wonderful.

Here are our goals for one summer:

1. Obedience with a good attitude. "Children, obey your parents in the Lord: for this is right. Honour thy father and mother; (which is the first command-

working out any glitches.
Kathy

I have finished the book and it was very well written and inspiring. J'Aimée

I am going to put together a Saturday schedule, for extra chores/projects. We don't usually do regular school on Saturdays, but there are larger jobs that need to be done, and I've been wondering how to schedule them in. I'm thinking I'll just allot two hours each Saturday for things like cleaning dressers and closets, cleaning out the van and garage (where we keep shoes and coats), maybe mopping floors, neatening up school supply shelves, etc. Most of this will be done by the older children, who are used to getting up early now (praise the Lord!).

Anyway, as an incentive, they are permitted to get up as early as they want (and I expect it to be early!) to do their chores and get them done, so they can play and do other projects or whatever on Saturdays. This will help me to not be tempted to do chores on Sundays, because I will know I'm going to have the time to do them during the week. And there will definitely be a hot cocoa treat involved!

I was really thrilled when I realized I had one whole day more than I was counting on. Debbie

I also appreciate how you emphasized the Lord as being the first priority in implementing our schedules. As you said, our schedules don't run as well as we would like without Him as the key, so I know that has been part of my problem—I'm making that area my first priority for improvement. Renée

ment with promise;) That it may be well with thee, and thou mayest live long on the earth" (Ephesians 6:1-3).

2. No complaining or arguing. "Do all things without murmurings and disputings: That ye may be blameless and harmless, the sons of God . . ." (Philippians 2:14,15).

3. Choose to be kind. "With all lowliness and meekness, with longsuffering, forbearing one another in love" (Ephesians 4:2).

These were lofty goals, but very necessary in our home. I need constant reminders and encouragement toward the behavior the Lord desires in me. It is the same with our children. "But exhort one another daily, while it is called To day; lest any of you be hardened through the deceitfulness of sin" (Hebrews 3:13).

In Conclusion

Summer could be a time for throwing out the schedule—if that seems beneficial to you and your family. Or it might be a time for a modified schedule, planned to meet the needs and goals you have for that summer. Whichever way you want to go, make it a prayed-about, thought-about, and discussed-with-your-husband decision!

Pauline's Activity Worksheet	
Quiet time	1/2 hr
Exercise/Shower	1 hr
Breakfast/Devotions	1 hr
Morning chores	1/2 hr
Lunch	1/2 hr
Prep for naps	1/2 hr
Rest	1/2 hr
Computer time	1/2 hr
Time with David and Prayer	1/2 hr
Sleep	7 hrs
Dinner prep	1 hr
Dinner	1 hr
Individual playtime with Mom	1/2 hr
Laundry folding	1/2 hr
Bath/Ready for bed or Playtime	1 hr
Nurse	3 hrs
School	4 1/2 hrs
Preschool 1/2 hr	
Hannah and Garrett 1 hr	
Phonics with Hannah and Garrett 1/2 hr	
Tutor Dustin 1 hr	
Voice of the Martyrs 1/2 hr	
Mom's free time	1/2 hr
Total	24 1/2 hrs

To find out how Pauline compensated for the extra time listed on her Activity Worksheet, you may want to look at her schedule in the Appendix.

Dear Friends, **October 24th**

We are Martin and Rebecca, parents of five: Emma (11), Caroline (8), Ben (6), Hannah (4), and Drew (1). We homeschool our children, and I also run a small business, mostly from the home. About the time we implemented this schedule, my husband started a new job, which was requiring longer hours than before. I had spent the months prior to finding this book feeling extremely overwhelmed. I was starting to wonder if my children would make it to adulthood! And if they did, would they be able to spell adulthood??? Would they know the true color of the bathroom floor??

We have not managed to be on our schedule ALL day long, but our mornings and evenings are in MUCH better shape, as is schooltime. What remains to conquer are the afternoon hours; it is so easy to just throw up my hands at that point and do whatever is calling to me, rather than what I am scheduled to do! The problem with that is that I end up catering to the urgent, rather than the important!! I run to the store INSTEAD of spending time with my four-year-old!

I have to say that putting the schedule together caused me to truly reevaluate my priorities in a way that nothing else could. Just as you apportion the money you have available each month, making your priorities painfully obvious, I was having to prioritize my time! The main change I made was spending far less time on business than I was before, and you know, business is still right where I want it! I believe God blesses us when we set our priorities following His will.

I will never be a super-clean, super-organized kind of person; however, I am getting ever so much more accomplished since implementing the schedule. It has truly been a blessing to our family!

From Rebecca

Chapter 11

Challenges to Scheduling

With all the benefits of scheduling extolled in this book, you are probably wondering if there are any challenges! Well, there are . . .

INFLEXIBILITY

The first obvious challenge to scheduling is a tendency to become inflexible. What do you do when your schedule says it is time for phonics and the child is sick? Or what about a regular outing with Grandma to deliver Meals-on-Wheels—regular, but not every week? The schedule is a tool. It helps us, setting the structure for our day. Generally it will work well, but there are times when you will change it for a special need that arises. In our example, a sick child can be released from his schedule to rest and recover from the illness. He can be nursed, loved, and cuddled close to Mom when possible, while she continues through her scheduled day. A regular outing like Meals-on-Wheels can be planned into the schedule, when the schedule is being set up, so it creates as little disruption as possible. The solution to inflexibility is to be willing to let go of the schedule when necessary. Start it again as soon as you can, but do not be upset when it has been changed for a short while.

SCHEDULE TOO FULL

Another disadvantage will occur if you have filled your schedule too full or not allowed enough time for each task. With this, you feel pressured and rushed all day, perhaps even frantic and harried. You will be pushing your family to keep up with the schedule. This is a most unpleasant way to live, for you and them.

If you have more activities than time on your schedule, you will need to do some rethinking. Start by praying. Ask the Lord for wisdom, to wisely use your time, and creativity, to properly arrange it. Just because it appears you have more to do than time to do it does not mean you have to despair. There are solutions.

There may be something scheduled every day that you could do every other day or even twice a week. For example, there might be time in your schedule for a daily read aloud session with the children, but not for a playtime with each one too. In that case, you might give each child a playtime with you every other day. Another possibility is that you could cutback on the amount of time given to an activity. In this same example, consider changing the playtime from one hour to one-half hour a day.

A Personal Word

I have a horrible tendency to make schedules that cram too much into a day. I feel defeated, and subsequently choose to "stick my head in the sand" and let my days schedule themselves. But at the end of the day (week, month, or year!), I find that a vital area, something that should be a priority, has been totally neglected. Ellen

Didn't realize just how busy I was till I saw it all on paper! Ricki

My schedule is working quite well and it has made a big difference around here even though we have not yet done a whole day of the schedule. My husband has been quite pleased with the results and has been advising and encouraging me not to cram too much in my day. Sally

I must be honest and say that I haven't followed the schedule to the letter with the times and such. BUT, after reading the book and preparing the schedule, I'm sure that I have accom-

Sometimes we find ourselves doing things with our time because we have always done it that way. It may be time to teach and train children to handle some of the household work that you are still doing.

Perhaps you are doing tasks that could be done less often. Washing sheets is an example from my life. As I grew up, my mother washed our sheets every week, so that is what I started out doing. With a growing family, this task took up more and more of my time, since the children were too little to do this themselves. Each week as I removed the sheets from the beds, I noticed they were not dirty nor did they smell bad. I began to wonder why I washed something that had no need of washing. Could it be tradition, based on an earlier generation's lesser frequency of bathing? So I began waiting to wash sheets until there was a need—smelly, wet, or dirty. This was a great time saver for me.

When you are feeling pushed by the schedule, this disadvantage is solved by putting more time in the schedule than the task requires. For example, when scheduling your one-on-one schooltime with a child put in extra flex time. This way you are relaxed while working with them and can peacefully deal with interruptions when they come, rather than being angry because they might keep you from finishing. If a child is having difficulty with a school subject, there will be extra time to work on it rather than feeling you must push on to keep the schedule.

What about outside commitments? If you don't have time to meet your home and family responsibilities, it is time to relieve yourself of some of those other commitments, which are not absolutely necessary. Even if they seem absolutely necessary, they may still need to go!

You can ask your husband for help in discerning what to eliminate, stream-line, or delegate, so you will have time for everything you need to do. No wonder many of us are frustrated when there are more tasks in our day than time to do them. You can absolutely not do more than there is time in the day, but you can absolutely be sure there is time to do everything God intends for you to do. However, if you don't limit your commitments, you may be burdened and pressured constantly; you will feel sorry for yourself, not having the peace and contentment the Lord intended you to have.

HUSBAND'S PREFERENCES

You are planning to develop a daily schedule. Where does your husband fit into this scheme? We need to recall that we are our husband's helpmeet—not the other way around. I would never attempt to schedule my husband's time. Does your husband have a plan for his time at home? If so, make sure you are cooperative. If he does not have a schedule, he may still give you direction concerning his desire for dinner time, family devotion time, and bedtimes; if you ask for his input. Then you can arrange your evening activities to accommodate his preferences.

My husband does not have a written schedule for his evenings or weekends, but he does have specific times for meals, exercise, family devotions, and bedtimes. I plan a schedule for the evening that involves the children and me. But, this schedule is open to variation depending on what Daddy is doing and who can be included with him. He has set 8:45 p.m. as the time for our family evening devotion. I make sure the children are all ready for bed so we can be prompt for Daddy's devotion.

Schedule Too Great a Focus

The last challenge is a possibility of focusing more on the schedule than the goals of the schedule. Once again, the schedule is a tool to help you accomplish what you believe God has called you to. We are dependent on Jesus Christ, not a schedule. We need to seek His help in implementing and adhering to our schedule, and His wisdom for determining if the situation calls for flexibility. We must consult Him when the schedule needs refining or additions. Keep the schedule as the tool and Jesus Christ as the Master Director. Then our focus will be right, and the schedule will be a help toward success in life.

In Conclusion

Each of the challenges to scheduling can be overcome. They are warning signs to cause reevaluation of where your heart is concerning your schedule. These challenges will drive you to the Lord, seeking His solutions. The solution may be as simple as rearranging a few pieces of the schedule or it may be as complex as learning to rest in your husband's leadership of the home. Whatever the case, scheduling challenges need not cause you to abandon the schedule, but rather to look for solutions, keeping your eyes on the benefits your schedule has afforded you and your family.

plished more than I would have without it—such as with school for Katie (seven years) and even with Hannah (four years) which I never would have done. My schedule helps me know the goals I have in mind during school hours. I'd like to implement more chores for the children, but they are already doing more than ever before, and they know that they do them after my shower and before school, even if it doesn't happen at exactly 8:30 a.m. I want you to know that we have not given up on the time part either. We have already achieved major improvements with what we're doing, and I plan to progress gradually to sticking to the time part of the schedule more as we go through the school year. Renée

Dear Friends,   October 20th

We are Dale and Renée Pratt. We have been married for nine years, going on forever. We have four children (so far): Katie Sue is 7, Hannah is 4, William is nearly 3, and Ben is 8 months. We met and married in Greeley, Colorado, where Dale went to college and I was born and raised. After we were married, we lived in Southern California for about six years. During that time, Katie and Hannah were born. The schools and lifestyle in Southern California helped to convince us that homeschooling was the best way to give our children the education they needed. We moved back to Greeley three years ago and have been happily reunited with my family and a slower pace. The community is more agreeable to our choices about parenting, but the schools still leave something to be desired.

We are strongly holding to our convictions to serve God first and foremost and raise our children with those same values. However, as our family has grown, so have our concerns about how to manage it all while maintaining everything else in life which demands attention. Needless to say, with four children, and more to come if God continues to bless us in that way, we have reached a high level of anxiety and frustration many times while trying to figure it all out. We have always had difficulty with discipline for schedules and getting things done in order of priority, instead of order of apparent need. On top of that, we really didn't know how to get started with scheduling. This is our first year of real, full-time homeschooling, and we were very concerned about managing the time with the other children and all the responsibilities of the home, while putting the necessary emphasis on Katie's schoolwork.

We had many conversations about how we would manage, and the level of frustration was rising. Dale read the MOMYS post from Teri first, mentioning the book plans and the request for volunteer families to test the system. He showed the post to me, and we were both immediately sure that Teri was a God-send and her scheduling book, the answer to our prayers. We were a bit concerned at first about the conflicts of scheduling for the older children with our convictions regarding not scheduling feedings for infants. We were, in a sense looking for the best of both worlds—a schedule structured in a way that would simplify the management of schooltime, chore time, rest time, etc. for the older children and still allow for the flexibility of interruptions from the younger. Although the book recommends the use of scheduling for each child, regardless of age, we have been able to customize it to our tastes and still reap the benefits of having a master plan. At first, our need to customize left us worried that we might not be very good volunteers, but Teri easily reassured us that she appreciated the variety and the fact that we could still benefit from the book without having to compromise our convictions. We expect to put the principles of the book to good use over the many years of schooling and home-management, with a large family, which are to come.

From Renée

Interruptions to a Schedule

What will you do when there are interruptions to your schedule? Perhaps the baby needs to be changed during morning Bible time. Or maybe two of the children are squabbling during their play-time together. There are dentist appointments in the middle of the morning or one of the children is sick and wants to sit on Mommy's lap all day. The phone rings; the doorbell rings; one of the other children interrupts to ask a question.

Interruptions are many and varied. They will come and disturb the very best of schedules. How do we view these interruptions? First, we want to see them as God's intervention in our day. "My times are in thy hand" (Psalm 31:15). "My brethren, count it all joy when ye fall into divers temptations; Knowing this, that the trying of your faith worketh patience. But let patience have her perfect work, that ye may be perfect and entire, wanting nothing" (James 1:2). If we know interruptions come from the Lord, then we do not need to be frustrated, impatient, or angry over them. We want to use them to accomplish their purpose not only in our lives but in the lives of our children. So much of this will simply come out of our attitude. Will we treat this interruption with a quiet and gentle spirit? As we are able to receive God's grace in this area, we will find our homes becoming the peaceful havens we desire them to be.

PLAN INTERRUPTIONS

Schedule routine appointments such as dental checkups when they will have the least impact on your school day. If your most intense school occurs in the morning, schedule these appointments for the afternoon. This also applies to shopping and running errands. Try as much as possible to keep these interruptions, that you can control, from coming during your school hours.

Avoid classes and activities that take you away from home during your school day. Often these will look enticing to homeschoolers, but they can rob you of the quality and quantity schooltime that you desire and need. A one hour class in the morning involves two hours by the time everyone gets ready to go, arrives at class, is in class, and returns home. The focus is off of school routine; Mom is tired, and the day is left to itself. This is acceptable once in a while, but on a weekly basis is certain to bring discouragement to a homeschooling mom's heart. Stay home during the day! Use evenings and weekends for being out and about. Your homeschool will benefit greatly from this decision. You will be amazed at how much more smoothly school will run if you stay home during school hours! Gauge how you use your time by the priorities God has called you to specifically.

A Personal Word

We haven't been real big on scheduling in the past because of our personal views on scheduling babies. However, I feel we can still hold our views for the babies and keep a structured schedule for the older children. We have already seen the children take to the schedule in a way that shows their need to have more of a routine. As we have more children, it's easy to see the value and necessity of scheduling. Renée

I have been prepping the children and they are excited. Hubby is excited too, as he is the "organized" one! I'm looking forward to feeling like I accomplished something every day. Kathy

I did end up with thirty hours for my day; might explain why I sometimes feel overwhelmed. Terri

My husband took the book to work today because he has a genuine desire to read it and also put himself on a schedule. That thrills me to no end. Understand that I

AVOID INTERRUPTIONS

There are practical ideas to help with interruptions. Caller ID, a phone service for about $5 per month, will allow you to see who is calling and decide whether to accept an interruption. We began Caller ID for another purpose, but have greatly benefitted by being able to read who is on the phone before we answer. Using an answering machine can work similarly but can be more of an interruption as everyone listens intently to the message being left.

It is a relatively easy process to install a switch on your doorbell so that you can turn it on and off. Use this to turn the doorbell off if there are times when it is likely to cause unwanted interruptions to school or nap time. Be sure to train yourself to turn it back on later!

HANDLING INTERRUPTIONS

Planning leeway time into your schedule was discussed in reference to relieving pressure caused by scheduling too much in too little time. Having a bit more time planned than an activity is likely to take will also help the interruption situation. When you have the time available, it is easier emotionally to take the break, deal with the interruption, and then go on. If the baby needs to be changed, taking five minutes from your one-on-one time with your first grader is fine because you have fifteen extra minutes built into your schedule just for such situations.

When you have a sick child, let him sit snuggling on your lap while you continue the school day. Allow a sick child to skip his schoolwork if needed, but consider, when possible, having him continue with some of his workbooks while lying in bed. Our family does not watch T.V., but we have a handful of educational videos that the children can watch when they are sick. This occupies a sick child, passing time for him while he is miserable. The rest of the schedule can continue on with him dropping out for the sick period.

When interruptions do occur, the key is to get back on the schedule track as soon as possible. If you have an emergency phone call, signal your children to continue on their own as much as they can. Then make the phone call as short as possible. When it is over, jump back into the schedule wherever you should be at the current time. Sometimes you may want to rearrange the schedule to pick up what was being worked on when the interruption occurred if that activity was high priority. Skip what is not so important and then get back on the schedule.

If a whole day or week were to be totally off schedule because of a major interruption, that is not a signal to give up on using a schedule. It does mean that you can return to the schedule as soon as it is feasible. In such a case, it is wise to have your children trained so they will continue on their individual daily schedule independently as much as they are able. This allows you to meet the needs that the interruption involves while the children remain directed and constructively occupied.

In Conclusion

Interruptions are unavoidable. They will come whether you are using a schedule or not. A schedule helps you be prepared to accept these interruptions. Plan for interruptions, eliminate those you can, and allow the Lord to teach you godly responses to interruptions. Dealing with the interruptions that come into your days in these ways will help the functioning of your home as you implement and use a daily schedule.

did not even ask him to do this, it was all of his own desire!!! PTL! Kristi

But using the schedule I can see some things that I will want to change around. For instance, scheduling the three youngest to play earlier with the child who has less patience with the little ones, before they get rowdy. Then my great baby-sitter can handle them before lunch and outside playtime! J'Aimée

Dear Friends,   October 24th

My name is Robyn Lee and I am married to Ken. We have six children at home: Timothy (11), Benjamin (9), Rebecca (5), Taylor (4), Brenden (2), and Daniel (5 months).

We homeschool our children, participating in two homeschool support groups which have monthly meetings. We also host a once-a-month family game night. In addition to that, our baby has continuing medical needs—so we have lots of doctor visits to squeeze into our schedule.

I tend to be a messy, unorganized person in the home. But, when I worked, everything there was as neat as a pin. As I have had more children, I have felt the need to keep things better organized and structured, because if I don't, things go to the complete-disaster designation amazingly fast. My big problem was in getting the homeschooling done while juggling all the little ones, which can be an incredibly frustrating experience.

This was my main reason for volunteering to be a test family for the scheduling book. The timing was perfect. I was starting school, and I knew I had to do something different. When I first read the book and then started filling out the Activity Worksheets, it terrified me. I actually had nightmares about this process! I just figured I could never get my schedule made. I persisted, but if it wasn't for those deadlines, I probably never would have gotten through putting my schedule together; I can put things off forever!

I worked my way through the scheduling steps and finally finished my schedule. I had posted the Master Schedule Worksheets on my kitchen cabinets, because it was big enough for the children to easily read, and we liked all the different colors. Then we tried to implement it. Complete disaster! By lunch time, on the second day of trying this crazy schedule, I found myself pulling things off it, chopping them up, writing new ones, and rearranging a good portion of it. That's the beauty of it though; I can do that!

The second schedule I came up with was more workable, but there were still problems with it. So, out came the scissors and the pen, and I rearranged things again. Now, the third time, I have a schedule that works well for all of us. It's so pleasant and easy I find myself thinking, "What am I doing wrong; this is too easy!" I was used to fighting constantly with everybody, and we are not doing that now. It is great!

We haven't gotten to where we are following the whole schedule, but we are working our way up to it. We are consistently doing things that always seemed to be left undone before. And what we aren't consistent about, yet, isn't critical.

This book is a wonderful resource. Its biggest strength is that it puts scheduling into a step-by-step process that anyone can handle, even people like me, who are incredibly resistant to being that organized!

From Robyn

Putting the Schedule Together

All the information about what to schedule is not very useful without hands-on, practical, step-by-step instructions for making a personalized schedule. The delightful aspect about schedules is that each one is uniquely designed to the needs of a particular family at a particular time. You should begin to enjoy "tweaking" your schedule as the needs of your family change. Those with babies will revise their schedules more frequently than a family with only older children. These changes will not require completely redoing the schedule but rearranging a piece here or there. Often the schedule is so well known and used by the family that these simple revisions will not even require rewriting the schedule.

You might as well know it now; the creation of your first schedule will take longer than the next one. With that in mind, it is time to begin the planning and organizing. Think of this as laying the foundation.

STEP ONE: ACTIVITY WORKSHEET FOR MOM

Think and pray about what you want and need to accomplish in a day. These thoughts should be written down on an **Activity Worksheet for Mom**, which is found in the **Scheduling Kit**. Not only will you list on this worksheet what you want to get done, but how long each item takes. Simply put, **Activity Worksheet for Mom** is a written list of all God has called you to do each day and the amount of time required to do it.

Don't hurry through; plan multiple sessions to accomplish this. Allow it to be an ongoing project that you work on for a while each day, perhaps over a week. This way you actually begin the planning process and avoid putting it off until you are able to devote a whole day to it (as if that would ever happen)!

This is a good time to refer to the Appendix in the back of the book. Here you will find many true life schedules of homeschooling moms just like you. Studying these schedules should give you excellent ideas for exactly which activities to put on your **Activity Worksheet for Mom**. The Appendix also contains an entire family's **Activity Worksheets** as samples for you to look over.

As you think through each part of your day, you might want to skim back through the chapter of this book that would apply. See if there are any ideas that will be useful to you. Ask the Lord to give you great creativity as you are in this phase. Your goal is to serve God and glorify Him through your daily time usage. He must be a part of the process each step of the way! Remember, your key to suc-

A Personal Word

So far, it has taken me a little time to get things right, but it's so worth the investment of my time. Tracy L.

It really does help to have all the little things broken down and itemized. You realize that these are the things we need to accomplish, and at least it's "easier" to look at them if they are all laid out nicely! It actually takes some of the fear and confusion out of things. Debbie

I completed my Activity Worksheet for Mom and the Activity Worksheet for my eldest two and then decided to take a break and get a perspective on it all. J'Aimée

The worksheets are GREAT! The book is great, reminding me along the way that we serve the Lord, not ourselves and NOT EVEN OUR SCHEDULE! I love being able to go through it one step at a time. I also like the reminder to pray over the Activity Worksheet, making sure these are the things God is calling me to

cessful scheduling is scheduling your daily quiet time with the Lord. List it on your **Activity Worksheet for Mom**. Also, recall the suggestions for scheduling of priorities.

Obviously, if you are going to have your school day scheduled, you need to decide how much time you can give to school and how you will budget that

Sample Activity Worksheet for Mom		
Personal Bible time/Dress		1 hour
Family morning devotion		½ hour
Walk/Shower		1 hour
Breakfast		½ hour
School:		5 hours
Preschool	1 hour	
Anna (K)	1 ½ hour	
John (2nd)	1 hour	
Joseph (4th)	½ hour	
Sarah (11th)	½ hour	
Bible	½ hour	
Lunch		½ hour
Prepare little ones for naps		½ hour
Writing		1 hour
Rest		½ hour
Reading to little ones		1 hour
Individual child playtime with Mom		½ hour
Dinner preparation		1 hour
Dinner		1 hour
Laundry folding		½ hour
Little ones baths or Playtime with Mom		1 hour
Evening family devotion		½ hour
Computer time		½ hour
Steve's backrub, Talking time, and Prayer		½ hour
Sleep		7 hours
Total		24 hours
Notes:		
Cleaning - 1 hour (Friday morning/no school)		
School planning/Record keeping - 1 ½ hours (Friday morning/no school)		
Ironing - 1 hour (Saturday morning)		
Date with Steve - 2 hours (Saturday afternoon)		

time. The sample **Activity Worksheet for Mom** in this step gives you an example of how to take a unit of time for school and break it up into the individual pieces for your worksheet. Remember, the actual time of day when each activity will be done is not being addressed in this step. It is simply a listing of the day's activities and their allotted time.

Spending several days with your **Activity Worksheet for Mom** will also allow you to read through your list during these days and pray over it. God may bring to mind items you did not think of at first, or perhaps He will eliminate some that are not necessary. You must place everything on your list that you want to accomplish and how long it takes. Your list will probably be longer than your day, but this is the starting point. (You mean there aren't 48 hours in a day?) You can see that if this step is rushed and unreliable information is assembled, the value of the entire schedule is questionable.

Take your time; do it right!

It is helpful if your husband will review the list with you. He can give insight into what he believes is important for you to accomplish. Sometimes we are busy doing things we think will please our husband only to find out, if we ask him, that he would rather have us use that time in another way. He can help with eliminating unnecessary items before specific times are worked into the schedule. He will view these decisions from a different perspective which can be very valuable to you.

At this point it may be apparent that the goals for your time usage are greater than the actual hours in a day. Here you have a realism check. If you do not have time in your schedule for all you want to do, you will have to pare down, eliminating some activities. Ecclesiastes 3:1 says, "To every thing there is a season, and a time to every purpose under the heaven . . ." Perhaps this is not the season for your children to be taking music lessons or to be involved in team sports. Maybe it is not the season for you to be teaching Sunday School. You have to know your priorities. If they are God, husband, children, ministry, then your time usage should reflect this. Don't eliminate time with your husband in order to have time to sew. And, don't forego your quiet time with the Lord so that you can help your neighbor by baby-sitting while she works.

We encourage you, at this point of your scheduling, to reread Chapter Eight, "Scheduling for Priorities" and Chapter Eleven's section, "Schedule Too Full." These will give insight into scheduling priorities and paring down a day that appears to have more activities than time. You need to tweak your **Activity Worksheet for Mom** so the activities add up to 24 hours or less.

accomplish each day. My hubby's input here has also been valuable! The way the schedule is assembled has kept me from being frustrated by any changes. Usually I am erasing and scribbling all over until I lose heart. This is so much easier! Thank you again for an opportunity to fine-tune my life to help me become the woman He wants me to be! Kathy

I have found that working on the worksheets every day for a week is very beneficial, even though I wanted to just blaze through them to get to the final product. As I prayed about the schedule, I thought of things that I had omitted and also felt God confirming the importance of other things. I am now comfortable with the things I have written down, and the initial feeling of being overwhelmed with all there was to accomplish has passed. I feel mentally capable of tackling the Master Schedule. Tracy W.

I am now done reading the book and have finished the third Child's Activity Worksheet! I am so excited, and I feel this is an excellent tool to have in the hands of homeschool moms! And,

believe me, I know! I am an organizational and schedule junkie! This is "the" fix for me! Corrie

It does take several days to work the Activity Worksheet. I worked on it for a while this morning, but had to stop and clear my thoughts. I'm having fun and can't wait to finish! Pauline

People have told me for years that I need a schedule, but every time I tried I couldn't get one to work. I always had problems with fitting everything that needed to be done into one day. With your system, I am actually accomplishing more and I have more time left over! The key to it is the great worksheets. They are invaluable. Sheri

I am so glad I did not give up on this schedule, Teri. It was so tempting, but most of the excuses I could think of were already listed in your book, with Scriptural rebuttals to boot! I would sit down to work on it, and just feel overwhelmed, wanting to get it done in that sitting, and then not being sure how to divide all those blocks of time. I am so grateful God

Don't necessarily eliminate activities, though, until you have tried to be creative in your arrangement of them.

Let your schedule help you toward the goals the Lord has given you for your life. You will have to make these decisions after prayerful consideration between you, your husband, and the Lord. There will likely be difficult decisions to make, but they are ones that will contribute toward the quiet and gentle spirit I Peter 3 says is of great worth in God's sight. It is the difficult decisions, left unresolved, that will sink a schedule. Make them; don't avoid them if you truly want to be successful.

There is always time in the day to complete what God wants you to do!

The actual making of your schedule comes only after you have spent much time in prayer, seeking the Lord for how to spend your time. Once these

Activity Worksheet for Child *Anna* Age *5* Grade *K*	
Wake up/Dress/Room chores	½ hour
Eat breakfast, Brush teeth, Clean sinks	½ hour
Preschool with Mom and little ones	½ hour
Phonics/Reading with Mom	1 ½ hours
Play with Jesse (4) and Mary (2)	½ hour
School Bible time	½ hour
Math with Sarah	½ hour
With Sarah for little ones playtime	½ hour
Play alone	½ hour
Lunch helper	½ hour
Lunch	½ hour
Workbook/Quiet activities	1 hour
Nap	1 ½ hour
Listen to Mom read	½ hour
Scripture Memory/Singing with Sarah	½ hour
Play or Dinner helper (one night/week)	1 hour
Dinner	½ hour
Bath or Playtime with Mom	1 hour
Evening family devotion	½ hour
Teeth brushing/Mom's goodnight and prayers	½ hour
Sleep	10
Total	23 1/2

decisions are made, you are ready to bring your scheduling process to fruition with a schedule.

STEP TWO: ACTIVITY WORKSHEET FOR CHILD

Once you have completed your **Activity Worksheet for Mom**, it is time to tackle an **Activity Worksheet for Child** for each child. These are found in the **Scheduling Kit**. This **Activity Worksheet for Child** will be similar to your **Activity Worksheet for Mom**, requiring time and prayer to finish. Simply put, each **Activity Worksheet for Child** is a written list of all you believe God has called that child to do each day and the amount of time required to do it.

Activity Worksheet for Child Joseph Age 9 Grade 4	
Rising/Room chores	½ hour
Breakfast/Teeth/Chores	½ hour
Piano practice	½ hour
Spelling/Handwriting	½ hour
Math	½ hour
Reading	½ hour
Science	½ hour
History	½ hour
One-on-one tutoring with Mom	½ hour
School Bible time	½ hour
Computer typing and Math drill	½ hour
Afternoon free time	½ hour
Playtime with the younger children	½ hour
Listen to Mom read	½ hour
Scripture memorization/Singing	½ hour
Lunch and Cleanup and Free	1 hour
Quiet afternoon free time	1 hour
Before dinner chore or Free	1 hour
Dinner and Cleanup	1 hour
Children's playtime with Mom	1 hour
Teeth brushing/Shower/Free	1 hour
Evening family devotion	½ hour
Sleep	10 hours
Total	24 hours

provided the motivation and the wisdom for me to get this done. Now, it is all worth it, and I am looking forward to developing the discipline to start and stop tasks at the appointed times. *Lisa*

It definitely does take more time to write each activity in everyone's schedule on a separate square, and then cut out each one, back it with "sticky tac" and stick it on, but the ease of rearranging "squares" (instead of erasing something and forgetting what it was before I had a chance to write it down again) is priceless! *Ellen*

I am now working on the Master Worksheet. The children applied the "sticky tac" to all the "squares" on the Master Worksheet. They begged to help so I gladly let them. *Pauline*

I love the way the Master Schedule Worksheets look when they are completed. And my husband was really impressed with the way the "sticky tac" works. I was showing him the finished product with all the little slips of paper in place. Upon explaining to him how our *day would run, we discovered that I had two children using the computer at the same time. What a simple thing to just swap that square with one from another location! Ellen*

Just thought you would like to know that I stayed up late and started pasting my "squares" on the Master Schedule Worksheets. I guess that was the only way that I could overcome my mental block. Seeing it made it much easier to figure out what was unrealistic and/or lacking! After seeing it all come together, I think it may actually be attainable; I was having my doubts. J'Aimée

I can't wait. Getting down to the nitty gritty of the schedule this morning was encouraging. I plugged in the main things first (waking, eating, chores, school, etc.) and then went from there. It was great fun! Pauline

Ironically, the Master Schedule Worksheets took me much longer than all of the other parts put together—it seemed like a REAL chore, figuring out how to apportion the day. Each time I got a bit tired or frustrated, I

If you have had a school-planning day with your husband (see Chapter Nine, "Planning For the School Year"), much of the background work for each **Activity Worksheet for Child** has been accomplished.

Referring to the schedules in the Appendix will give you insight into the activities, and their corresponding amounts of time, that other mothers have used for their children. Please don't use these sample schedules as a basis of comparison. Each one is a real-life schedule that a mom has used, but the Lord has called us all to slightly different circumstances. The sample schedules are simply for you to evaluate and glean ideas from.

Hints to remember:

Use older children to teach and supervise younger children or babies. (See Chapters Three and Four)

Assign two specific children playtime together in a designated area. (See Chapter Three)

Make use of individual playtimes. (See Chapters Three and Five)

Have a preschool time for younger children with Mom. (See Chapters Three and Four)

List specific chore times. (See Chapter Three and Six)

Include younger children in some group schooltime. (See Chapter Four)

Upon finishing the **Activity Worksheets for Child**, if your husband is willing, it would be wise for you to get his feedback on what you are planning for each child to do. Is this list reasonable for this child? Is his day too full, too empty, or just right?

STEP THREE: MOM'S PREPARATION WORKSHEET

For Step Three, again return to the **Scheduling Kit**. Choose a **Preparation Worksheet** color for yourself. Each color has **Preparation Worksheets** with ½ hour slots and hour slots. Label "your color" pages with "Mom," "Mommy," or whatever your family refers to you as, in the box by the title.

Take your **Activity Worksheet for Mom** that you prepared in Step One. Write each activity from it onto an appropriately sized box of your color **Preparation Worksheet**. Order and timing are not important for this step, because you will be cutting these pages apart to use like pieces of a puzzle. The smaller slots are for ½ hour activities. If the activity is a ½ hour activity, write it in one of the ½ hour slots. If it is an hour activity, choose one of the hour boxes to write it in.

To keep your first schedule from being too complicated the smallest increment we will use is 1/2 hour. If you need only fifteen minutes for an item, you might try either combining it with another fifteen minute activity or using the extra fifteen minutes as a buffer.

It is easiest to schedule the same activity at the same time each day, therefore, we recommend trying to consistently schedule every weekday. You might find this is not possible with the demands on your time. You can also choose to vary activities within a given block; for example, an hour could look like this:

> M - Correspondence
> T - Phone calls
> W - Grocery planning
> Th - Cleaning
> F - Cleaning

Or perhaps you have school Monday through Thursday with a normal schedule, but on Friday you have the children work independently while you spend the day cleaning and school planning. In this case, you would plan your schedule for Monday through Thursday, placing a note at the end of your schedule to indicate an alternate Friday plan. If you needed more detail for Friday, you could fill out separate **Preparation Worksheets** for the day that will have the alternative schedule.

STEP FOUR: CHILD'S PREPARATION WORKSHEET

Step Four sends you back to the **Scheduling Kit**. Designate a different color **Preparation Worksheet** for each child. Title the top with the child's name and fill in the individual boxes with each of that child's activities from their **Activity Worksheet for Child** just as you did for yourself. Pay close attention to writing the activity in the appropriately sized box for the amount of time it will take, either ½ hour or hour slots.

STEP FIVE: MASTER SCHEDULE WORKSHEETS

You have now completed the background steps and are ready to dive into the meat of your schedule! In the **Scheduling Kit**, you will find a set of the **Master Schedule Worksheets**. This set consists of three, 11 x 17 inch pieces of paper (Morning, Midday, and Evening) that fit together to make a large blank schedule.

For this step, you will need the **Master Schedule Worksheets** and each of your colored **Preparation Worksheets**. Cut apart the individual "squares"

just put it away and got it back out the next night. Amazingly, it finished itself up almost effortlessly! VERY helpful system! Rebecca

I actually started cutting out pieces and putting the schedule together yesterday. It was fun! I did what you said and started with the easy stuff that we all do together (and that we already do, meals, etc). Robyn

I love the schedule. I would recommend it to anyone. The greatest thing about it is that finally we "Mothers of Many" will be able to answer that oft repeated question: "What do you do with the younger ones when you homeschool?" I can't wait to whip out my Master Schedule Worksheets in all their pink, gold, yellow, and green splendor. Sally

I just finished the Master Schedule Worksheets! What a sense of accomplishment. It took me several hours but I had fun doing it. Pauline

that are filled in from your **Preparation Worksheets** and the accompanying name at the top. (Remember paper dolls?) You need three name rectangles for each person on your **Master Schedule Worksheets**, so there is an extra name rectangle provided on one of the two **Preparation Worksheets** in each color. The **Preparation Worksheets** are color coded so you can easily remember which activities go with which person as you arrange your schedule.

Begin organizing these individual "squares" on your **Master Schedule Worksheets**. The **Master Schedule Worksheets** let you creatively work at designing your schedule, much like you would fit a puzzle together. Note: If you are scheduling more than eight, use two sets of **Master Schedule Worksheets**, side by side. To help with viewing continuity, tuck the margins and side titles underneath your first set of **Master Schedule Worksheets**. (To order an additional **Scheduling Kit** see the Registration Form and Order Form in the back of the book.)

Your **Master Schedule Worksheets** and **Preparation Worksheets** allow you trial and error in producing your schedule. When you use these schedule worksheets and cut the pieces apart, you have a moveable table that frees you to easily rework when a conflict arises in your scheduling process. You can creatively try different scheduling scenarios.

"Sticky tac" will keep your **Preparation Worksheet** blocks in place as you put other blocks on the **Master Schedule Worksheets**. Take a section of *"sticky tac"* and peel the plastic away from both sides. With sharp scissors cut a 1/8 inch strip from the side. Then take the strip and cut off tiny 1/16 inch or 1/8 inch pieces. If you prefer, you can just pinch small pieces off the large strip. Press the small piece of *"sticky tac"* flat between your thumb and finger. Firmly place a piece in each square you think you will be using on your **Master Schedule Worksheets**. If you are brave and live in a wind free, childless environment, you can choose to forego the *"sticky tac."* But be warned! Without the use of *"sticky tac,"* a sudden breeze at the end of your scheduling process may reduce you to tears.

Place the names across the header row: Mom in the column next to the time, and then each of the children to the right of hers. Now, begin placing the individual activity pieces.

TIPS ON COMPLETING THE MASTER SCHEDULE WORKSHEETS

If scheduling a whole day sounds intimidating to you, start by working with the morning only. This step, just as the previous steps, does not have to be completed in one sitting. It would be beneficial to plan to devote yourself to it for a set amount of uninterrupted time each day, over several days.

The Master Schedule looks incredible!!! My husband was so impressed!!! Kristi

Well, I have completed our Master Schedule and I am very pleased at how it all fell into place! When I was done with the Activity Worksheets, I felt panic and discouragement at the thought of trying to fit it all into the Master Schedule. I kept praying as I went that God would direct my thoughts and keep me going. It was much less difficult than I thought it would be, and I cannot tell you how excited I was to see it complete! Connie

I made the mistake of trying to fine-tune on the final copy, which I had typed on the computer, without using the Preparation Worksheet "squares." BIG MISTAKE! I am not as frustrated when I don't have to think about resizing cells on the computer schedule at the same time. I am still praying over the whole thing and know the Lord will guide me through the difficult parts. I think I may be still struggling with wanting to do things I don't NEED to be doing. Back to

Between scheduling sessions, the Lord will perk your thinking so that you are fine-tuning your schedule while still in the process of making it up.

Scheduling of some activities will be easily determined; start here. You probably already have fairly consistent bedtimes and wake up times. Stick those "squares" on the appropriate place on the **Master Schedule Worksheets**. If these times are not yet determined, this is the place in the scheduling process to do so. Meals and chore times will likely be at the same time for everyone. If you have a nursing baby, remember to plan for his needs first and then work the family around him.

At this stage it is also good to take into consideration any regular outings or activities that will affect your schedule. For us, one of our children accompanies Grandma to deliver Meals-on-Wheels every other Monday. They are gone from 10:30 a.m. to 1:30 p.m. I try to have what I need to accomplish with them scheduled before 10:30 a.m., so that when they are gone we don't get behind on anything critical to our school schedule. They can make up their individual work on their own. However, you can see if I had planned time with them during Meals-on-Wheels, not only is their schedule impacted, but mine as well.

During this assembly phase, you will want to consult the sample schedules from the Appendix again. You can consider how other mothers used their older children with their younger ones, how they delegated responsibilities, and how they divided their time usage. Looking at these schedules and evaluating them should give you added insight and creativity as you design your schedule.

Figuring out the final details of a schedule is like putting a puzzle together or working a logic problem. If Sarah is practicing the piano from 9:30 to 10:00 a.m., she cannot be assigned to play with the little ones during that time, nor can Joseph have his practicing time then. If the baby naps from 10 to 11 a.m. in the room next to the piano, you will probably not schedule any piano practicing from 10 to 11 a.m. Experiment by moving the pieces around.

You may think you have all the pieces perfectly fitted together only to find you have a child scheduled for something that is impossible at that time. As you rearrange, be aware that a perfect schedule may not be possible. Ask yourself if the one you have created is at least workable. If it is, use it, and in time you may be able to fine-tune it toward perfection. For example, I do not like to have the children break a thirty minute school subject into two fifteen minute parts, but one year, for one of our children, there was no other option to make the schedule work. So that's the way it was!

It may not always be possible to arrange the pieces of your schedule as easily as sitting down with your **Master Schedule Worksheets** and plugging in

*my Activity Worksheet.
Kathy*

I got the morning and most of the afternoon plugged in today. Once you get your hands on it and get going, it makes so much sense! If you are a hands-on visual person, this is for you! The different colors really help with visually separating each child. You can tell who's who at a glance. Pauline

I have completed the Activity Worksheets for myself and each child. Last night I was cutting out the Preparation Worksheet "squares" and sticking them on the Master Schedule Worksheets, and I got that finished. Dale reviewed the schedule list with me and thought it looked great.

I guess the bottom line is that we're both pretty satisfied with the schedule and being able to fit everything into one day. Overall, the process has been good for us by making us think in terms of organization, and just getting everything down on paper makes it seem much less overwhelming. Renée

Thank you for your encouragement and please stress in your book that it may take a while to get to do your exact schedule but at least you are aiming for something and will accomplish more than you think. J'Aimée

Oh, today is even more smooth than yesterday, at least where the schooling is concerned. I also got soup made, hung out laundry, and we took our walk before lunch. How nice to come in from the fresh air to the homey smell of soup simmering. Lisa

Here is one of the good things we have experienced this week. Even though we began about four and a half hours of schooling each day, with me fully involved, I did not feel overwhelmed. Before using my schedule, I felt overwhelmed when I had the whole day to get stuff done. Now we schedule to have the house cleaned, schoolwork done, our major meal at noon, and the kitchen cleaned by 1:00 p.m. Therefore, even if I want to veg-out the rest of the day (which when pregnant, I

the various activities. The complexity of scheduling increases proportionately to the size of the family, but so do the benefits. Therefore, we encourage you to apply yourself to the task of making your schedule and not be daunted by its difficulty. Enlist the support of your husband to encourage and help you through any perceived impasse.

If you think you need a different schedule for every day of the week, try to get as much as possible on one Master Schedule. By this I mean that you schedule the different day's activities by listing the day and the activity (M/W Read aloud, T/Th Art, F Piano lessons) all in the appropriate time block or blocks.

If the basics need to be totally moved around each day, then making different Master Schedules is an option. You might photo copy the **Master Schedule Worksheets** (if you have registered your book—see last page of this book for registration details) and then only redo the parts that will vary. Much of the day will probably be the same. For example, I have an alternate Friday schedule. The only parts that change are from 8:30 to 12 noon so I just cut that much out of a **Master Schedule Worksheet**, work out the schedule, and post it on the wall.

There are two sample schedules (Ellen and Debbie) to reference in making up schedules for various days' needs. Debbie's has a M/W/F schedule and a T/Th schedule. If you evaluate her schedules, you will notice she did this to accommodate her school subjects. However, you can glean from what she did, and apply it to your particular need for more than one schedule.

Ellen started her schedule when her husband had a consistent work time. Then he was promoted and had different shifts. Ellen thought she could mentally rearrange the pieces of her schedule for the days when her husband left for work in the afternoon rather than the morning. That wasn't successful. She decided to invest the time in making up her second schedule, which didn't take her nearly as long as the first. Ellen was quite pleased with the results and functioned better when she could actually look at the schedule she needed to use for the day.

Not having consistency from day to day does make the scheduling process more time consuming. However, the benefits gained from those schedules will be invaluable. It may take longer to memorize your schedules when they aren't the same each day, but as long as the schedules are there, they can be easily consulted.

You may need to rework and rework and rework your **Master Schedule Worksheets**. Please, please persevere. Again, the difficulty of generating your schedule is indicative of the need and the potential usefulness of your schedule. The investment of persevering through the difficulties will be rewarded by smoothly-running, efficient days.

Sometimes the actual schedule production is so complicated that it does require several time periods of prayer, thinking, and creatively rearranging your "squares." This does not mean you should give up in frustration; it only confirms the great need you have for scheduling. The more difficult it is to make up a schedule, the more factors you have that need to be controlled, planned, and managed.

The last school schedule I worked on for our family was so complicated—with seven people I needed to schedule—that I had knots in my stomach when I began to move things here and there. Whereas, I usually enjoy the actual schedule making, this one seemed like it would be impossible. I played with it for a half-hour a day for four days and finally had my schedule. It was not perfect, but it would meet our requirements. My anxiety over developing that schedule was wasted. The Lord met the need as He says He always will.

STEP SIX: TRANSFERRING MASTER SCHEDULE WORKSHEETS INTO FINAL SCHEDULE

After you have generated your schedule with the colored cut-out pieces on the **Master Schedule Worksheets**, it is time to post them in a central location in your home. Or you may transcribe them onto the smaller **Final Schedule** we have provided for this step, if this would be more convenient for your general use. Now you are ready to photocopy the schedule for each person using it and implement it.

You can also choose to put your schedule on the computer. All word processors have a "table" feature. This is usually found on a drop down menu at the top of the screen. The number of rows and columns needed for your schedule table can be determined by consulting your **Master Schedule Worksheets**. Once you have created a blank table you can fill the individual "squares" by typing the information in, just as you would write it out by hand on the **Master Schedule Worksheets**.

IN CONCLUSION

Are you excited? Are you pleased? Can you believe, if you have always wanted to have a schedule but never been able to, that you are now looking at your own schedule?

Having the schedule completed should give you great satisfaction. It is the result of God's working, consultation with your husband, and persistence in wanting to manage your home in the best way possible. Your schedule will allow you to pursue the goals and direction the Lord has set for you as a wife, mother, and teacher. Now, enjoy the benefits it will bring to your life and the lives of the members of your family.

often feel like doing!!) I don't feel guilty because the major work of the day is all done. I have the rest of the day to enjoy my family. Kathleen

Our school schedule is very helpful. I'm surprised at how well it is working, though I'm sure it will be changed periodically. I'm already seeing jobs that I need to shift (giving some children "promotions!"). Debbie

Dear Friends,   October 26th

Hello, my name is Sheri, and I am an reforming "messie." I am married to a wonderful man named Dale, and we have five children: Michael (10 years old), David (6 years old), Andrew (4 years old), Joshua (3 years old), and our little Tirzah (she's 5 months).

We have homeschooled for five years now. I have tried schedules in the past, and they never worked. I couldn't get all the details figured out, and I ended up frustrated, in worse shape than when I had begun. My self esteem was badly bruised from all my failures.

One morning I was praying to the Lord for an answer to the desire of my heart, which was to have a tidy house, clean and happy children, and a husband who looked forward to coming home. Just after my prayer, I had the opportunity to join the test group with the Maxwells. I knew it was an answer to prayer, and was I excited. The schedule kit and book arrived, and with great fear, I began to read. I started to worry that I would fail again, but I had a peace as I read the book.

Next came the making of the schedule. I had to "capture each thought" of fear and give it to the Lord. My husband and I had a grand time creating our schedule. But alas, as we started using our first schedule, we found it to be greatly lacking, and we had to redo it. That was a little discouraging, but I knew it could work out, for the Lord was in it.

After revising our schedule, we posted this second schedule and started to use it. Once again, a snag. The schedule "flushed out" all sorts of obedience problems with our children. My children hadn't known how to clean things and put them away, because I had never taught them properly. We took a couple of days "off" our schedule to do some training, and when we went back to it, things went much smoother.

We have been implementing the schedule full force for three weeks now, and the changes are amazing. My husband is happier when he comes home, because he feels confident that there won't be any "disasters" awaiting him. The children fight less and are more content. I have time to do a few things that I enjoy, plus all those projects with the children (you know the ones I said we would do "next week" for a year). Anyway, making and using a schedule can help you. It has helped me, and there were people who thought I was hopeless. I now know the "secret recipe" . . . God and His timing + the Maxwell's wonderful system + "sticky tac" = Success!

From Sheri

Implementing a Schedule

So! Your schedule is committed to paper and you are ready to implement it. Thinking through and preparing for the start of using a new schedule will be helpful. Change is often accompanied by difficulties.

Any change takes time; it takes adjusting to; and often it involves some problems. It just might not "feel" right for a while. Recently our church moved from a gymnasium to a college's performing arts center. The new facilities were much nicer than the old, but the change was emotional. We left what was familiar to us. Within a few months our new meeting place felt like home, but it did take time.

Through this implementation step of your scheduling project, I want to remind you of Philippians 4:6-7, "Be careful for nothing; but in every thing by prayer and supplication with thanksgiving let your requests be made known unto God. And the peace of God, which passeth all understanding, shall keep your hearts and minds through Christ Jesus." We serve a God Who knows the number of hairs on our heads and Who cares about the details of how we arrange our days. We desire to bring Him glory by how we use our time.

Each family member who is involved in the schedule, and can read, needs a copy of the schedule. You will also want to post it in at least one central location in your home for easy reference by everyone. Little ones will need to be directed at each change of activity, but you will be surprised how quickly they learn the sequence of the schedule even if they cannot read the exact time.

It will be helpful to go through the schedule with each person who will be participating in it. You can let them know what they will be doing at each specified time. This will allow them time to think through what the changes will mean to them and be prepared. Questions will surface that are easier to answer before you start the schedule than they would be on your first day.

Since you have worked to make a reasonable schedule, the transition should be smoother than if you are pushing too much into too little time. If you have over filled the schedule, you will be frustrated and your family will be too.

IMPLEMENT GRADUALLY

We highly recommend making the adjustment to a schedule gradually, particularly if scheduling is new to you. Since change can be hard, taking it in small increments will make it easier.

A Personal Word

I will be easing into it slowly. I am a perfectionist, and I just know I will be all in a lather if I try to do the WHOLE thing and no one cooperates! Corrie

Just wanted to let you know we are starting our schedule today. I have been gradually doing the baby's schedule already, and it has been wonderful. It felt so good to get out of bed and know that I had a game plan. Not just a game plan but a well thought out and prayed over plan! I didn't feel overwhelmed anymore but excited about facing a new day! Even if things don't go smoothly I know that we can always get back on track. I have been feeling so overwhelmed with the arrival of baby number six, but those feelings have been going away since starting the scheduling process. Pauline

As I was trying to implement my schedule, I felt discouraged that I would never be able to implement all of the things I had written down. Then, I decided to

You could start with implementing one portion of the day at a time, perhaps adding a new part of your schedule every few days. For example, the first three days, only implement the morning through 9:00 a.m. That is it! Finish your day just as you always have. Then for the next three days, add the scheduled hour, 9 to 10 a.m., to the scheduled morning you are already doing. Three days later, if things are starting to roll smoothly, from 10 a.m. to noon could be implemented.

It will be easier on you to start your schedule gradually. You will flush out your children's character issues a little bit at a time and be able to use your "unscheduled" rest of the day to deal with them. You may be surprised, after sending your children for their scheduled half-hour to make beds and get dressed, that they have done neither when you call them to breakfast.

Another schedule implementation idea would be to have two weeks for getting the wake up time, chore time, mealtime, and bedtime schedule down. Then the hours that would normally go for other activities could be used for child training or discipline refreshing.

A child who is not obedient will be a great hindrance to the schedule. Two excellent books on child training and discipline are listed in the Resource section of the Appendix. If obedience, diligence, and responsibility are character areas that need attention in your home, you will want to read these books before your training weeks. After those two weeks using only the "basics" schedule, then add school and other activities.

Beginning life on a schedule is a major lifestyle change. Allow yourself those small steps toward implementing your schedule. If you have gone this long without a schedule, you can afford the time of easing into it in a way that will lend itself to eventual success.

AN IMPLEMENTATION KEY

There is a major key to implementing your schedule that you will want to utilize. This key is the discipline to make yourself get up at your scheduled time each morning, whether you feel like it or not. In our family, we have family devotions at 6:25 a.m. Because of that daily appointment, I am willing to wake up at 5:30 so I can have time for my own Bible reading and prayer.

If you foresee rising at your scheduled time might present a stumbling block for you, here are a few suggestions to help. Ask your husband to hold you accountable to your wake up time for two weeks. Ask him to sweetly, with great compassion and encouragement, pull, push, or kick you out of the warm covers. After two weeks, he doesn't have to coddle you; you'll be on your own. Or ask Mom or a friend for a daily wake up call to help you follow through on your commitment to stick with the schedule. Or promise yourself some reward for beginning the day as planned.

BEGINNING EXPECTATIONS

Generally though, when you have a schedule you will be anxious to get the whole thing started right away. If you begin your schedule full force including school, you may be surprised at the deficiencies you see in your children. You need to be prepared for this, and, even though the schedule is going, have low expectations for actually accomplishing what the scheduled slot was set for. Have high expectations for spending much of the first week with discipline and training issues.

Don't see this as a negative but as a positive. Character is at the heart of what we desire for our children. It won't take long for your children to catch on to the schedule, what they are doing independently, and what they now have time limitations on. But if you are expecting, on that first day, to spend each slot on your schedule as it is designated, you may be disappointed. If you expect to spend time teaching and training toward schedule "compliancy," then you can feel excited about being on the schedule, making the planned changes of activity, and accept any discipline and training needs you must deal with. It will be as important to work with these issues as it will be to cover a math lesson.

Changes to a routine take time. Give yourself and the schedule that time. Do not feel that whatever didn't go well the first day is a disaster. Recently we decided to have our oldest daughter begin to work with two of the little ones on Scripture memorization. We scheduled this at 4:15 in the afternoon. The first day was fine, but most of that week we forgot all about Scripture memorization. It was not yet a part of our plan and routine. Several days would go by and one of us would say, "Oh, no! We have not been doing John and Anna's memorization time." We gradually got to where we forgot less and less. After a few weeks, Scripture memorization became a remembered part of our schedule. Was it a failure that it took us several weeks to be consistent with the new schedule? Did we say we couldn't make it work because we kept forgetting? No! We just kept trying and eventually were successful.

SCHEDULE REVISION

Don't be afraid to revise the schedule! Most schedules will need some fine-tuning once they have been put into use. Give your full schedule two or three weeks, and then evaluate rough areas that may need changing. Your schedule is a tool not your slave driver. You must be willing to adjust it to meet your needs and the needs of the family.

allow myself one week of adjustment for each child. That gave me six weeks to get my schedule running smoothly! I found that each week was easier than the week before, and that, indeed, after six weeks, things were really going as I had envisioned them. I am so glad I did not give up after the second week! Your encouragement kept me going. Tracy W.

I am not always able to do exactly what my schedule calls for, but we are on the right track, now, and have a direction. It is my hope that as each new week comes I will be able to add something more in until I am getting everything accomplished that I would like to be! Corrie

I have to be honest and tell you that I am very excited and nervous at the same time. As I have been reading I feel that this is an answer to a long time prayer. Pauline

Now that I am using a schedule, I don't feel so bad about sitting down to "do nothing." I am getting my work done and keeping the house in better shape. Trish

I need help getting up, since I know I really don't HAVE to get up like I did when I had to be to work at a certain time. I still should be at work managing my family at the appropriate time, but you know how it is. Your example of the office manager arriving to work at a different time each day is GREAT!!! Tracy W.

The schedule is extremely beneficial. It helps, even after we've gone astray, to come back and pick up with what we should be doing. Kathy

I definitely need to tweak a few things—need a bit more time for math and a little less for read alouds, but I'm going to see this week through before I decide to make some changes. Rebecca

My first week of my schedule went well. I was quite pleased with the results: house cleaner, dinner on time, bedtimes on schedule, and knowing what I wanted to accomplish next. I managed to stay on schedule most of the day that week. Sheila

You have to evaluate whether the areas of difficulty are due to the schedule or character issues that the schedule will flush out. These character deficiencies may be in either the children or yourself. For example, if you are having difficulty changing activities at the scheduled time, the schedule only needs to be revised if you believe you have not allowed adequate time for the activity. But, it could be that you need to develop the self-discipline to end the activity at the assigned time and pick it up the next day. Here is another example. You have planned a playtime alone for your toddler, and he cries through it. The schedule only needs to be rearranged if you have put that playtime at a bad time for the toddler, perhaps just before a meal. Otherwise, you have an issue of teaching him to be content and quiet even though he is alone.

Last school year, I revised our school schedule in December. I was having preschool at 11 a.m., but my back would hurt so much by then that I was not able to enjoy the time with our little ones or have the patience I wanted to have with them. As I prayed about this problem, the Lord directed me to redo the morning schedule. I moved preschool to right after breakfast, before my back began to hurt. Then I had other school activities that were not so hard on my back scheduled for later in the morning. The revision worked great; it solved the problem!

It may take two or three revisions to find the schedule that is right for your family. These revisions are relatively simple with your **Preparation Worksheet** pieces and **Master Schedule Worksheets**. Just rearrange the pieces to allow you to find a more workable schedule.

In Conclusion

Remember, a schedule is a plan to help you function efficiently. If you are not accustomed to using a schedule, you will need to be patient with yourself and your family as you make the necessary adjustments. A day that the schedule falls apart is not a day for discouragement or abandoning the schedule. You will just want to pick up your routine the next day and move on. Even if there is a whole week where there are so many unforeseen disruptions to your plan that it is totally forsaken, you can still choose to go back to it when you are able.

Implementing a schedule is the culmination of much prayer, thinking, planning, and just plain hard work in putting the schedule together. This final stage of your ongoing process of scheduling should be filled with a great sense of accomplishment. And it should produce all the fruit we discussed in Chapter One that were benefits of scheduling. Remember, even at this point, not to rely on yourself or the schedule, but keep your trust in the Lord.

Sheri's Activity Worksheet	
Nursing:	3 hrs
Early morning (6 a.m.) 1/2 hr	
Late morning (9 a.m.) 1/2 hr	
Noon 1/2 hr	
Early afternoon (3 p.m.) 1/2 hr	
Late afternoon (6 p.m.) 1/2 hr	
Evening (9 p.m.) 1/2 hr	
Personal devotion and Prayer time	1/2 hr
Exercise	1/2 hr
Shower and Dress	1/2 hr
Family morning devotions	1/2 hr
Help little ones dress	1/2 hr
Breakfast	1/2 hr
Morning chores	1/2 hr
School:	3 hrs
Preschool 1/2 hr	
David (1st) 1 hr	
Michael (3rd) 1 hr	
Bible 1/2 hr	
Lunch	1 hr
Ready children for nap or Quiet time	1/2 hr
Rest or Write or Read	1/2 hr
Individual time with older children	1/2 hr
Reading with children	1/2 hr
Chore time (afternoon)	1/2 hr
Dinner preparation	1/2 hr
Dinner and Cleanup	1 hr
Laundry folding and Putting away	1/2 hr
Evening family time	2 hrs
Computer time	1/2 hr
Bath time for children	1 hr
Dale's time (talking and prayer)	1/2 hr
Sleep	7 hrs
Total	26 hrs

Weekly:
    School planning
    Errands (Sat.)
    Bills with Dale

To find out how Sheri compensated for the extra hours listed on her Activity Worksheet, you may want to look at her schedule in the Appendix.

Dear Friends,   November 11th

My family has truly benefited from learning to use a schedule. I am not completely there, using it all the time, but the basics are getting done regularly, and my guilt is subsiding. I used to know what needed to be done but got sidetracked so easily. I still tend to slide there, but the written schedule pulls me back, and I stay close to the target.

My non-reading six-year-old has even taught himself to read the schedule. I was going to spend time teaching him but have not implemented that yet. Instead, he loves the schedule, learned to read it, and keeps us all on track—especially the fun times!! He would be deemed ADHD in a public school setting, so a routine benefits him greatly. I have even seen an amazing calmness in him lately.

My older boys have, also, become much more responsible. They know what is expected and know if they are doing it or not. So discipline is a much easier thing—not so much sliding through the cracks, because we weren't sure who was supposed to be doing what. My baby started sleeping longer almost immediately and never wakes up during the night.

I still have some catching up to do for many years of unplanned activity, but feel so much better about it all. I was even praised by a friend when I told her, "No, I cannot help with the baby shower." And there was no guilt—I could see I did not have the time. So I told her that and suggested another lady, who was thrilled to help, had great ideas, and actually wanted to help all along. So many times before, I would have felt obligated, served with less joy, and would have caused my family to suffer. God truly led me to learn to say "no" and, also, provided the replacement, helping me to learn that He takes care of ALL! It is not up to me. I just need to follow Him and be faithful. Others will appreciate that I don't give them less than my best but am honest and say when I cannot help.

I really believe in this book and think that it will help any family that struggles, but desires to do right. It is so simple to follow. My own family will continue to implement it completely. My husband is also very pleased with what he has seen and has made his own changes for himself.

I do already need to make some changes because the baby is nursing less and has given up the morning nap, but it will be easy to make the changes. It is very user friendly! Thank you for sharing it with me.

From Terri

Questions and Answers

CHILDREN'S ACTIVITIES

"I'm unclear on how you schedule your time alone with each child. I know they each have some individual time during the week with you. Does this time come at the same time every day or does it vary by day? Do the children alternate days?"

My individual time with the children does come at the same time each day, and they alternate days. The time is at 4:30 in the afternoon and listed as "Fun School with Joseph/John or Visit Meme" on my schedule. Joseph has his half-hour on Monday; on Tuesday I take one child with me to visit my 90-year-old grandmother, Meme, and make dinner for her; on Wednesday there isn't a child scheduled for that time; on Thursday it is John's playtime with me; and on Friday it is free time for me again.

I wanted to have individual time with each of my children, but it never happened. We would be too busy or, if there was time, I would be too tired to motivate myself to play with them. It would be easier for me to go to the computer or sit in my chair. So I planned a half-hour each week for individual time with Joseph (9) and with John (7). We called it fun schooltime on the schedule because it came when the child outgrew preschool time with me. That had been so special for them that I wanted to continue a "play" time that was educational and individual.

Anna (5), Jesse (3), and Mary (2) share their Mom's time during preschool time. They elected to have one choose the activity and the others participate each day rather than having their time rotate individually with Mom. This has worked fine, but I am thinking about including them in the afternoon individual time so they get a little of that each week too.

Once a month, when I am getting ready for the homeschool meeting that we lead, Joseph doesn't get his individual playtime since we eat dinner early. That week he and John share individual playtime on John's Thursday afternoon. We do something they both agree on.

"When scheduling activities for children, you have them on ½ hour increments. I personally think that is too short for some activities. I know the schedule needs to be adjusted to fit our own personal needs. I just wanted to know your thoughts on playtime with siblings and quiet alone time being more like forty-five minutes or an hour."

No problem with longer increments for activities. You can put together ½ hour and one hour blocks to make what you want. If you look at our sample schedule for the 98/99 school year, you will see

A Personal Word

Just as we were all so into the swing of our schedule, my husband had to change shifts. He is now working afternoons from 2 - 10 p.m. BUT, he still has to work days sometimes: Thursday and Friday this week, maybe Monday and Wednesday next week, Tuesday the week after. Well, you get the picture, confusing and frustrating.

Despite our optimism that our schedule would still work, we have found it IMPOSSIBLE to do our normal routine with Dad at home. After a week and a half of pulling my hair out trying to stick by the "old" schedule, I finally gave in and made an "alternate" schedule to use when my husband is home in the mornings and gone in the afternoon. Wow!!! I actually had the tools to do something other than throw up my hands in despair! I just got out those handy-dandy Master Schedule Worksheets and rearranged the little "squares" until everything worked! I'm so excited again.

Now, when my husband says, "Oh, by the way, honey, I'm working middle shift tomorrow," I can pull out the

that Sarah has her school subjects in forty-five minute increments, but I keep the times on the schedule in ½ hours blocks. So she has some ½ hour blocks that say something like "History/English." We both know that she spends the first fifteen minutes of that slot finishing up history and the other fifteen minutes starting English.

The playtimes with siblings and quiet time alone can be lengthened. You know your children and their capacities. The two things to consider are: changing an activity after a half-hour will often prevent problems such as sibling squabbles or boredom; a longer time may be difficult for them if the activity is not as enjoyable as other activities—say a social child that is spending time alone.

We use the half-hour increments quite frequently because we have so much we want to work in and would rather do a little of all of them, than have more time in fewer. Each family varies, so your schedule will obviously reflect how you would like to arrange your activities and time. It will work just fine. Having it planned and plugged into your schedule will help guarantee that it is happening.

"The kindergarten/preschooler has several 'free time' spaces. Should I fill these in with something more definite (like coloring or craft time) so he will have more direction or just let him 'float' during these times? 'Floaters' get into trouble, though, don't they?"

I would define your kindergarten/preschooler's time as much as possible; it will be helpful. This also depends on the personality of the child. I have children who do fine on their own and others whom we supervise more! It is true; floaters do tend to get into trouble. When my kindergarten daughter has her individual playtime, she is allowed to "hang" around the living room where I am doing individual schooltime with a child. She will sometimes choose to do this. As soon as she starts talking, she has to go back to her room or the playroom, whichever she is assigned to play in. You know little girls; this happens regularly!

If you give them craft time, you will need to make sure they can get supplies out and cleanup themselves or have someone available to help. If you are planning some other schooltime for yourself and other children, and this child keeps interrupting for help with his supplies, you will be frustrated.

"How many 'free' half-hours, maximum, do you suggest for each age group? I think the more details we know from an experienced mom about how our schedules can best be set up, the better our discipline will go, and the less frustrated we will be as we embark on what, for us, is uncharted territory for our families."

Hmmm. I have not considered coming up with a rule of thumb. I like to have my children, whom I schedule for, have at least a couple of hours each day that are entirely free for them to play. I schedule playtime in the evening when I will play with all of them together so this is free time for them. I gauge the amount of free time for each child by how they are handling their free time. If free time is leading to lots of bickering and squabbles, I am more likely to find ways to fill it up. During schooltime, I like to have another child or myself with the toddlers and babies all the time, except for that half-hour I have them play alone. So during the school morning, I have no scheduled "free" time for the children, but it is "free" time in the sense that one child is playing with younger children.

The time that they can all be together is late afternoon and evening. I have done this because I am more available mentally and emotionally to deal with the character issues that erupt when they all play together. I could interrupt schooltime to deal with discipline issues, but it is easier for me to do this in the late afternoon or evening.

SCHEDULING CHORES

"My question would be that you clarify at what times during the week it is appropriate to schedule big cleaning jobs. All of my children are six and under, and I'm really unsure about allowing them to do things like the bathrooms and other BIG cleaning jobs."

I agree that I would not want a young child working with the cleaning chemicals, used in bathroom cleaning, or having to do jobs too hard for them. I personally like schooling four days a week year round with some two week breaks. This leaves Friday for my weekly cleaning. I keep the children on a semi-school schedule on Fridays, but during the time I would normally spend one-on-one tutoring them, they are free while I clean. That makes it seem like a vacation day to them. They have some weekly chores such as dusting, cleaning out the van, and "dust-busting" the stairs, but they usually do these on Saturday morning.

I have known several who have really liked scheduling a cleaning time each day. They tackle one of the big cleaning jobs during that time. The disadvantage is that the house is never all clean at one time. But they have liked being able to get these jobs done with a little effort each day. It is not so tiring and is often more easily scheduled than doing it all at once.

Before I had big children to share cleaning jobs with me, I sometimes scheduled cleaning when Steve was available to oversee the children during an evening or Saturday morning. It was very hard for me to be in the middle of scrubbing the toilet and hear screaming begin between the children. It

"alternate" schedule and we're all set! Even if during breakfast he says, "Um, I have to go to work this morning!" it's still no problem. Just turn back to the "regular" schedule. I do have to know by the end of breakfast, though, or it's a little tougher to shift gears. Ellen (See the Appendix for Ellen's two schedules.)

I schedule a half-hour every day, totally devoted to my husband's needs. I keep a list of his comments, suggestions, and requests for me, and during that half-hour I work on them.

Usually, these are things like making phone calls, typing or writing letters, paying a bill, making a card on the computer, praying for something, or meditating on a verse. But, it can extend to addressing comments like, "The back of the van is sure messy!" or "This is not a good place to stack all the bills," or "Grandma would sure like to have pictures sent to her," or "It would be nice to send that family a meal."

This way, I can have the peace to enjoy being a "helpmeet" and a blessing to my husband, without feeling like he has been too demanding or like I am failing him as a wife. I could feel that way if his requests and preferences seem to interfere with the schedule, and I have no extra time. After I complete everything on the list, if I still have some time left at the end of the week, I like to write him notes to surprise him, bake something special for him, clean and straighten his drawers or possessions, or spend that time in additional prayer for him—nice things that I might otherwise feel totally incapable of doing.

The list is excellent, too, because I forget his requests very seldom now, something I was always doing before and was so embarrassed about. I know some women might not think they have a half-hour to devote to this— fifteen minutes might do. It has been such a blessing to me, my husband, and the whole family, I'd like to at least make the suggestion. Sherri M.

Whatever we are learning during the preschool time, I try to put this in his play-time too. For instance, we just recently did a community workers theme so I looked for some little plastic people (postman, nurse, etc.), and I allowed him to play with those. Or, if we are covering a particular letter, I'll add

would also be difficult for me to keep the toddlers back from the cleaning solutions. When I had to do cleaning this way, it was not as reliable because there were often "unscheduled" activities that came up for our evenings or Saturdays.

"Do you actually clean your house in just one hour on Friday morning????? Please tell me how???? I spend soooo much time cleaning!"

Our main house cleaning tasks are divided between four adults: myself and three children ages 16, 19, and 21. Our 21-year-old son is "affluent" enough that he now hires his 16-year-old sister to do his chores, but they are still his responsibility. So, my hour of cleaning time would be at least four hours if I were doing it by myself. I vacuum and dust the upstairs, while others have the bathroom cleaning and downstairs vacuuming. We try to keep up with the kitchen each day by scheduling extra kitchen chores throughout the week.

"I just read the chores section and this is an area we are really struggling with right now. Scheduling the chores isn't the problem; getting the children to do them and to do them correctly is a big problem. How do you train your children to do their chores? What kind of consequences do you impose for doing a lousy job or 'forgetting' to do a part of their job? My two oldest boys (ages nine and eleven) do a good job when I'm standing over them, training them, but as soon as I'm not right there, telling them every single step, the job gets done progressively worse and worse until it's a complete disaster. I'd really appreciate any advice you could offer."

I can understand your frustration with the chore situation in your home. This can be an area of challenge in our home too. I have found the biggest key to this is my consistency. When I make particular chores my focus—reteaching, then checking the job every time, it improves greatly. It is not unusual for the quality to slip as I begin checking less.

A rule or responsibility means nothing unless there are significant consequences for neglecting it. I do best if I write down consequences for not doing a chore or for doing a poor job. We have these notes on the white board right now.

1. No morning teeth brushed - no dessert for two days.

2. No schoolwork - no dinner until it is done.

3. No Saturday chores - no lunch.

4. Breakfast dishes not put in dishwasher - breakfast cleanup for a week.

5. Table not dried - Fine of $0.25.

6. If table/floor has to be redone - 15 minutes sitting on the chair.

We try to think of consequences that are appropriate and motivational. I also try to encourage myself that this is as important a part of my childrearing as homeschooling is. Most of the chore issues are truly character related and are where I want my focus to be. I have to keep telling myself this, because I tend to react emotionally to failures in our children in the area of their chores. We make better progress when I deal with it all in a calm manner but have the courage to let the consequences be enforced consistently.

I would suggest that you have a time scheduled in your day when you check on the chores and evaluate them. My frustration usually comes when we start school and I walk by the dining room table to discover it hasn't been washed. If I have on my plan during the breakfast half-hour to check chores, then I can deal with them and allow the consequences to come. I have trained myself to stop by the bedrooms before breakfast and have not allowed a child to eat breakfast until the room passes my inspection. Sometimes that means I have to go back and look again.

May I also encourage you that it seems to be more difficult to train boys in the chore area than girls. My older boys will do what they are assigned chore-wise, and as adults, still living in our home, they do a good job. But they do not "see" areas of need outside their assigned chores. They are much like the majority of men, from what I have found in talking with women. Our teen-age daughter does see, and is sensitive to, these extra needs. All three children were raised in the same home with the same requirements for helping. We still encourage the big boys to look for needs at home and meet them, as we know what a blessing this will be for a future wife!

"I have time for chores so that the house gets cleaned each day, however, I am not sure how to 'work' that time block. In order for our lives to run smoothly the house must be kept clean. I would love a system to help with chore time to make sure everything that needs to be done is getting accomplished. I have a ten-year-old boy and the rest are five and under, so most of the work falls to me. Any ideas or helps? I would love a worksheet or something to help this specific area. As you can guess, I have an extremely difficult time coming up with a system myself, but can use one if someone gives it to me and shows me how to set it up."

Since you are getting your schedule pinned down, I think you could do the same for your chore schedule. I have found the only way for me to keep track of this chore area is to write it all down. Our chore system has been in place for many years, but occasionally it will have an item added to it.

things to his playtime that begin with that letter for him to play with. I think that it really reinforces what we're learning, and it's EASY!! Tracy L.

Thanks so much for doing this book. I am loving it. Rebecca

For those people who have unmitigating circumstances crop up, I have a message: Don't give up! For those people who feel they may be failing at scheduling and making their family goals a reality, I have a message: You aren't the only one! For those relaxed homeschoolers who want to implement some scheduling changes, but are finding your plan difficult to follow, my message is: don't stress yourself out, give it some time. Sheila

Just a word of warning for those who have computers. Schedule your computer time and try to stick to it. I can easily spend hours at my computer, and I believe this has been the biggest source to keep me off schedule. As a reward for accomplishing some work early, I will hop on the computer for a few minutes. With this schedule,

it is good, though, because I know that I have to get back off quickly enough to start the next job. Unfortunately, I will confess that I haven't been doing this like I should. Also getting to bed and rising early has to be another main key to my schedule. The reward is great when I do. Cindy

We had been having such a struggle with breakfast in the mornings. Either I didn't have time to slap anything but cold cereal on the table, or I cooked a nice breakfast but lost time in my schedule. I get lunch, and sometimes supper too, on their way during our "breakfast" time in order to keep "on schedule" the rest of the day.

Anyway, I recently discovered make-ahead breakfasts! I did an Internet search on breakfasts and quickly came up with at least a dozen easy, cost-effective recipes that can sit in the fridge overnight and be popped in the oven the next morning! Evenings before bedtime are much less hectic for me than the mornings, so it's not so tough to find ten or so extra minutes to throw together a pan of breakfast food! We've had strata, Mexican casserole, baked oatmeal, and French toast. English muffin

Because of the need indicated by our test group of families in the area of chore assignments, we have developed chore worksheets and step-by-step instructions for the determination of chores and chore assignments. You will find these in Chapter Six, "Scheduling Chores."

SCHEDULING BABIES

"I have a question about a nursing baby's first scheduled time for nursing. My baby is a month old, and I nurse him when he wakes up during the night. Last night he nursed at 4:00 a.m. and then was too full and sleepy to nurse at his scheduled time of 6:00 a.m. I was hesitant to try to wake him up by changing his diaper, in case he wouldn't go back to sleep, and then I wouldn't be able to do my planned morning things. I'm not sure what to do since moving his nursing time up an hour just for today would disrupt the whole schedule I spent so long adjusting to be 'just right.' If I skip the 6:00 a.m., I doubt that he could go five hours until the next scheduled feeding at 9:00 a.m. Any ideas? I'm sure this has happened to you too."

This age is a tricky time for a schedule and a baby. It is a good problem because the baby is stretching his night out just as you want him to do. Here are a couple of things I have tried:

1. Wait to see when he does wake up again and is hungry. Sometimes mine have slept through until that nine o'clock morning feeding, even when I thought they wouldn't.

2. If he wakes up before that, have your morning routine such that you can accommodate. For example, if you are scheduled to nurse at 6:00 a.m., then scheduled to have your devotion time, you could go ahead and have your devotion time at 6:00 a.m. Then you could do anything else that you could manage to do early on your schedule. This might include some prep on breakfast or some of your chores. It is hard to be really specific since I don't know what your early morning schedule is. The things you are going to do from 6:00 a.m. until 9:00 a.m. will be the same, they would just change order. If he were up at 7:00 a.m. to nurse, you could nurse him and put him back to bed. Then try to get him to nurse again at 9:00 a.m., his normal time. If he won't go back to sleep at 7:00 a.m., then just carry him around for what you are doing in your morning routine. Newborns sleep so much that he will probably go back to sleep for a while before his 9:00 a.m. nursing and have to be awakened then.

3. The third possibility is to split the difference between 4 and 9 a.m. and not even try to get him to nurse until 6:30 a.m. or even 7:00 a.m. You might have more success just that little bit later. Again, this means rearranging

some of your early morning schedule. As he gets nearer the six o'clock nursing some of these issues go away. If he wakes up to nurse at 5:30 a.m., he will probably be able to go until 9:00 a.m.

4. Flexibility will be key for these next two or three weeks as he stretches out the night. You have a plan of what to do and times set on the schedule, but you may have to move some of those pieces around to accommodate him—not physically on the schedule but mentally in your mind. It shouldn't take him long to stretch his night to 5:30 or 6:00 a.m. I hope this doesn't discourage you on your schedule; it is challenging, but very temporary.

"Do you wake the baby back up if she falls asleep nursing?"

No, if my baby falls asleep nursing and the next thing she is to do is sleep, I just put her down. Most of my babies wake up when I put them down even if they were asleep while nursing, so they usually seem to be put to bed awake. In our schedule, some nursing times come before a sleep time but others don't, so the baby is going to sleep both ways—just after nursing and also later on.

"Another thing I have been wondering about. You don't mention how church activity times affect your schedule. Do you intentionally schedule baby nursing times around church meeting times so that you won't be routinely missing services to nurse the baby?"

I do take our church schedule into consideration with the nursing, but more often, since it is only one day a week for us (no Wednesday night service at our church) I make my nursing plan around our daily schedule, not the church times. My preference is to not have to nurse at church, but we have a forty-five minute drive to church, so we leave at 8:00 a.m. and are not home until 12 noon. When we arrived at church, I nursed at 9:00 a.m. just when the service was beginning, and again when we arrived home. We are generally gone from home for three hours in the evening for the service. I would nurse at 7:00 p.m. when the evening service had just ended and our family was fellowshipping. It was a little early from the usual 7:15 p.m. nursing Mary had for several months, but a few minutes variation from the schedule once in a while was certainly no big deal.

I suggest you look at your nursing times and on Sunday nights nurse before choir and after church, if that is close to the normal nursing time. The same with your Wednesday evening service, nurse before it starts and after you get home, if the baby can wait. As you look at the possibilities—when the baby normally nurses, and when it is most convenient for you to nurse, you will see ways to work the baby's schedule around those two or three times. It will probably be close to his normal schedule but perhaps not exactly.

pizzas, refrigerator bran muffins, breakfast burritos, and crock pot cobbler are soon to come! The children can wake up to a hot, filling tasty meal instead of boring, expensive cereal, and I can feel like I'm really "doing" something for breakfast! Ellen

Dad's desire for more children, too, is affected by the order of the household. If time is effectively scheduled, children can accomplish many tasks that normally fall to him. Sally

In retrospect, having used the book, I would have paid one hundred dollars for it, if I could have known beforehand the tremendous benefits I would gain: peace in my busy home and the ability my schedule gives me to accomplish the things I feel God wants me to do in my family. Tracy W.

Some things that I'd like to implement into my schedule that I learned from the book:

1. Rotating children's playtimes with other children or the baby. The children are loving this! Their faces light up when they can stop their "seat work" and play with another child. I think maybe, though, I need to have something in mind for them to do (something fun), because the playtime sometimes runs ragged toward the end of the half-hour.

2. One-on-one tutor time with each school age child. I had been doing the "school teacher" routine, walking around the classroom, waiting for questions. I love having the half-hour to teach just one-on-one. It just never occurred to me before, except in the case of teaching phonics and how to read.

3. Scheduling with more flexibility. I tend to schedule the minimum time it takes to get something done, not the maximum. This never left any room for discipline, interruptions, or emergencies, and left me anxious and "pushing" the children as the day would progress.

4. Planned training time. Never thought of that before, and it is fun! I'm so much more patient and kind with the children, NOT trying to "push" or "hurry up"! The Bible doesn't really have good things to say about hurrying, does it? So, I ask myself all the time, "Why do I say 'hurry!' to my children several times every day?"
Sherri M.

"I assume that even though you drop the schedule for weekends you still have to maintain the baby's nursing schedule so as not to cause confusion for the infant. Is this correct?"

Yes, yes! The baby stays on his schedule throughout the weekend even if we do not have as much structure to our days. The nursing and napping schedule, in and of, itself makes structure for the weekend.

"How do you adjust for growth spurts?"

I have not found a need to adjust for growth spurts. My only explanation is that the baby takes more milk when in a growth spurt and then I produce more. I can't remember a baby just being fussy and me feeling that he needed to nurse more frequently. We do make that allowance for a sick baby, and we would if we felt he was in a growth spurt and had extra needs. But, again, that has not been my experience. The babies have just been happy and grown nicely.

"Have you ever had to supplement with formula?"

No. Our babies have nothing except breast milk until they are about eight months old. I will often try at six months to see if they are interested in eating solid foods, but they haven't been. I have never had a problem with my milk supply.

"Do you ever nurse in between if just nothing else settles the baby down?"

Yes, if I have had a young infant who wakes early from a nap I will sometimes try nursing him to see if he will be coaxed back to sleep. This doesn't happen very often. Usually our babies are fussy from getting tired, not from being hungry.

"What about if they want to nurse in the night?"

I nurse them at night until they seem ready to drop that feeding. For our last five babies that has been between two and three months of age. If they seem close to going through the night, but aren't quite there, we may try letting them cry. This decision is reached between my husband and me with much prayer and discussion. Mary, at two months of age, cried for forty minutes one night. It was agony for me, but once I had let her cry a while, I felt committed to not wasting the time she had already cried, and I stuck with it. She only did that one night and has slept through every night since, except one or two when she was sick. We have had babies that slept through the night at this age on their own and others who have cried for a night or two, but that forty minutes for Mary was the longest crying session I remember.

I know many do not feel they can make the choice to let their babies cry at night. I understand and respect that decision. For us that night of crying was difficult, but we have felt the dividends in a rested, sweeter Mommy for the whole family was worth any sacrifice Mary might have made. It is debatable, in my mind, whether it was a sacrifice versus ultimately being better for her. She has always been a good sleeper and continues to be. A pediatrician told a friend of mine, who was seeking his advice on how to get her baby to sleep through the night, to let the baby cry. He said it was as important for a baby to have an undisturbed night's sleep as it is for an adult.

I have shared the information on babies and family schedules with you from my experience and how it has worked for our babies, our home, and our schedule.

It seems necessary, if a family wants to have a schedule, that the baby should have one too. Whether it is a two hour nursing schedule, two and a half-hour schedule, three hour, or longer. It just has to be determined and planned as part of the schedule. With a baby it will change. For our babies the three hour schedule accommodated them from two weeks until weaning time—well over one year of age. The only part of the schedule that changed was their sleeping times, unless they were nearing weaning and beginning to drop nursings.

"I see I need to set the nursing time to begin at the same time every day and keep it pretty consistent."

Yes, this is key to the schedule for a baby and for every person in your family. Make this waking up time realistic. For our babies, I nurse them early in the morning and put them right back down. I want them to sleep until eight because I am out of the house walking from 7:00 to 7:45 a.m. I don't want other family members to have to give up their devotion and chore time to care for the baby. But if I were home and making breakfast earlier in the morning, I might get the baby up earlier, so he would take a longer nap in the morning when we would like to have some less disrupted schooltime.

Are you getting a picture of how a schedule is your plan for your family, for your particular needs? Are you seeing how it is like a puzzle, with many little pieces that need to be meshed together for the greatest efficiency of your home?

INTERRUPTIONS

"I have a question. This comes up a lot, and I'm sure its just something I have to learn to deal with continually, but maybe you have some ideas.

RAINY DAY activities: (for when you have outside time scheduled and it RAINS!!!)

Play dough

Color

Paint

Bake cookies

Draw

Indoor scavenger hunt

Read an extra book

Make a tent to play in

Small children could put on their swim suits and pretend to swim together in bath tub.

Make cards to send to relatives to let them know you are thinking of them.

Learn an extra Bible story, act it out (maybe even video tape it for Dad to see when he gets home).

Play Legos at the kitchen table with Mom.

Play dress up with some of Mom and Dad's old clothes.

Make a tape of the children singing Christmas carols for Grandparent's for Christmas (my children think this is really a lot of fun, especially when it's a 100 degree day and humid!!).
Tracy L.

It is neat now that the schedule is in my head, to know what to do next! Even my little ones are learning their schedules. I cannot "skip" Jesse's pre-K time. If he sees me try to start the twins' phonics, he jumps in his high chair, shoves crayons and his learning to color book at me, and says, "Sing, Mama, sing." He KNOWS he comes first! Lisa

I have added a thirty minute time period each morning where my older children will do chores that require a good chunk of time. Zak vacuums upstairs or downstairs, Abi organizes pots, pans, or Tupperware; Ben folds laundry. They can do these things without supervision, and they are not in the same room, so they don't distract each other. Then, I don't have to have a big chunk of time later that they are unavailable for school. Debbie

After school the schedule gets a little more flakey. A lot of it is free time of course, but I will be working on structuring some of the earlier afternoon. I have a music/art/Spanish period

I seem to be constantly running into situations where I am doing a task, and I then notice a new mess that someone has made (e.g. they have dumped out something that belongs to me—a special pen or paper from my desk—not anything too big). So I have to stop what I am doing, and what they are doing, and have them pick up whatever it is. It gets to be very confusing to remember what they were supposed to be doing before then.

Another thing is when I later notice that something wasn't cleaned properly after lunch, and now they are out mowing the lawn or something. I do try to check before they go on, because I don't want them learning bad work habits. Right now, it seems my nine-year-old can sweep after every meal, but still leave so much behind that it doesn't seem he swept at all! Most things he does really well.

Anyway, we are all in the school room, and I notice a big mess on the floor. So we stop, and they work on that. Meanwhile, time is ticking away.

My seven children are all ages nine and under, and while they are very helpful, it is mind-boggling to keep up with what they are all supposed to be doing. I seem to give them so many instructions, it's hard to remember what they are supposed to be doing.

Looking at neat little boxes with labels really seems to be scary though. Mostly because I know that we seem to do a lot of backtracking while training them."

First, may I assure you that I would be surprised if there is one of us who could not relate to all you shared. Several ideas do come to mind. With your schedule and all those "neat little boxes with labels" you should have an easier time remembering who is to be doing what, when you get side-tracked. It is all written down and can be consulted. I think after two weeks of using the schedule you won't be looking at it anymore, nor will your children. Even your three and four-year-olds will know the order of their activities, though they do need to be told when to change activities.

Some messes we deal with right away, but some we leave until a more convenient time. If I were to notice a toy mess on the floor during schooltime, I would let it go until lunch. I might have one of the younger children work at picking it up if they were responsible for making it, but not have too high expectations because they are better "picker uppers" with Mom's coaching. At lunch time, I would assign a child who didn't have other responsibilities to pick up the mess or have us all pitch in to work on it.

If the mess was water that had been dumped all over the bathroom floor by one of the little children, I would leave the child to clean it up or send another child I felt was capable, to do it. I would come back to the schooltime, jumping in where the schedule said I was to be.

There will be regular occurrences of distractions and interruptions. A schedule keeps me on track. It assures me that I am having phonics time with my five-year-old every day. If I must break from that phonics time to discipline or deal with a minor catastrophe, it will not require all of that time every day. I will still be making good, regular headway with this child, in phonics. If I did not have that time scheduled for her, I would likely keep myself busy with other school tasks, discipline issues, or housework, and feel guilty or discouraged through the year that I was not getting around to phonics with her.

Do you see the polarity I am trying to describe? On the one hand I have scheduled the activities and times to accomplish what God has called me to, and take the interruptions as they come, getting back on track as soon as possible. On the other hand, without a schedule, I am driven by these interruptions and somehow never seem to get to what I have felt are my priorities, but rather these priorities begin to seem like burdens.

Sometimes, I do not stop school to deal with a discipline issue. If I am having preschool with the little ones, and the seven and nine-year-olds are fussing with each other, I may send them to separate rooms to do their schoolwork, and deal with discipline at lunch time or after school. If two of my preschoolers are assigned to play together during the school morning and they are squabbling with each other, I have them spend the next few minutes of their playtime sitting on dining room chairs. Then I let them try again. It is a simple discipline, but it separates them, has them quiet, and motivates them to want to get along. If it happens again, they go back to the chairs for a longer time!

When I let a mess or a discipline issue go, I may write notes on paper or the whiteboard, as a reminder to myself. Yesterday when I put Jesse down for his nap, the closet light was on. When I turned it out, I noticed quite a large mess that needed to be cleaned up. That was not the time to call the culprits to task. When I went upstairs, I wrote a note. Yesterday afternoon when I would have had Joseph and John pick up in their closet, they were gone with their daddy to Kansas City. The evening was filled with dinner, cleanup, and grocery shopping. But my note is still on the counter. When their playtime with Sarah is finished this morning, their first task is to cleanup their closet. Then they can enjoy their free time.

scheduled after lunch, which may really need to be moved to the end of the schooling time to be more effective. It's very hard to get back to things—and since we're starting school at 7 a.m. (a natural time for me), we have been finishing up by 11 a.m. anyway, so continuing to 11:30 won't be that big a deal. Rebecca

I also forgot to tell you in my last message, your reply to my panic really helped me. The part that helped the most was where you talked about your first day of school and how most of what you do the first couple of weeks is training and adjusting to the schedule. This encouraged me to look at the whole process differently. I told my big boys that for the next couple of weeks we weren't going to worry about how much school we get done, but more about training everybody to work with the schedule and deal with character issues that are getting in the way. This has caused me to feel better because my priorities are different. I think this is going to work in the long run. Robyn

I began fine-tuning my final schedule. I was plan-

ning on getting up at 6:30 for exercise and then my shower. 7:00 dress and clean bathroom, 7:30 nurse Abigail.

I was going to begin today with my wake up time. Guess what? I didn't get up. I was awake but I just didn't want to get out of bed to exercise. I realized that 6:30 a.m. to exercise is not going to be realistic for me. But I also realized that I like to lie in bed for a while and think about my day. What I decided to do is to make my first twenty-five minutes a prayer time. Then I will get up and exercise for twenty minutes and finish out the 7:00 time slot with a quick shower and cleanup in the bathroom. I can then nurse the baby at 7:30 and do my quiet time.

I also worked out a dinner time that I think we can live with. I had wanted to eat at 5:00, but I had to admit that it wasn't a realistic time either. I talked with my husband and decided 5:30 would be better.

Well, I changed a few more things and am very excited with the final outcome. I know we will probably make other changes as we actually start using the schedule, but I am pretty confident that most things are going to work. Cindy

We are becoming a family decorated in modern whiteboard. We have found whiteboards to be such wonderful reminders. We have one in the kitchen where I list discipline consequences. How often have I said, "If you slam a door again, you will have to practice closing it quietly twenty times for every time you slam." But if I don't write it down, I quickly forget and just repeat the "threat" the next time the door is slammed. If I write it down and see it regularly, the next time the door is slammed, I call the slammer to practice. If the time isn't good to practice then, I write a note so it can be dealt with later.

When I am consistent at checking the children's work and calling them back to redo it if necessary, it improves. Then I let down my vigilance, and so do they. I truly believe that my continued perseverance in not growing weary in these child training issues will be blessed by our faithful God. Sometimes I think I want to quit and let it all go. Is there any possibility of the children becoming orderly, responsible, diligent, obedient workers if I did? Certainly God could miraculously do this, but since He has given my husband and me that task, I expect, if in my disobedience to God, I quit, He would let me live with the consequences. I don't think I would be any happier with that than I am with the constancy of teaching and training our children.

Summed up, a schedule will help you know when to deal with "messes" right away and when to put them off to a more convenient time. It should help you get more accomplished so distractions and interruptions are less of a difficulty to your overall efficiency. Making notes will help keep those thoughts of what needs to be dealt with later from escaping your mind. Plus, you don't have to work on remembering them, since they are written down as reminders.

"How do you handle phone calls that come in all afternoon? I've already put in a time slot for them; should I also plan activities I can do while I talk on the phone?"

I can think of a couple of ideas for phone calls that cannot be scheduled. One is what you mentioned in having scheduled activities that you can do while you are on the phone. Then if there are no phone calls, you can just do what you have planned anyway.

Another is to have a scheduled time when you can return calls. This fits in with the previous idea because while you can schedule your outgoing calls, you can't schedule the incoming ones. I have callback time from 1:30 to 2:30 p.m. and 9:30 p.m., after the little children are in bed. These times are "scheduled" for other activities such as sewing, writing, and computer. But they are activities that are not mandatory to our life maintenance. I can forego them when I need to return phone calls. The older children know this is the time I return calls and will tell the caller these times, seeing if that is acceptable to them. That way they know I haven't forgotten them if I don't return the call until 9:30 p.m.

I do like to double this time if I can, so I often fold clothes (which is scheduled for another time), one of the few things I can manage to do acceptably while on the phone. If I get my clothes folded while on the phone, I have scheduled "clothes folding time" as a bonus free time that day.

I prefer to make phone calls while the little ones are in bed. I do not like the distraction if the children are misbehaving, and I don't like having to ask someone to hold while I settle a problem or discipline.

I try very hard not to answer the phone. If one of the older children answer it, often a quick message will be left, whereas if I answer the phone, it can easily turn into a ten minute or more conversation. We have older children to answer the phone, but I would use an answering machine if we didn't.

"I seem to discipline and instruct children all day. Do you just have time 'buffered' into your schedule to allow for this? You certainly can't schedule it. I know by the time I instruct, discipline, pray, and love the culprit, I've spent at least five minutes with a little one, and if the culprit happens to be a 'big' one it usually takes a little longer."

Yes, I have tried to make my scheduled times for various activities generous enough to allow for discipline time. You are very right; it does take at least five minutes and maybe more. Often in our home while I am in disciplining one, I come out to another situation that has happened while I was gone from the room, that now requires discipline too. So back into the bedroom I go again. There have been days I felt like we were living in there! Does that happen at your house? Of course, my schedule does not have that much time allowed for disciplining. Then I have to remind myself that the schedule is my tool, my helper; it directs and organizes my time. If there are discipline needs, those come before some parts of my schedule. I will let go of schooltime to discipline, but I will not make a baby wait to nurse if he is hungry. In that case, I make the child wait for his discipline.

The main goal with our children is godly character. That is brought out in being willing to leave a scheduled activity to teach, instruct, and discipline when needed.

It is also good when we can have a scheduled time for focusing on particular character training we desire for our children. I have to say I don't have this in my schedule right now, but I have seen the benefits it brings. When I had a half-hour a day for this, I could work with my children all together in a character area. Or I could have one child that was struggling that I could

So on Monday this week we started back in and have tried to do our schedule every day. It does really help to have the outline so I do not get distracted. Many character flaws have bared their ugly head in myself as well as the children. Terri

My biggest problem that I can foresee is going to be checking up on the chores. I am planning to use some detailed, posted instructions, with self-checking questions already on the list, so the children will remember exactly what is expected of them. I have some instructions I had written up for other chores, like the exact method for washing dishes since we have no automatic dishwasher. That is really helpful, and Abi has already memorized it. I was never taught how to wash dishes when I was young, so I was constantly told to wash them over. She is almost eight, and really does well. Debbie

How many times, as a young wife, with ever increasing numbers of children, did I look around and say to myself, "I HAVE TO CHANGE THE WAY I DO

THINGS." And then, as soon as my husband came home I said, "Okay Honey, this is what we are going to do."

It has only been by the infinite grace of God (and the near infinite grace of Tom) that I finally discovered Who was in charge, and who was second in command. Now, many years later, I am continually delighted by Tom's ability to listen to my esoteric descriptions of household glitches and conflicts and to come up with a very perceptive solution.

And why does he go to all the effort to come up with a reply to my minor questions? Well, first, he knows it pleases his God to tend to the needs of his flock. And, secondly, he knows I'm really waiting for the answer and haven't wandered off in my own direction in the meantime.

It is such an exciting thing to see, every day, in my own home a small likeness of Jesus' love and care for His people. Sally

One of the problems was that I didn't have enough time to get my chores done in the mornings in the short block of time I allowed for that. So, I put in a half-hour

work with and share Scriptures in their area of need. Perhaps having a scheduled time for this character focus would help prevent some of the unscheduled discipline issues.

"How do you get back on schedule when you are off due to waking up late, discipline problem, cleaning up messes, or anything else? Do you pick up at whatever time it is and miss doing the things before that, or do you start at the beginning and just do everything at a later time? Are you following me? We should have started school at 9:00, but it is 9:30, and we haven't even done the chores and devotions yet."

I do pick up the schedule wherever it is and go on from there. But this would only be occasionally necessary. I seldom let the children sleep late. I go ahead and get them up at their normal time, assuming they will catch up on sleep at nap time or the next night. So there aren't very many times when we are behind on our morning schedule.

If you start the schedule at a later time than called for, something will have to be left out. You can make these decisions, since you know what are the most crucial parts of your schedule. I let some of the early morning chores go until lunch or after school, to start the school day on time. I also look at the morning schooltime and decide what is least important and eliminate that first. For us that is preschool time (one-half hour), half of John's meeting with me (one-half hour), and our school Bible time (one-half hour). Those I would let go first.

When I am dealing with a situation that is short term but needs my attention such as cleaning up a mess, I tell everyone to go ahead and start what they are to be doing while I cleanup. Then I join where I am supposed to be. If I have a one-on-one time with a child, I have them go ahead and do anything they can while they wait, such as drill work or reading out loud.

"If for some reason you miss your cleaning day, perhaps because of illness, do you have an alternate schedule, or do you wait until the next week to clean?"

For me, the answer would be that it depends on the circumstances. If I am sick, the cleaning just gets missed until the next week unless my family pitches in and does it for me. Usually they will do this. If the children are sick, I can often manage to work in my cleaning around taking care of them. I might take an evening that would have been "free" time to do it or fit it in on Saturday. I will let some of the cleaning go that might not matter so much and only do the necessities. At this stage of my parenting, it isn't so crucial because most of the weekly cleaning is divided between four adults (a 21, 19, 16-year-old, and myself). If I can't get my cleaning done, only one-fourth of it is left undone. When another family member is gone, who has cleaning responsibilities, or is ill, we all pitch in to cover for them.

SCHEDULING CHALLENGES

"The evening schedule? We will have this fall, AWANA on Mondays, prayer meeting on Wednesdays, my husband is taking a college course Thursdays (so no family devotions with him that night), and then there's the weekend. All of these activities have fairly regular time slots (just not the same time slots). Would you suggest we have a different schedule for each night or just make our evening schedule 'loose' to accommodate the varying conditions?"

I would suggest a basic evening schedule that can be dropped the nights you are not there. So, in other words, I would not plan to fold my laundry in the evening if I had two nights a week when I was not home. I would have my laundry folding late in the afternoon, perhaps, or have a child take it over, if possible, since I do laundry almost every day, and it needs to be folded and distributed each day.

"What about scheduling Saturdays?"

We do not have a Saturday schedule. I know what I need to do, and I start in the morning working through my "to do" list. The children are usually involved with Daddy so they also have a few areas of responsibility but mostly are free to be free. There are "benchmarks" to our weekend—exercise, nursing home ministry, Steve and my date, mealtimes, and devotion time. But the time in between is not scheduled. If your husband is not home on Saturdays, a schedule would certainly be helpful for keeping up with basic Saturday chores and projects. But I expect for most of us, Saturday is a family day with Dad home and in charge.

If you are just beginning to schedule your days, I would not encourage you to schedule Saturdays. Work on your basic weekday schedule. If that routine and schedule is helpful and going well, then consider a more rigid Saturday schedule. But not now.

"I had asked you about our 'predictably irregular' evenings. I think I have it figured out, and I'm so excited I just had to write and tell you about it!!

I did a combination of what you told me about not cramming the schedule too full (cushioning scheduled activities with lots of extra time) and actually planning in 'extra time.' With all of our children so young yet, I think this might work.

of independent work for the older boys and free time for the little ones, to allow myself enough time to get my work done, before we start our time together. Robyn

We are trying to figure out how to make this work with our family situation. Up until now, we have been committed to breast-feeding on demand, and I have always been loose with nap times. We take naps, but it could start anywhere between 1:30-3:30. I have never watched the clock that closely. That also goes for feeding times.

I can see the benefit of knowing when the baby will be ready to eat and sleep. So this week I have been observing seven month old Ben to see when he normally sleeps and eats. We have a general bedtime, but because of our different activities, that can vary as well. You probably think we have a long way to go.

I have been praying this week, watching, and observing, so when I make my schedule, it will be more reality based, and we will be able to stick to it. We have started a few of your sugges-

tions. I know we have a ways to go. Renée

One thing I'll mention that I wouldn't have thought to do without the scheduling project. I bought a Timex Triathalon watch that has a timer and stopwatch on it. I set the timer for fifteen minutes, and I can start it anytime. I'm thinking about setting it for thirty minutes instead. A little alarm goes off to help signal when it's time to change activities. It has been a great help for all sorts of things. "Mom, how many minutes until we leave for church?"

I had planned to buy an electronic timer for the schoolroom, but realized I needed a new watch anyway, so I decided to put those two needs together. The watch was just under $30, and so far, well worth it! It does keep time by the way, as well as keep the date where I can see it. Rebecca

I asked the one child who was really excited about the schedule, "Why?" He said because he wanted to stay on track (he's eleven).

He also said, "I don't know; I just thought it would be fun."

What I've done is to plan in 1 ½ hours each evening of what I call 'Family Events.' This includes AWANA, ball games, church services, visiting, family movie and game nights, and hospitality. Some things will take longer than 1 ½ hours (like AWANA, for example, which takes 2 ½ hours from the time we leave the house until we arrive back home). But, since I've cushioned supper with some extra time and those nights the children won't be taking baths, it should still work great! I'm so excited!! Is this what you meant? Am I getting the idea?"

That's exactly it!

"When occasional (but regularly scheduled) activities occur, have you found it best to do a shortened version of your normal schedule or just eliminate some items. For instance, once per month we have home-school activity day. When we get home after noon, should we try to run through our usual morning schedule in quick time or pick up with whatever the schedule says when we arrive home?"

Pick up with whatever the schedule says when you get home. If you try to squeeze in a usual morning schedule in quick time, you will be frustrated and pushing your family. Being away from home and coming back has its own stresses. Your schedule should help you with this because you, and the rest of the family, know what to do when you get home.

If you have a regular weekly outing, perhaps a morning ladies' Bible study at church, you could drop some of the scheduled afternoon activities—particularly for school age children—and substitute the most important core of morning activities. I have found a varied schedule for one of the weekdays is workable, but if you have this for too many days, you are undermining one of the strengths of a schedule, and that is everyone knowing what to do and when to do it. On our cleaning and school planning Fridays, I have to do much more directing of the children, because we are not on our normal schedule.

"How do you work in spending time with friends? We usually have friends over once a week, and it normally gets late. We encourage and challenge one another in the Lord, and I really don't want to see this go. It would be hard to rise early after a 1 a.m. or 2 a.m. fellowship. Any suggestions? We normally do this on Friday or Saturday night."

When we get together with friends, it is on weekend nights for us too, but our evening with them usually ends around nine, when we put the little ones to bed. But, Steve and I stay up until midnight on Friday and Saturday nights. We just sleep later on Saturday morning. On Sunday, we have to get up at 6:30 a.m. to get to church by 9:00 a.m. We all take naps on Sunday afternoon—all ten of us—for at least two hours. That helps us catch up on the sleep lost to late weekend nights.

You would seem to have two choices for your mornings after late nights. You either go ahead and get up at your normal wake up time, perhaps taking a nap in the afternoon. Or you push everything back on your schedule and get up later. Since your late nights are on the weekends, I am wondering if you are planning a structured schedule for Saturdays and Sundays. If you are, then you could schedule for a later rising time on the weekend. If your weekends are less "scheduled" then it wouldn't matter so much when you got up.

"When do you run errands and go shopping?"

Steve and I run errands on our Saturday afternoon date. He also does many errands when in Kansas City, during the week, on business. He has taken over the grocery shopping the past few years and does that on Thursday nights. It is a special time for him and the children. He takes all the little ones and one of the older children. I know most moms do not enjoy this luxury and need to plan that time into their week.

I have begun a monthly outing with Sarah (16) on the first Tuesday of the month. I had to set a time for this, tell her, and be accountable to it, or I found I never got around to spending special time with her. I keep a list, through the month, of things I need that don't have to be purchased right away. She and I eat at a fast food restaurant and then go shopping together. It has become a meaningful part of our relationship.

We have two boys of driving age who often frequent places I need items from, so I have a "to buy" list in my notebook organizer on a sticky note. When they are going, they ask if I need anything. I can tell them very easily if I do.

It may seem like an eternity until your children are old enough to do some of your errands, but it really isn't. Look forward to those days. They are truly a delight to my mother's heart. Usually the big boys will invite a little one to accompany them on their errands. They will buy the little one a treat and make it a special time. Those relationships are very sweet between them and dear for me to watch.

You need to plan your errand and grocery shopping into the schedule. Develop organizational skills, such as having "to buy" lists and "errands" lists. I have a friend who has a master grocery list with space down the side for her to list other errands and items to purchase at other stores. When she has a shopping afternoon, she does not have to worry about forgetting any-

I think the other children were a little excited because it was something new, and we have things scheduled that we don't usually get to do. Robyn

There were a few little things that didn't go smoothly, like my kindergartner wasn't scheduled to do any school until after lunch and rest time. She "bugged" me all morning about when would she get to do school, so I need to rethink that. My two preschoolers need more time from me in the morning too, so I need to revise the schedule a little. I figured I'd try it for a week like it is and then do any revisions this weekend. Ricki

I don't even talk on the phone like I used to. I am feeling more able to focus all my attention at home, and I'm not as easily distracted. What an awesome feeling. The children love the schedule too. They are always looking at it telling me what they are supposed to be doing. If they miss their time to play with the baby, they sure let me know! Pauline

I finally got up on time today. PTL!! I have NEVER

been an early riser. God is giving me the strength, and I already see His blessings. The children got brand new alarm clocks yesterday as a reward for their willingness to make this work. They were so excited. Josh slept through his alarm this morning. I knew I should have gotten a BIG BEN!!! He'll get it eventually. We actually started and finished breakfast early! Off to chore time. We have extra time to finish. This is so wonderful!!! Kristi

Lunchtime, and so far, so good! One thing I didn't work into the schedule and naively thought wouldn't be necessary was time to prepare lunch. But if it's not written down, I have a tendency not to do it, so today when noon (lunchtime is from 12:00 to 12:30) rolled around, and I saw "Lunch" on the schedule, I said, "Oops!" and ran out to get the chicken nuggets out of the deep freeze and get the pan of water boiling for macaroni. (May I borrow a teenager for meal prep, please?) Hmmm, how do I fit in time to make lunch? The rest of the morning went just "great" schedule-wise, so I hate to change anything! Ellen

thing. She has kept a running list through the week, on her master grocery list, of what she needs to do while out.

If you do errands on a weekday afternoon, you may need a variable schedule for that afternoon. There are sample schedules in the Appendix that make use of different activities on different weekdays for the same time block. Try to keep your errands limited to one time per week.

PUTTING THE SCHEDULE TOGETHER

"I started on the children's Activity Worksheets beginning with the baby's first. This is where I got confused. Do you do an Activity Worksheet for the baby? It seems you do their schedule around everyone else's. Does this mean I do others first, start putting it together, and then do the baby last, after the times are set?"

Maybe it is easier to start with the older children's worksheets first since more of what they do is determined, such as: school, meals, chores, and bedtimes. Don't be afraid to leave things off at the start. Take a first cut at everyone's worksheets—what you know they will be doing. Then you can "tweak" them by adding other activities if there is available time. Some of this you may not know or figure out until you start plugging in your "squares" from the **Preparation Worksheets**. Every hour of the day does not have to be planned on the **Activity Worksheet**, only what you already know. There will probably be extra time in the children's **Activity Worksheets**; they will not add up to 24 hours (yours will likely be full right away!). The extra time will either be free, or you will come up with activities. For example, if Child #1 has six extra hours a day, you might assign him to look at books with Child #3 and Child #4 while you are making dinner.

Yes, do an **Activity Worksheet** for the baby, but it won't be as detailed or full as yours. How many times a day are you feeding the baby? I imagine it is at least every three hours. If it is 6 a.m., 9 a.m., 12 noon, 4 p.m., 7 p.m., and 10 p.m., then you would fill in your activity worksheet: "Baby nursings - 3 hours," if you average one-half hour each time you nurse. When you go to your **Preparation Worksheet** you fill in "nurse" on six of the ½ hour blocks of Baby's color.

I would write down "nap" on your **Activity Worksheet** but not bother with an amount of time. When you go to the **Preparation Worksheets**, you could fill in several hour and ½ hour blocks for napping and place them onto your **Master Schedule Worksheets** at the appropriate time.

What else will Baby do? Will your older children each have a playtime with him? Then, on Baby's **Activity Worksheet** list, "Time with Child #1, ½ hour." If Child #1 will have two times to be with Baby, you would put, "Time with Baby, ½ hour, ½ hour" or "1 hour" if you can remember it is two separate times. If you don't know how much time Child #1 will have with Baby, don't fill that time in until you have worked on Child #1's worksheet. If Child #2 is going to have a playtime with Baby, on Baby's worksheet you list, "Time with Child #2, ½ hour."

Here is another idea. If you are finding this step difficult, don't allow yourself to get bogged down with your **Activity Worksheets**; fill out what you know. You probably have somewhat set meal, nap, and chore times. Figure out how much time for school and you have the skeleton for your schedule. Put those activities on your **Preparation Worksheets**, cut out and plug them into your **Master Schedule Worksheets**.

Then look at your holes on the **Master Schedule Worksheets**. What do you still want to accomplish? What do you want the children to accomplish? Go back to your **Activity Worksheets** and fill in some of these. Now again, back to your **Preparation Worksheets**; write them in; cut them out; and put them onto the **Master Schedule Worksheets**. See if that gets you going, making progress.

"On the sample 'Activity Worksheet for Mom' you list breakfast and lunch as ½ hour. Does this include preparation and cleanup time?"

No, my **Activity Worksheet** does not include breakfast and lunch preparation or cleanup, because I don't do that, others do. Assuming you do not have others in the family to do these tasks, you need to schedule more time for them.

"I hate getting up in the morning, but I think that after six children I need to get used to the idea."

If you hate to get up in the morning, by all means, do not schedule to get up at 5:30 a.m. You will gain more from consistently getting up at 7:00 a.m. than to put in your schedule a 5:30 a.m. wake up, do it once, and dislike it so much you can't make yourself keep it up. You will defeat your schedule before you start. Make it realistic, based on what you know of yourself and the family.

If you are getting up later in the morning, it means you are staying up later at night. See if it will work to schedule that late nighttime when your children are in bed for some of the things you want to do that are hard when the children are around. Examples might be: your devotion time (if you are not getting up early enough to do it in the morning), sewing, schoolwork grading and planning, computer, and e-mail time. It is harder to have a schedule in the evening because of husbands being home and our desire to spend

We are implementing the chores part, but have not put together the school schedule. We are deciding who does what as far as school activities is concerned.

Implementing just the chores schedule is an interim measure, so we have some structure while working on the full schedule. The chores still take lots of interaction, with me teaching and correcting.

We are pretty settled on the chores part of the Children's Activity worksheets. But I haven't touched the Master Schedule Worksheets, yet. Dave and I will talk tonight about the Activity Worksheets for several of the children, including their schoolwork. Once we have that together, I can start working on the Preparation Worksheets and Master Schedule Worksheets. Debbie

It will be some work for us as we are so spontaneous, and will really take some effort to change the "whole" family, if you know what I mean. I am looking forward to results. I have already started breaking things into smaller time chunks and not

allowing the children to go do a job and forget about getting back to them to see if they are doing it. I thank you for putting so much time into this. It is a testimony to it, that you had the time to write a book with all your children. Terri

I've read the book and so much makes sense to me. I am sharing a lot of tips you've given throughout the book to just about anyone who wants to listen. Renée

It looked great on paper but, we were having difficulty in real life. I ran into trouble also because I was planning on having Mitchell and Caleb doing phonics and reading together. As we began, I realized that the curriculum was too hard for Mitchell. I decided to split them up. YIKES! That gave me even less time.

But I also found out that I was scheduling too much time for other things. Thankfully, it takes about half the time to do science and history. I didn't find this out until this week since things were taking longer because of some behavioral problems I had to deal with.

time with them. But there will be evenings when they are involved in their projects, and then we can have our plan too. The evening schedule will help direct you when you are tired and might not make use of that time. If you are realistic, choosing activities that you look forward to, you will find yourself willing to keep using the schedule even later in the evening.

"I really tweaked my Activity Worksheets a lot until everything fit, and I think I can skip the cutting out colored 'squares' step and just fill in the final schedule (in pencil of course!). Is this okay, or do you think I will miss a real benefit? My schedule is probably less complicated than many because my husband is home during the day, so we have some fairly large blocks of 'free time' with Dad."

There is no problem with filling in the **Master Schedule Worksheets** without using the **Preparation Worksheet** "squares" if your scheduling needs are not so complicated. If that doesn't work, you can revert to the "squares." I just wouldn't want you to skip using the "squares," find it complicated to work out the schedule by penciling the **Master Schedule Worksheets** in, and then want to give up. The benefit in the colored blocks is that you can see your pieces and rearrange them easily, without erasing and rewriting. It is true that there are some schedules that won't need this step because they aren't as complicated as others.

"I was also wondering how many years you have used a schedule. Were you doing this when you only had 'little ones' and no big helpers? I would really like to see an example of that kind of schedule."

To be honest, I can't remember if I had a written schedule when the older ones were little, but I suspect I did. I certainly would if I had it to do over! I did not use the computer then, so I don't have copies of the schedules. I think my schedules have become more rigid and demanding as our family has grown. That has been out of necessity, because I have not been able to keep up without having a daily plan to guide me. Something as simple as reading out loud to the children used to be a burden, because I wanted to do it but just didn't get around to it. Now that it is a part of my schedule, it happens. That doesn't mean there are never any variations to our schedule. For example, there are occasional days when I have to be gone in the afternoon. The children may miss their scheduled reading time, or whoever is caring for them may follow the schedule and read to them. But the vast majority of days, I am able to read to them.

We now have many examples of schedules where Mom has only little ones and no bigger helpers. Look through the Appendix for them, with children's ages listed on each schedule.

IMPLEMENTATION

"Now, do you suggest looking at the completed schedule and mulling it over for a couple of days or jumping right in and prayerfully trying it out? It doesn't really look too intimidating to try all at once, but should you try to get as many bugs as possible worked out beforehand or work them out as you go? Or both?"

As far as implementing the schedule, I suggest you talk through the schedule with each child, showing them what they will be doing and when, before starting. I do this before the school year begins, detailing any schoolwork that the child will be doing on his own. With the prayer, planning, and discussion that went into making the schedule, you could be ready to run with it. If school isn't starting at your house yet, consider beginning the schedule with the schooltime blocks left open; that would ease you into your schedule more gradually.

I don't think you will get bugs worked out until you try it, unless it is something like discovering the computer is double-booked! Remember to give your schedule some adjustment time. What looks like a bug the first day may not be so by the second week; it may only be a problem with the transition. For us change is difficult, but before long it is routine!

"Do you have days when you just blow off the schedule all together? For example, my littlest one was sick the last two days, and I spent the night on the couch, up a lot. He and I slept until 9 a.m., and I was basically worthless the rest of the day. Do you do this, or do you always discipline yourself to get up and be on schedule no matter what your night was like?"

You asked if we had days when we dropped the schedule. We have such days, but not many. They are usually planned in advance as a "vacation" day. Occasionally illness causes us to leave the schedule. Usually, when we have illness, those who are able to do school continue on their schedule, while the others cough, blow their noses, and are miserable lying on the couch!

For the most part, I choose to get up and get going in the morning, even after a hard night. I have some circumstances that figure into this. One is that I can't sleep when the children are up and making noise. Another is that I meet my mom in front of my house at 7:00 a.m. to walk. That accountability causes me to get up and get going. When we have illness in our home, Steve frequently will allow the sick child to miss early morning family devotions, which includes only the older children, anyway. If enough are sick or we have had a very late night, he cancels that devotion and lets us

This week has been much better, and I feel much more encouraged. I switched some things around. I didn't do this until this week though. I would have a good day, and then the rest of the week would be terrible. We would get our schoolwork done, but because of the interruptions we were finishing things through the day. I told my husband that it was taking all day to get schooling done. But it has been much better!!!! Cindy

It occurred to me that I have far less worries about the arrival of our sixth child in January than I have had with any other baby. I know from reading your book and the testimonials that a new baby can become a part of a large homeschooling family, peacefully, and the world can go on. That is wonderful encouragement, and helps me to look forward to that exciting day when, Lord willing, I hold my sixth child for the first time! Sherri M.

We are definitely planning to implement a schedule using the worksheets which you've supplied. We're trying to adjust our thinking to that frame of mind, and every day we have discus-

sions about what we can do. When Dale read today, he was pleased with the ideas you were presenting and is eager to put them in place.

We realize that more structured feeding times will be beneficial for scheduling, and with our seven-month-old we will be trying to do that to some extent—at least to space them farther apart and make the timing more convenient. However, we probably will not go to scheduled feedings completely for Ben, and when God blesses us with another baby we will probably not go to scheduling feedings to any extent until the baby is about six months old (unless God changes our conviction on that issue in the future). Renée

So the whole schedule is in place, but I need to work out the specifics of some of it. For example, I need to structure Hannah a bit more, at least during the morning, and I need to get some specific things listed to do during chore times. Rebecca

Our transition times are going much better. I usually have everyone start cleaning up at five minutes before the

sleep. If I am tired that afternoon, I let my scheduled time go, for what I usually do while the children are napping, and will sleep myself.

I have found that everything goes much more smoothly when we are on our schedule. Therefore, when I am tired, it is even more beneficial to keep it going. I have fewer decisions to make, fewer children's squabbles, and less catch-up to do the following day—all of which would be more difficult to deal with if I were tired. The schedule is your tool. If there are days you will manage better without it, let it go. Get back to it the next day, or the next, when the baby is feeling better, and you are rested. If you find the schedule is very beneficial, you may decide, as I have, it is easier to keep on it even on "tired" days.

"What would you do with your schedule in the event of an extended illness of the mother, particularly morning sickness. I was just wondering because I know about many mothers who go through these trying times in their lives. I go through three to five months of severe morning and emotional sickness with each child, though the Lord in His mercy has delivered me from this on one occasion."

When Mom has an extended illness, having a schedule in place, beforehand, makes this time easier since the household knows how to function. There will be, as is only logical, some things that are not going to get done. Mom can't function as she normally does, or there wouldn't be a problem in the first place. I encourage letting go of whatever you can, accepting the state of the house when you can't give it as much attention as usual, and asking for more help from the family. For example, I would skip getting up for my personal devotion, family devotion, and walking. I'd try to keep the morning school going—from flat on the couch—if necessary. I would drop any writing or sewing in the afternoon, having a short devotion time, and rest. Having a plan for the day will help, whether Mom can function at full capacity or has to cutback, because the benefits a schedule provides hold for the rest of the family, and even for Mom, budgeting what time and energy she does have.

"We tried to start our schedule today, and it was pretty much a disaster. What do you do with a completely uncooperative two-year-old? We are working on serious discipline issues with him right now, and he totally wrecked our schooltime today. I don't have people scheduled to be with him, because we just don't have enough hours in the day to get things accomplished. I know I'm going to have to change that, but I have a feeling that he will still be trouble. He either wants to be with me or doing whatever someone else is doing, not what I have him scheduled to do. I had him working right under my arm, so I could supervise him, but he kept taking off and jumping in the middle of everyone else's

stuff. I'm praying, and I asked my husband to help, but any suggestions you could offer would also be appreciated."

It may have seemed pretty much a disaster on this first day of your schedule, but I assure you that is not uncommon. I have had years that on the first day of school, on a schedule, I would give this "glowing" report to Steve in the evening: "We didn't do anything except get everyone in their place, get things out, put things away, deal with attitudes and discipline issues. How will we ever get any school done?" But the next day would be better, and the next, and the next. With little children it never becomes absolutely smooth sailing, but it is manageable.

Much of what you were sharing would be a problem whether you were using a schedule or not, because you would be doing school with your other children and have a two-year-old in the middle. Obviously, this change of routine is going to take your two-year-old some getting used to. If you are expecting him to sit quietly while you do school all morning, that would be unrealistic for a two-year-old. It will greatly help to have him assigned to older brothers and sisters throughout the morning, or even off and on through the morning. I expect, if he has been "hanging out" with you, he will be happy to have a playmate.

I would change my mindset for the next two weeks from "getting everything done on my schedule" to "changing activities at the right time and training the two-year-old." With consistent effort and discipline, day after day, he will begin to cooperate. His training is an area you are working on anyway, so if the expectation is that this is to be a focus for several days, it won't be so difficult to break what you're doing to deal with him. Be mentally ready and even looking for infractions to work on. You want to teach him to be able to be around Mom and the other children, who are doing school, and not be so totally disruptive. You may as well set your mind to doing it now!

I would have some toys, near where you are working, that he enjoys, if that is where you are going to have him. Maybe try the rotating toys routine. They can be a pain to get out and pick up, but they will help keep him occupied while you are trying to do school.

Make sure you have a preschool playtime scheduled in the middle of the morning for you and the two-year-old, giving him some individual attention. He will need it, since he will be getting his fair share of discipline.

"I am struggling with making myself get up in the mornings. Most days I have gotten up in time to fix my husband's lunch—a new thing for us as he used to come home every day. But, I often go back to bed after-

next time block. When they are done, we all stand in front of the schedule, and I read off what everyone is supposed to do next, and where they are to do that activity. Everyone trots off one by one as I read what they are to do. Tracy W.

I don't think I allowed enough time for housework. I already had chore charts made up that allowed us to do general housecleaning, a little every day, so we don't have to spend Saturday cleaning, but we had trouble doing those chores and just keeping picked up in the time I had allowed.

In my schedule I had chore time in the afternoon followed by a short amount of free time which the children never got because we didn't get chores done. Ricki

Since we had the chore schedule up and running before Rebekah Eunice arrived, Dave had a game plan to keep the house running while I was lounging around. It was soooo nice to have the laundry caught up and the kitchen relatively clean. Usually, I would just be doing things off the top of my head. Dave didn't have a

clue, things would snowball, and HE would wind up doing all the work. Debbie

Teri and Steve, thanks so much for doing this book. I am loving it. I also have an e-mail loop of gals, who are doing the same homeschool curriculum that I am, who are VERY interested in what I am doing. I have been mostly keeping them in suspense, but I will share my schedule with them when I have it worked out. Many of them are very organized gals already, but some of them are more like me—definitely RAW material!!! Rebecca

I have been using the schedule, and when I have not, the children ask for it!! They love the time set aside for them. They have not been balking the way they were about the work time. Lisa

I am looking forward to my schedule allowing me to put more effort in my own character growth and spend more time in His Word: reading, memorizing, and meditating. Cindy

wards, and then I have a hard time getting up again and on track. Another place I need to tweak the schedule, I think."

Yes, you might want to do some tweaking on that morning wake up time. Morning wake up time needs to be something you can live with, a time when you will realistically get yourself up.

If you are getting up to make your hubby's lunch, it seems that would be a good motivation to stay up. Could you take a shower before, or after, making lunch? That might stimulate enough to keep you up. I suspect what you are missing, by going back to bed, is time with the Lord. That is your most needful time of the day! I encourage you to push yourself to not go back to bed. Think of ways to motivate yourself to stay up. Maybe make the bed right when you get up that first time. Or put on a cup of tea when you are making lunch so you will want to drink it while you have a quiet time.

You do have to make sure the schedule allows for an adequate amount of sleep so you can keep up with the day and children. If you have scheduled seven hours for sleep and are up twice in the night with the baby, then it wouldn't be surprising that you are having trouble staying up in the morning. Do you have an afternoon nap worked into your schedule? I can get by with much less nighttime sleep if I can have a half-hour nap in the afternoon.

"What do you do if your husband is very supportive, in words, of your schedule? However, in practice he brings many disturbances to it."

I shared this question with Steve to get his counsel and input before I responded.

We believe that communication between you and your husband is key to this concern. Since your husband has gone over the schedule and is supportive, he may not be keyed into the fact that some of the things he is doing cause difficulty for you and your scheduled day with the children.

Can you discuss this with your husband? I find these discussions are best when we can have them at a neutral time. For example, Steve and I have a date each Saturday, so I will keep a running list of things I need to discuss with him. You probably have some talking times with your husband and could bring this topic up during one of them. If he is supportive of your schedule and feels it will be beneficial to you and the family, then you need to discuss how you are to handle it when he brings interruptions to the schedule. He should be able to give you his direction and then you can follow his desires. Steve said often men don't think about how their actions impact others, unless it is brought to their attention. It seems like, as you discuss this problem, he will say one of three things.

1. He is still supportive of the schedule, didn't realize the impact he is making, and will work with you.

2. He is still supportive of the schedule, but wants to have the freedom to make interruptions. Then, it is up to you to figure out what needs to be made up and what doesn't. You will have to pray for the Lord to give you creativity and a spirit that can deal with the uncertainties this will present. Having the schedule in force much of the time should help with these interruptions when they come, but it will take a quiet and gentle spirit on your part.

3. He hasn't liked life with the schedule and really wants to not continue using it. Then, of course, ditch the schedule and go back to what you were doing before.

When Steve asks me to do a project for him during the day, I will say something like, "This is my phonics time with Anna. Do you want me to do it now or may I do it later?" Then he is aware of the impact and can make the choice as to the importance of his request.

I don't have any "pat" answers for you. These are areas I can struggle with on a daily basis; how do I submit to my husband; how do I respect him; when do I speak up; when am I to be quiet? I pray the Lord will give you wisdom as you seek Him in this area. If I am to err, I prefer to err on the side of being quiet, rather than being controlling toward my husband. I fail in this so often though. I will have the very best of resolves to be quiet and end up blurting out what I didn't want to say. Maybe the Lord would have you bear these difficulties with patience and make the best of it, allowing Him to work in His time if He chooses.

With my oldest, Zak, we decided his lawn mowing could be done "early" in the morning. It's actually a paid job, so by having that out of the way early, he will be able to do his normal day's activities without being absent for a few hours twice a week. So that will be done before breakfast, ideally. We'll try that out at least. Debbie

The times I had little ones playing with little ones didn't go well. They are not used to playing with each other without a big guy to entertain them. I guess this isn't really a schedule problem though! Ricki

Dear Friends,   October 24th

My name is Tracy. I'm married to Paul, and we've been blessed by the Lord with Courtney (6), Joshua (4), Jacob (3), Jessica (1), and a new blessing due in June. We are both believers and attend a church in the area where we teach a pre-teen Bible study.

My husband and I have reached a place in our lives where God has led us to homeschool. We are currently teaching 2nd grade and K5. I'm an assistant to the support group leader of our homeschool group as well as helping my husband run the web page for our school. It does take lots of time, but it all has great benefits!

Aside from the top two activities listed, Paul and I have also started a business in our area creating web pages, building computers, and assisting businesses in their computer needs. My husband's full time work schedule is from 6 a.m. - 2 p.m., and then he works on our business until 6 p.m. and half a day on Saturdays.

When I saw the request to work on this book, I thought that it must be too good to be true. I had just asked my church to pray for me. My request was that I might be able to get myself organized enough so that I could get the needed things done in the house and still have time to spend with my husband and children. I knew when Maxwell's request was sent out that God had literally answered my prayers; little did I know at the time what an answer it would be!

The day I received my scheduling package, I rushed in and read the entire book that afternoon! Over the next week to week and a half, I began to work on the schedule itself. The "squares" are great, because they actually make you look at all of the time that you are using and not miss a thing! It also makes the job a little intimidating.

Once I got my first schedule made, I began to implement it a little at a time. At first I only went until 9 a.m., and then 11 a.m., and so on. I was so amazed! I could get more done by 9 a.m. on my schedule than I could all day on a normal day.

I began to see results immediately! The first thing was that there was a lot less arguing among my children. Because they each had a place to be and something to be doing all day, they really didn't have anything to fuss about or any time to.

The next BIG advantage was the night someone in my support group stopped by WITHOUT CALLING first. My house was so neat; I just invited her in! I've always expected my home to be a place of ministry, and for the first time it actually was. I was thrilled to say the least!

I hope that everyone tries this schedule. It's meant to fit all lifestyles. It's the first book I've tried that I can really say that about, and I've tried LOTS of them!

From Tracy L.

Chapter *16*

Choosing to Schedule

We realize there are those who may say, "Scheduling is just not for me. It is too structured and too rigid." This is for each individual to decide, but if God is a God of order, and a God Who has set times and seasons in place, could that possibly mean He wants order in our lives too? "To every thing there is a season, and a time to every purpose under the heaven . . ." (Ecclesiastes 3:1). "Let all things be done decently and in order" (I Corinthians 14:40). Do you resist because that lifestyle doesn't please you? "For though I be absent in the flesh, yet am I with you in the spirit, joying and beholding your order, and the stedfastness of your faith in Christ" (Colossians 2:5). If that is the case, then you have to decide if the principles here are Scriptural. If they are, then it doesn't necessarily leave a choice in the matter. "Jesus answered and said unto him, If a man love me, he will keep my words" (John 14:23a). It may be that God is calling you to "put a plan and order" together for your days!

Others may say they do not want to live according to a schedule, because they do not want to have to develop the self-discipline necessary to adhere to it. "For God hath not given us the spirit of fear; but of power, and of love, and of a sound mind" (II Timothy 1:7). Here again, we must ask ourselves some questions. Do we desire to do all the Lord has called us to? What kind of example do we want to set for our children? Why would we not choose this area of self-discipline? "All things are lawful for me, but all things are not expedient: all things are lawful for me, but all things edify not. Let no man seek his own, but every man another's wealth" (I Corinthians 10:23).

If you are able to keep up with your responsibilities and do not believe God is speaking to you in the area of scheduling, you, obviously, have the freedom to choose against it. There will be families, particularly with fewer children, who can manage their homes and homeschooling without using a schedule. This does not mean that they would not be more efficient, or accomplish more, if they decided to live within the framework of a schedule.

We want homeschooling families to enjoy the life that they have chosen as they follow the Lord's leading. This is only possible if the mother can keep up with her God-given responsibilities. We, as women, are prone to discouragement. When the house is a mess, the laundry is piled high, the meals are haphazard, and school is in shambles, we are not joyful mothers of children! Learning to generate and implement a schedule for your family can be used by the Lord to free you from these areas that can cause you to feel downhearted.

A Personal Word

Benefits from my schedule: regularity in the children's schoolwork; a relaxed time to teach my children desired character traits and life skills; adequate rest for myself and all my children; a relaxed time to nurse the baby that is not during mealtime; time to play outside with my children; daily time learning a Scripture verse and a hymn; and time and patience for the "extras" like playdough and painting that I was never able to get to before. Tracy W.

Recall again with me Paul's mandate to the young widows in I Timothy 5:14, "I will therefore that the younger women marry, bear children, guide the house, give none occasion to the adversary to speak reproachfully." Your completion and implementation of the daily schedule is the fulfillment of this mandate. You have chosen to manage your home rather then letting it manage you!

IN CONCLUSION

We challenge you to consider what has been written in this book and determine to test the methods set forth here. We are certain you will find a new sense of peace and joy in accomplishing what the Lord has called you to do. "And also that every man should eat and drink, and enjoy the good of all his labour, it is the gift of God. Wherefore I perceive that there is nothing better, than that a man should rejoice in his own works; for that is his portion" (Ecclesiastes 3:13, 22). Our hearts' delight as Christians, wives, mothers, and homeschoolers is in serving our Lord Jesus Christ. Therefore, our goal is to discover ways to fulfill what He has given to us as responsibilities. May scheduling be an exciting adventure, challenge, and calling as you continue to follow Christ Jesus.

Tracy L.'s Activity Worksheet	
Sewing	1/2 hr
Quiet/Devotion time	1/2 hr
Dress/Personal grooming	1/2 hr
Reading/Writing	1/2 hr
Laundry	1/2 hr
Make bed/Straighten bedroom	1/2 hr
Nurse baby	3 1/2 hrs
Bathing children	1 hr
Homeschool support group	1/2 hr
Sunday School prep	1/2 hr
Computer time	1/2 hr
Evening family devotions	1/4 hr
Breakfast	1/2 hr
School:	2 hrs
Preschool (Jessica and Jacob) 1/2 hr	
K-5 (Joshua) 3/4 hr	
2nd grade (Courtney) 3/4 hr	
Prepare children for naps	1/2 hr
Rest	1/2 hr
Reading to children	1/2 hr
Individual playtime with children	1/2 hr
Dinner preparation	1 hr
Lunch	1/2 hr
Dinner	1 hr
Laundry folding	3/4 hr
Paul's time	1-2 hrs
Sleep	7 hrs
Cleaning/Organizing	1 hr
School planning and Record keeping	1/2 hr
Personal finances	1/2 hr
Exercise	1/2 hr
Pet care/Lawn care	1/2 hr
Total	28-29 hr

To find out how Tracy compensated for the extra hours listed on her Activity Worksheet, you may want to look at her schedule in the Appendix.

Dear Friends,   *November 1st*

Over the past several years, God has caused me to think of many important things I need to do with my children. Of greatest importance is to teach them to know the one, true, living God; the Maker of all things. I also want to teach them how to live in harmony with each other; have self-control in times of difficult situations; and how to use their innate curiosity to find out about the world around them. These ideals were deep longings in my heart; but with each wonderful new baby, I despaired of ever being able to even begin working toward any of these desires. With six children, ages seven and under, on most days my basic goal was to keep everyone alive and fed.

I asked the Lord to help me as I began this school year with two in school, two preschoolers, and two babies. How on earth would I get any of my goals accomplished when: my two grade schoolers were unable to work on their own due to their beginning reading skills, my energetic preschoolers needed to play, my toddler needed my supervision to keep her from destroying the house, and my new baby needed to be nursed and held! And then there were the household tasks of meals and laundry and cleaning and . . .

I had thought of making a schedule before, but I did not believe that it was possible to make a workable schedule for six children, ages seven and under. Bless the LORD! I managed to read the draft of this book while I nursed my three-week-old baby, and then I began to fill out the worksheets in the evenings. I prayed and asked God to show me what was important for this year, knowing that next year would find me in different circumstances. Then I asked God to show me when to do each of these things. I also prayed for help to follow the new schedule as this represented a whole new way of living for my family.

God enabled me to persevere, and now our day is running smoothly. Our days are not idyllic or perfect, but every day I know there is a time to do all the things we need to do. If our morning is interrupted by an unexpected visitor, a major cleanup due to a wet bed, or the need to answer questions like, "Mommy, what if God forgets to make somebody get better?" I know that we will get back to the regularly scheduled activity the next day. I can enjoy the task at hand instead of worrying about all the things I am not getting done. The child I am with at the moment can enjoy my attention, without having a distracted, vacant Mommy. The Lord is faithful to enable us to accomplish the things He has called us to do in our families. "And let the beauty of the LORD our God be upon us: and establish thou the work of our hands upon us; yea, the work of our hands establish thou it" (Psalm 90:17).

From Tracy W.

Managers of "His" Home: A Chapter for Dads

In the tenth chapter of John, we read that the Shepherd lays down His life for the sheep, while the hired hand flees. The Shepherd does this because He loves the sheep and is responsible for them. In the same way, God has entrusted our families to us to love and be responsible for their care and training. Fathers, we will answer to God for how we have led our families. Truly, it is an incredible honor and trust God has given us.

The father is responsible for every aspect that relates to his family. The only way he can accomplish it all is by relying on his God-given helpmate. His wife is a precious gift from God; together they are able to fulfill God's calling for their family. If your wife will prayerfully go through the recommended steps in completing and implementing a schedule, there will be great improvements in:

your wife's peace and satisfaction with her role as mother and helpmeet,

what is accomplished in your children's school,

the children's time together,

the orderliness of the home,

and many other areas.

I maintain such a confident opinion based on the glowing feedback we have received from the families who tested this book and scheduling kit. If you have doubts, read the sidebars in earlier chapters. You will be amazed at what God has been doing in these homes. It is not because of the greatness of *Managers of Their Homes*, but because God is a God of order. When order is implemented, there are many benefits. Are there needs in your home that cry out for improvement? If so, read on, and ask the Lord Jesus what He would have you do to help your wife create and implement a schedule. You have nothing to lose and much to gain.

Our experience has been: most wives breeze through the book, seek God's guidance, ask their husband's counsel, and then proceed with great enthusiasm. But, I'm convinced there are some wives who will never succeed in managing their homes without the patient, steady leading of their husbands. They need extra help. In those homes, the father's role is absolutely critical to the mom's success.

Regardless of the amount of help your wife needs, there are a number of key points that will help you, help her. Please read them carefully, and ask the Lord Jesus what He requires of you.

A Personal Word

This whole scheduling adventure has been a gift from God to my family. At first I was a bit skeptical, thinking this was just the latest homeschooler's "silver bullet." "Just buy this book and life will be perfect." Boy, was I wrong! Scheduling isn't a gimmick; it's just a logical way of doing what God has given us to do, in the time He has given us to do it. Dave

As my wife was planning her schedule, my role was not all that demanding. Renée didn't need or want me to do the work for her— she really only needed my confirmation and support. I read most of the book, gave recommendations regarding trouble spots, confirmed ideas, gave suggestions, and reviewed the process at several stages. It was enough for Renée to know that I cared about the project, and I was going to support her. Dale

Even my very "together" wife, with significant organizational skills, can use some help juggling the responsibilities of being a loving wife,

RESPONSIBLE

Dads must own the fact that, if the management of the home is lacking, he is ultimately responsible. If a shepherd had a sheep with a habit of wandering off, he would take steps to guard and protect that sheep. He would not stand around complaining to the Lord about his sheep's poor performance. Like the Good Shepherd, if there are areas where a husband can facilitate his wife, he needs to step forward, doing what he can.

I pray that a husband would never, never criticize his wife's home management practices to her or to others. You know what I mean. We have probably all heard a husband criticizing his wife's abilities. This wounds a wife's spirit deeply and reflects negatively on her husband. If Teri is failing, I am failing in that same area. It is up to me to find out what I can do to help her. Galatians 6:2 says, "Bear ye one another's burdens, and so fulfil the law of Christ." If Teri is stumbling under the load, God calls me to lift her up.

Years ago, when the difficulty of setting up a school schedule was seeming like an impossible task, I took a more active part. It was then we started having a yearly planning day, and it became one of Teri's most special days of the year. Why was she so excited? Primarily because this day was devoted to crying out to God for guidance for the upcoming year. Also, she had my full attention in discussing the issues that needed direction. She saw that her "life" was truly important to me, and I would work with her until goals were set and problems resolved. She felt special and loved.

Each husband reading this chapter has a unique opportunity to show his wife how important she is to him. As she undertakes to develop a schedule, he can lift her continually in prayer, and ask how he could help. If she would like to spend time discussing issues, he makes it a priority to be available. If it means a day away for just the two of them, he must do it. Whatever it takes, he should invest it!

Another way to own responsibility for everything in the home is for fathers to hold their children accountable to staying on the schedule. Dad must not undermine his wife's authority with the children by allowing them excuses for not adhering to their schedule. The schedule must have the full force of his approval, as rebellion against the schedule becomes rebellion against the father.

COMMITTED

The husband must be committed to his wife's success, particularly her desire to make and implement a schedule. Is he committed enough to his wife implementing a schedule that he is willing to invest time and effort in areas she needs help? I heard one dad share how his wife was drowning under her workload—to the point of a nervous breakdown. As she was getting more discouraged, he kept trying to encourage her. He finally said, "I couldn't have been more encouraging, but it never occurred to me to offer help."

I know of a couple dads who do dishes, most of the time, for their families. They know it is something they can do in the evening to free their wives for other activities, such as housekeeping, grading schoolwork, personal development, or just some quiet time alone!

It is easy for me to encourage Teri with words, but I know there are times my actions have not been consistent with my words. There is a good reason for that. I don't care for many of her tasks! However, I know she does them because they need to be done, not because she likes them all. I have found tasks which greatly relieve Teri's burden, and I actually look forward to them.

I have purposed to not ask Teri to do any errands. I do all of them for the family, to include grocery shopping. For errands and shopping, which I do in the evening, I take the five younger children with me. It's great "fathering time," and it allows Teri to be undisturbed at home. I also cut all of the hair in the home (except mine), which saves us a significant amount of money, and I love the one-on-one time with each of my family members.

Your wife may need some extra time while she reads the book and creates a schedule. May I encourage (and challenge) you to look for ways you can free up an hour for her each day—as she works through this book? Ask her what issues she is struggling with so you may spend additional time praying for those. Then, patiently listen to her describe her scheduling or implementation problems and help her work toward solutions.

What if the solution was to impact you, would you graciously receive it and cheerfully be inconvenienced? Your commitment to your wife's success, in creating and implementing a schedule, will yield tremendous dividends of blessings through the years. A husband must be committed to his wife's success. How would the Lord have you demonstrate this commitment?

TWO ARE BETTER THAN ONE

There are times when I have been involved in some work on the computer, for a client, and not been able to get beyond a roadblock. I've discussed it with Teri, and innocently, she has offered up the solution. In the same way, she comes to me when there is a schedule problem, and I listen as she relates the particulars. Often we pray about it and together come up with a solution.

homemaker, mother of six children under eight years old, homeschooling the two oldest, and working part time at home for the local charter school. She implemented the scheduling system at a time when things were reaching critical mass in our home, and almost immediately, I noticed a calming effect. When I first get home and look into my wife's eyes, there is a noticeable decrease not only in the droop of fatigue but also the blank stare of being overwhelmed. Gray

My advice to other dads is to first realize how important this is. Managing his home well is one of the requirements given for overseers and deacons (1 Timothy 3). Even if your wife does most of the day to day work, she is only doing it by delegation. It's still your job, your responsibility. Next reread and even memorize Ephesians 5:25. Working through the scheduling process can be a great opportunity to practice loving our wives as Christ loves the church. Dave

The greatest impact on me personally, as a Dad, has been a much improved level

of confidence, less frustration, and greater peace regarding Renée's frame of mind. I now know that she knows that she can do it. She has guidelines and a plan in place that gives her confidence. Her confidence decreases my anxiety and frustration because when she's at peace, our home's at peace. Regardless of what actually gets accomplished at home in any given day, I know things aren't out of control. Renée's greatest benefit is confidence—she knows that it CAN actually all fit into one day. Dale

Dads instinctively know that their wives need to feel a sense of teamwork on a practical level. I have found it immensely helpful to look for a household job that I can do every day to communicate my dedication to teamwork and uniquely ease my wife's responsibilities. My activity of choice has been to cleanup the kitchen after dinner and take care of the dishes. Of course older children can do this task, but I can do it quickly, properly, and best of all unsupervised! Gray

With a schedule we are able to make sure that the

Several years ago, when Teri was struggling with the complexity of scheduling eight people in our family, the Lord had me suggest the idea of writing the tasks down on squares of paper so she could move them around like a big puzzle. That was not my wisdom, but the Lord's. I believe He delights in helping a husband meet his wife's needs when that man cares enough to be involved!

WILLING TO LIMIT MY FREEDOM

A schedule is a framework that provides stability for the family's daytime (and nighttime if desired) activities. Even when a "storm" of interruption rains on the wife's schedule, she is much better prepared to deal with it than if she did not have a schedule. Once the storm passes, she is able to jump back into her schedule and continue. However, picture a hurricane that lands and does not move on—mass destruction! This is what a dad could do to his wife's effort to induce structure into the home. How?

I have found I must be sensitive to what Teri has scheduled for herself and the children. For example, I know there are times when a telephone call from me is a schedule wrecker. If this is her time to help Anna with phonics, and I call Teri, I'm not owning the responsibility of our children learning to read. I'm putting my interests ahead of our child's reading. I'm being selfish and impatient, because I know there are better times when I can talk to Teri during the day. Certainly, I can call when necessary, even if it is inconvenient, but what I'm referring to is the flagrant disregard for Teri's need to carry out what God has called her to do during the day. The question I must consider is, "Am I aware of what she is doing, and willing to limit my freedom, so as to not hinder her implementation of the goals the Lord and I have given her for the family?"

KNOW YOUR FAMILY

The husband is the shepherd of his family. He is to go out before them and know them as our Lord knows us. Again, in the tenth chapter of John, we will read that the Shepherd calls His sheep by name; that is a picture of closeness. With intimacy, comes the knowledge of strengths and weaknesses. If you were to take "inventory" of your wife, where would she excel and where could she use growth? The strengths are easy, but how are you attempting to nurture areas that need strengthening? Are you praying for her in those areas? Are you seeking ways to help her overcome these weaknesses?

What a tremendous opportunity you have to bless your wife. Struggles can be depressing and discouraging for her. When you come alongside to help physically, emotionally, or spirtually, and she has success; the weight is lifted and her joy returns.

It is not likely a wife will come to her husband and say, "I'm struggling with slothfulness, I need help." It is for the husband to see the need and nurture growth. Certainly the first step is prayer. May I never be so arrogant as to think I can train my wife! It is the Lord Jesus who works in hearts, and we must seek Him first.

However, a word of caution. I must be prepared for the possibility there is something in my life the Lord wants to get my attention in, first. As dads, we can be an insensitive crew, and often we won't get involved unless something really rocks the boat, disturbing our comfort zone. A wife in constant tears, no clean clothes, the house a mess, skyscrapers of dirty dishes—really gets a dad's attention. I am ashamed of how many times the Lord has had to use Teri to wake me up and cause me to cry out to Him. Then, to my chagrin, it was I who needed to change. Once my problem was taken care of, He dealt with the speck of sawdust in her eye. I'm sure she was glad the plank was finally out of my eye!

So when the husband is confronted with what he believes is a weakness in his wife, I think he should cry out to the Lord and ask Him if there is an area in his life that needs attention. Next, he needs to see how the Lord would have him lead the way out of the problem.

For example, what if a spouse had a terrible time getting out of bed, in the morning, at the proper time. The husband could post Scripture around the home about the benefits of rising early and put notes about it on her pillow. I expect we can readily agree that would be a bad idea. After praying, let's assume the Lord showed this husband that he should be leading a time of family worship in the morning. He would then share with his wife that he would like to begin having family devotions before going to work. He would explain when he would like family worship to begin, enlisting her help. He might be the one to help things get started by waking everyone. Can you see the picture of the shepherd leading his flock in this way?

This probably means the husband would have to get up earlier to have his devotion first and get ready for work, but that is a small price to pay for having the family up and going in the right direction. Are we really willing to die for our family? Not only did Christ die on the cross, but He died daily to self. Therein lies my greatest difficulty, and some of you may share this same challenge. It is much harder to die to self by humbly leading, versus telling my wife where she is failing and needs to improve. Ugh, can you believe a loving husband would do that? I know it's true in my life, and maybe it is true in yours as well. But, how gracious our Lord Jesus is, if we but call out to Him for direction in how to lead.

In Conclusion

Husbands—you are key to the success of your wife being able to create and implement a schedule. If you will be supportive in word and deed, you will observe many positive changes in your home. May God bless you as you endeavor to serve Him.

time we spend on something is in line with the importance we place on it

Now with the schedule in place, we are seeing the ongoing benefits of getting more accomplished with less stress. My wife is more "in control" of her day than I have ever seen her. The differences were noticeable around the house immediately. Life isn't perfect, but it is much more productive and much less chaotic. It's also much easier for me to help now, since I am able to know what the kids are supposed to be doing. Dave

Have patience with your wife through her scheduling process; don't be tyrannical. Offer support constantly— not just in words, but in involvement. Give positive feedback (or feedback in a positive way) as often as possible, and especially when asked. Dale

APPENDIX

Contents

Maxwell's School Schedule (1)

Time	Mom	Sarah (16) 11th Grade	Joseph (9) 4th Grade	John (7) 2nd Grade	Anna (6) K	Jesse (4) Preschool	Mary (2) Preschool
5:30 am	Bible	Sleep	Sleep	Sleep	Sleep	Sleep	Sleep
6:00	Prayer/Praise Dress	Sleep	Sleep	Sleep	Sleep	Sleep	Sleep
6:30	Family devotion	Family devotion	Sleep	Sleep	Sleep	Sleep	Sleep
7:00	Walk	Personal devotion	Sleep	Sleep	Sleep	Sleep	Sleep
7:30	Walk/Shower	Chores/Make breakfast	Wake up/Room chores	Wake up/Room chores	Wake up/Room chores	Wake up/Room chores	Sleep
8:00	Eat/Cleanup	English 11	Eat/Teeth/Chores	Eat/Teeth/Chores	Eat/Teeth/Chores	Eat/Teeth	Eat/Teeth
8:30	Preschool with Anna, Jesse, and Mary	English 11/World History	Science	Typing/Computer math drill	Preschool with Mom	Preschool	Preschool
9:00	Phonics/Reading with Anna	World History	Piano	With Mary/Jesse	With Mom Phonics/Reading	With John	With John
9:30	Algebra II with Sarah	Algebra II with Mom	History	Science/History	Mary/Jesse	With Anna	With Anna
10:00	Bible	Bible	Bible	Bible	Bible	Bible	Bible
10:30	School with Joseph – Math, Reading, English	Playtime with little ones	W/Mom/Math Reading/English	Play with Sarah	Play with Sarah	Play with Sarah	Play with Sarah
11:00	School with John Math, English	Bible	Handwriting/Spelling	w/Mom/Math English	Play alone	Play alone	Play alone
11:30	School with John Phonics, Reading	Math with Anna	With Mary, Jesse, and Anna	w/Mom/Phonics Reading	Math with Sarah	With Joseph	With Joseph
12:00 pm	Lunch	Make lunch/Eat	Lunch	Lunch	Lunch helper/Eat	Lunch	Lunch
12:30	Lunch/Reading with Anna	Eat/Free	Eat/Cleanup	Eat/Cleanup	Eat/Mom	Eat/Free	Eat/Free
1:00	Phonics w/Anna	Health	Math	Math/Write/Spell	Phonics w/Mom	Prepare for nap	Prepare for nap
1:30	Sew or Write	Health/AlgebraII	Reading/Bible	Reading/Phonics	Read	Nap	Nap

Time	Mom	Sarah (16) 11th Grade	Joseph (9) 4th Grade	John (7) 2nd Grade	Anna (6) K	Jesse (4) Preschool	Mary (2) Preschool
2:00	Sew or Write	Algebra II	Quiet	Rest	Nap	Nap	Nap
2:30	Rest	Rest	Quiet	Rest	Nap	Nap	Nap
3:00	Check school work	Projects	Art/Read	Rest/Stories	Nap	Nap	Nap
3:30	Read to Jos/Jh Read to A, Jesse	Projects	Mom reads aloud/Math drill	Mom reads aloud	Nap/Listen to Mom read	Nap/Listen to Mom read	Nap
4:00	John reads/Mom reads to Jesse, M	Projects/Lead memory time	Typing/Memory	Read to Mom/ Memory	Listen to John read/Memory	Listen to John/Mom read	Nap/Listen to Mom read
4:30	Fun school J/J or visit Meme	Free	Free or Fun school w/Mom	Free or Fun school w/Mom	Free	Free	Free
5:00	Start dinner	Free	Helping jobs	Helping jobs	Free	Free	Free
6:00	Dinner	Dinner	Dinner	Dinner	Dinner	Dinner	Dinner
6:30	Dinner	Dinner/Cleanup	Dinner/Cleanup	Dinner/Cleanup	Dinner	Dinner	Dinner
7:00	Laundry folding	Free	Free	Free	Free	Free	Free
7:30	Play with little ones or Baths	Free	Free	Free	Free/Bath	Free/Bath	Free/Bath
8:00	Play with little ones or Baths	Free	Free/Shower	Free/Shower	Free/Bath	Free/Bath	Free/Bath
8:30	Family devotion	Family devotion	Brush teeth Family devotion	Brush teeth Family devotion	Brush teeth Family devotion	Brush teeth Family devotion	Brush teeth Family devotion
9:00	Good nights	Good nights	Good nights	Good nights	Good nights	Good nights	Sleep
9:30	Computer time	Sleep	Sleep	Sleep	Sleep	Sleep	Sleep
10:30	Bedtime	Sleep	Sleep	Sleep	Sleep	Sleep	Sleep

NOTES:

1. Laundry in the washer and moved to dryer throughout the morning when we change activities.
2. Cleaning and school planning/record keeping on Friday mornings. We have light school through the summer (math, reading, and Bible) so we can have light school days on Fridays. I spend the morning cleaning and doing school planning and record keeping rather than schooling.

Maxwell's School Schedule (2)

Time	Mom	Sarah (15)	Joseph (8)	John (6)	Anna (4)	Jesse (3)	Mary (1)
5:30 a.m.	Nurse	Sleep	Sleep	Sleep	Sleep	Sleep	Nurse
6:00	Devotion	Shower	Sleep	Sleep	Sleep	Sleep	Sleep
6:30	Bible with Dad	Bible with Dad	Sleep	Sleep	Sleep	Sleep	Sleep
7:00	Walk	Devotion	Sleep	Sleep	Sleep	Sleep	Sleep
7:30	Walk Shower	Make breakfast	Room chores	Room chores	Wake up	Wake up	Sleep
8:00	Eat	English	Eat/Chores	Eat/Teeth	Eat/Teeth	Eat/Teeth	Eat
8:30	School with Joseph	English/Time w/Little ones	School with Mom	With Mary With Sarah	With Jesse With Sarah	With Anna With Sarah	With John With Sarah
9:00	School with Joseph Nurse Mary	With little ones Science	School w/Mom Handwriting	With Sarah ABC's w/Anna	With Sarah ABC's w/John	With Sarah Alone	With Sarah Nurse (9:15)
9:30	School with John	Science	Piano	School with Mom	Alone With Jesse	Alone With Anna	Play alone
10:00	Bible	Bible	Bible	Bible	Bible	Bible	Bible
10:30	School with Sarah	School with Mom	Science	With Jesse and Anna	With John	With John	Nap
11:00	Preschool	Bible study	Help John with phonics workbk/ Spelling	Phonics workbk/ Joseph helps	Preschool with Mom	Preschool with Mom	Nap
11:30	School with John	Bible study	History	School with Mom	With Joseph	With Joseph	With Joseph
12:00 p.m.	Lunch	Make lunch/Eat	Lunch	Lunch	Lunch	Lunch	Lunch
12:30	Nurse	Cleanup	Cleanup	Cleanup	Free	Free	Nurse
1:00	Read with John	Geography	Math	Read to Mom	With Mary	Free	Anna
1:30	Sew	Geography/ Algebra	English	Math	Look at books	Nap	Nap
2:00	Pray/Bible	Algebra	Reading/Bible	Rest	Rest	Nap	Nap
2:30	Rest	Rest	Rest	Rest	Rest	Nap	Nap
3:00	Check school	Projects	Rest/Story	Rest/Story	Rest	Nap	Nap
3:30	Read to Jos/John Read to Anna and John	Projects	Mom reads Math drill	Listen to Mom read	Rest Mom reads	Nap	Nap

Time	Mom	Sarah (15)	Joseph (8)	John (6)	Anna (4)	Jesse (3)	Mary (1)
4:00	Phonics with John/Read to Jesse	Projects Lead Scripture memory	Typing Scripture memory	Phonics with Mom/Scripture memory	Free Scripture memory	Nap Read with Mom	Nap
4:30	Nurse/Time with Joseph or John	Free	Free Time with Mom	Free Time with Mom	Free	Free	Nurse Play
5:00	Start dinner	Free	Free	Free	Free	Free	Joseph
5:30	Time with Steve Finish dinner	Free	Free	Free	Free	Free	Free
6:00	Eat	Eat	Eat	Eat	Eat	Eat	Eat
6:30	Eat/Cleanup	Eat/Cleanup	Eat/Cleanup	Eat/Cleanup	Eat	Eat	Eat
7:30	Fold laundry	Free	Free/Bath	Free/Bath	Free/Bath	Free/Bath	Free/Bath
8:00	Teeth brushing	Free	Teeth	Teeth	Teeth	Teeth	Free
8:30	Nurse/Evening Bible	Evening Bible with Dad	Evening Bible with Dad	Evening Bible with Dad	Evening Bible with Dad	Evening Bible with Dad	Nurse
9:00	Good night	Bedtime	Bedtime	Bedtime	Bedtime	Bedtime	Sleep
9:30	Bible/Projects	Sleep	Sleep	Sleep	Sleep	Sleep	Sleep
10:30	Bedtime	Sleep	Sleep	Sleep	Sleep	Sleep	Sleep

NOTES:
1. Laundry in the washer and moved to dryer throughout the morning when we change activities.
2. Cleaning and school planning/record keeping on Friday mornings. We have light school through the summer (math, reading, and Bible) so we can have light school days on Fridays. I spend the morning cleaning and doing school planning and record keeping rather than schooling.

Maxwell's School Schedule (3)

Time	Mom	Christopher (17)	Sarah (14)	Joseph (7)	John (5)	Anna (4)	Jesse (2)	Mary (Baby)
5:00 a.m.	Nurse/Bible	Sleep	Sleep	Sleep	Sleep	Sleep	Sleep	Nurse
6:30	Family devotions	Family devotions	Family devotions	Sleep	Sleep	Sleep	Sleep	Sleep
7:00	Walk	Breakfast	Breakfast Devotion	Sleep	Sleep	Sleep	Sleep	Sleep
7:30	Walk Shower	Computer	Get Anna up	Dress/Room chores	Dress/Room chores	7:45 Rise/Dress	7:45 Rise	Rise
8:00	Breakfast	Computer	Wisdom Booklets	Breakfast	Breakfast helper	Breakfast	Breakfast/Dress	With Mom
8:30	Dress Mary, Jesse/Bathe Mary/Lndry	Practice piano	Wisdom Booklets	Breakfast/Chores	Breakfast	Teeth/Play	Teeth/Play	Dress/MTH Bath
9:00	Nurse Mary	Practice piano	Play with little ones	With Sarah	With Sarah	With Sarah	With Sarah	Nurse
9:30	Play w/Jesse, Phonics/John	Journal/Diploma quiz	Math with Joseph	Math with Sarah	Phonics w/ Mom/15min	With Mom	With Mom	With Mom
10:00	School with Sarah	Play with little ones	Meeting with Mom	With Christopher	With Christopher	With Christopher	With Christopher	10:15 Nap
10:30	School with Joseph	Math with John	Letter/MWF Journal/TTH	Math with Mom	Math with Christopher	Play with Jesse	Play with Anna	Nap
11:00	School with Joseph	Wisdom Booklets	Math	Reading/Spelling with Mom	Play with Jesse	Play alone	Play with John	Nap
11:30	Preschool MW - Anna TTH - John	Wisdom Booklets	Math	Piano/ Handwriting	Preschool TTH with Mom	Preschool MW with Mom	Play alone in crib	Get up
12:00 p.m.	Phonics/John Lunch/Nurse	Lunch/Cleanup	Lunch	Lunch	Phonics/ Lunch	Lunch	Lunch	12:45 Nurse
1:00	John reads/ Prepare naps	Write letter	English	Math/Reading Seatwork	Read to Mom	Play	Prepare for naps	With Mom
1:30	Sew	Journal/Diploma Quiz/MWF	Computer/TTH Journal/MWF	Dabbler	Ready for nap/Read	Read in bed	Nap	Nap

Time	Mom	Christopher (17)	Sarah (14)	Joseph (7)	John (5)	Anna (4)	Jesse (2)	Mary (Baby)
2:00	Read/Write	Journal/Diploma Quiz/MWF	Computer	Seatwork/Read	Nap	Nap	Nap	Nap
2:30	Rest	Mowing	Projects/Sewing, Newsletter, Dinner prep, Stamp art	Rest	Nap	Nap	Nap	Nap
3:00	Check school work	Mowing	Projects continued	Rest/Stories of Great Christians	Nap/Stories of Great Christians	Nap	Nap	Nap
3:30	Read to Joseph/John	Mowing	Projects continued	Read with Mom	Read with Mom	3:45 read with Mom	Nap	Nap
4:00	Phonics with John Nurse baby	Mowing	Free	Typing/Personal devotion	Phonics w/ Mom/15min	Play	Nap	4:15 Nurse
4:30	Read to Jesse Dinner prep	Mowing	Free/Walk with little ones	Piano/Free	Free	Play	Read with Mom	Play
5:00	Dinner prep/ Fold laundry	Mowing	Free	Free	Free	Play	Play	Play
5:30	Dad home	Mowing	Free	Free	Free	Play	Play	15 min. play alone in crib
6:00	Dinner prep Dinner	Mowing Dinner	Sarah helps Mom Dinner	Dinner	Dinner	Dinner	Dinner	With family
6:30	Dinner	Dinner/Cleanup	Dinner/Cleanup	Dinner/Cleanup	Dinner	Dinner	Dinner	With family
7:00	Nurse	Free	Free	Free	Free	Free	Free	Nurse
7:30	Fold laundry	Free	Free	Free/Bath	Free/Bath	Free/Bath	Free/Bath	Free
8:00			Get little ones ready for bed. One older one per week brushes teeth. Mom gets Jesse and Mary ready.					
8:30			Family devotions in little boys bedroom. All participate except Mary.					
9:00	Nurse Mary							
9:30	Catch up							
10:30	Bedtime					Bedtime		

NOTES:

1. Laundry in the washer and moved to dryer throughout the morning when we change activities. 2. Cleaning and school planning/record keeping on Friday mornings. We have light school through the summer (math, reading, and Bible) so we can have light school days on Fridays. I spend the morning cleaning and doing school planning and record keeping rather than schooling.

Maxwell's Summer Schedule

Time	Mom/Mary (baby)	Sarah (15)	Joseph (8)	John (6)	Anna (4)	Jesse (2)
5:30 a.m.	Nurse/Bible	Sleep	Sleep	Sleep	Sleep	Sleep
6:00	Prayer/Praise	Rise	Sleep	Sleep	Sleep	Sleep
6:30	Family devotion	Family devotion	Sleep	Sleep	Sleep	Sleep
7:00	Walk	Bible	Sleep	Sleep	Sleep	Sleep
7:30	Walk/Shower	Make breakfast	Dress/Room	Dress/Bfst helper	Dress/Room	Rise
8:00	Eat/Cleanup	Eat/Dress Mary	Eat/Teeth/Chores	Eat/Teeth	Eat/Teeth	Eat/Teeth
8:30	Clean/Organize	Walk w/little ones	With Sarah	With Sarah	With Sarah	With Sarah
9:00	Organize/Nurse	Sentence Analysis	With Christopher	With Christopher	With Christopher	With Christopher
9:30	Phonics with John	Sentence Analysis	Piano	Phonics with Mom	Play with Mary	Play Alone
10:00	School with Joseph	Faith Journal	With Mom	Play with Mary	Play with Mary	Play with Anna
10:30	Anna/MW Jess/TTh	Faith Journal	Play w/Anna/Jesse	Play alone	With Mom/Joseph	With Mom/Joseph
11:00	Bible time	Bible time	Bible time	Bible time	Bible time	Bible time
11:30	Jos/MW John/TTh	Little ones	With Mom or Sarah	With Mom or Sarah	With Sarah	With Sarah
12:00 p.m.	Lunch	Make lunch/Lunch	Lunch helper/Lunch	Phonics	Free	With Mom
12:30	Lunch/Nurse Mary	Lunch/Cleanup	Lunch/Cleanup	Lunch/Cleanup	Lunch/Free	Lunch/Free
1:00	John read/Nap prep	Geography	Reading/Math	Phonics	Free	Free
1:30	Sew	Geography	Math	Read to self	Look at books	Listen to tape in bed
1:45	Sew	Algebra I	Reading/Bible	Read to self	Look at books	Nap
2:00	Prayer/Bible	Algebra I	Reading/Bible	Nap	Nap	Nap
2:30	Rest	Rest	Rest	Nap	Nap	Nap
3:00	Read/Write	Read Female Piety	Rest	Nap	Nap	Nap
3:30	Read to Jos/Jhn/An	Free	Listen to Mom	Listen to Mom	Nap	Nap
4:00	w/John/Read to Jess	Memory/John/Anna	Free	Phonics/Memory	Free/Memory	Nap/Read w/Mom
4:30	Nurse Mary	Free	Free	Free	Free	Free
5:00	Dinner prep	Playroom cleanup	Playroom cleanup	Playroom cleanup	Playroom cleanup	Playroom cleanup
5:30	Talk w/Steve	Free	Free	Free	Free	Free
6:00	Eat/Cleanup	Eat/Cleanup	Eat/Cleanup	Eat/Cleanup	Eat	Eat
7:00	Evening activities	Evening activities	Evening activities	Evening activities	Evening activities	Evening activities
8:30	Nurse/Bible	Teeth/Family Bible	Teeth/Family Bible	Teeth/Family Bible	Teeth/Family Bible	Teeth/Family Bible
9:30	Catch up	Bedtime	Bedtime	Bedtime	Bedtime	Bedtime
10:00	Prepare for bed	Sleep	Sleep	Sleep	Sleep	Sleep
10:30	Bed time	Sleep	Sleep	Sleep	Sleep	Sleep

Amy's Schedule

Time	Mom	Amber (7)	Lucas (6)	Ricky (6)	Shawn (5)	Eric (4)	James (4)	Raven (1)
5:00 am	Personal hygiene				Sleep			Sleep
5:30	Prayer/Bible							
6:00	Quiet time			Personal hygiene				Bottle/Dressed
6:30				Walk				
7:00				Family Bible time				Portacrib play
7:30	Meal prep							Free time
8:00				Morning chores				
8:30				Breakfast				
9:00	Instruct Amber	Cursive writing		Outside				Free time
9:30	Instruct Lucas	Math	Math with Mom	Outside				
10:00	Preschool	Reading	Workbook	Preschool with Mom (Ricky/T, Shawn/W, Eric/TH, James/F) or Outside				Portacrib play
10:30	Read	Reading	Play w/Ricky Family room	Play w/Lucas Family room	Play w/Raven Shawn's room	Play w/James Eric's room	Play w/Eric Eric's room	Play w/Shawn Shawn's room
11:00	Cleaning/MTW	Essay writing	Play w/Eric Room	Play w/James James' room	Play alone Room	Play w/Lucas Room	Play w/Ricky James' room	Portacrib play
11:30	Make bread/THF	Play w/Raven Amber's room	Play w/James Family room	Play alone Room	Play w/Eric Eric's room	Play w/Shawn Eric's room	Play w/Lucas Family room	Play w/Amber Amber's room
12:00 pm	Meal prep	Play w/James	Play alone	Play w/Shawn	Play w/Ricky	Play w/Raven	Play w/Amber	Play w/Eric
12:30				Lunch				
1:00	Rest	Rest				Nap		
1:30		Finish school work						
2:00	Quilt/Sew							
2:30								
3:00				Five in a Row				
3:30	Computer	Play w/Lucas	Play w/Amber	Play w/Eric	Play w/James	Play w/Ricky	Play w/Shawn	Free
4:00	House projects				Bikes/Outside			
4:30								
5:00	Dinner prep/Bible cassette tape			Bible video				Free
5:30		Bath w/Raven			Books			Bath w/Amber
6:00				Dinner				
6:30				Kitchen cleanup				
7:00	Bathe boys	Bed		Baths				Free
7:30	Kid time with Mom and Dad			Kid time with Dad and Mom or Bed (M – Lucas/T – Ricky/W – Shawn/TH – Eric/F – James/Sat – Amber)				Bed
8:00								
8:30	Time with Steve			Sleep				
10:00	News							
10:30	Bed							

Corrie's Schedule

Time	Mom	Adam (13)	Arielle (8)	Chloe (6)	Lillie (4)	Olivia (2)	Seth (1)
5:30 a.m.	Quiet time/Dress				Sleep		
6:00							
6:30	Exercise/Shower						
7:00		Room chores/Quiet time/Shower/Dress			Room chores/Dress		Sleep
7:30	Breakfast/Nurse					Dress	Nurse
8:00	Chores		Breakfast/Teeth/Chores (Olivia help Mommy)				With Family
8:30			School Bible time				
9:00	Math w/Ar, L	Math	Math	Writing/Phonics	Math	Play alone	
9:30	Math w/Chloe		Spell/Write/Voc	Math	Bible movie		Playtime with Adam
10:00	Phonics with girls	With Olivia, Seth		Phonics/Reading		Playtime with Adam	
10:30	w/Adam/Nurse Seth	Shurley Grammar	Reading	With Olivia	Computer	Playtime with Chloe	Nurse/Nap
11:00	With Arielle	Spell/Write/Voc	Shurley Grammar	Computer	With Olivia	Playtime with Lillie	Nap
11:30	Story time w/O, S	Science	Typing/Math drills	Reading/Workbook/Quiet activities		Story time with Mommy	
12:00 p.m.		Lunch (Lillie-lunch helper)/Cleanup (Adam, Arielle, Chloe)/Piano practice (Adam)					
12:30							
1:00			History			Quiet play/Puzzles	Quiet play
1:30					Rest		
2:00	Housework/Projects		Quiet activities			Nap	Nap
2:30		Latin/Thinking skills					
3:00		5 in a Row (MWF 1st week, TTH 2nd week)/Science (TTH 1st week, MWF 2nd week)					With Mommy
3:30	Cleanup school		Chores				Video/Play
4:00	Phone/Laundry		Free time				
4:30	Read/Mail/Play						
5:00	Dinner preparation		Before dinner chores or Free		Dinner helper MWF Or Playtime	Playtime	With Mommy
5:30			Dinner and Cleanup				
6:00						Dinner and Play	
6:30							Nurse / Play
7:00	With little ones	Computer	Teeth brushing				Bath time or Playtime with Mommy
7:30		Free	Ready for bed				
8:00			Family devotions				
8:30	Nurse		Teeth brushing/Ready for bed/Goodnight/Prayers				Nurse
9:00	Final cleanup				Sleep		
9:30	Time with Curt						
10:00	Computer time						
10:30	Ready for bed						
11:00	Bedtime						

Debbie's Schedule for M/W/F

Time	Mom	Zak (9)	Abi (8)	Ben (6)	Sarah (5)	Solomon (4)	Hannah (2) Joe (1)	Rebekah (2 mo)
5:30 a.m.	Dress/Rm/Nurse	Sleep					Sleep	Nurse/Sleep
6:00	Q.T./Planner	Early A.M. chores		Sleep	Play with babies	Quiet play/Book in room/Chores	Sleep	Sleep
6:30	Start laundry	Breakfast prep	Quiet time		A.M. Chores			
7:00	Babies/Ck chores		A.M. Chores			Mom dresses	Mom dresses	
7:30		Breakfast and Bible time						
8:00	Preschool Bible/Nurse/Chk chores	Kitchen chores			Pick up/Play w/babies	Preschool Bible time/Play		Nurse/Play
8:30	B/S Scribe/Check Zak Bible study	Genesis Bible Study		Scribe and Handwriting		Video		Play
9:00	Assignment w/A	Ed game w/Ben	With Mom	Ed game w/Zak	Color w/Solomon	Color with Sarah	Play in family room	Play
9:30	Assignment w/Z	With Mom	Ed game w/Sarah	Legos w/Solomon	Ed game w/Abi	Legos with Ben		Sleep
10:00	Nurse/Math w/B		Math	Math	Play with babies	Designated toys		Nurse/Crib
10:30	Math w/Sarah			Reading lesson	Math	Play - Family room		
11:00	Reading w/Ben	Writing lesson		Reading lesson		A.M. Pick up		Play
11:30	Reading w/Sarah	Lunch prep	Clean work area		Reading lesson	Video		
12:00 p.m.		Lunch						
12:30	Put H/J/Sol down	Kitchen chores		Kitchen chores	Kitchen chores			Play
1:00	Check kitchen chores/Nap/Nurse		Laundry folding					
1:30			P.E. video			Nap or Book time		Nurse/Nap
2:00	Review time/Zak	Review w/Mom					Nap	
2:30	Review time/Abi							
3:00	Nurse	Free	Free	Free	Free	Playtime	Playtime	
3:30	Weaver activity				Weaver activity			Nurse/Crib
4:00	School prep			Free	Free			
4:30	Computer time							
5:00	Nurse		P.M. Cleanup					Nurse
5:30	Dinner prep	Video/Book or Dinner prep M (Abi), W (Sarah), F (Zak)				Video	Video	
6:00		Dinner						
6:30	Misc. activities	Kitchen chores						Play
7:00	Babies/Ck chores	Evening chores						Nurse
7:30	Nurse	Free						
8:00		Bible time						
8:30	Put children down	Bedtime						Play
9:00	Nurse	Sleep						Nurse
9:30	Free							
10:00	Bedtime							Sleep

Debbie's Schedule for T/Th

Time	Mom	Zak (9)	Abi (8)	Ben (6)	Sarah (5)	Solomon (4)	Hannah (2) Joe (1)	Rebekah (2 mo)
5:30 a.m.	Dress/Q.T./Nurse			Sleep				Nurse/Sleep
6:00	Q.T./Planner	Q.T./Chores	Early A.M. chores / Q.T.				Sleep	
6:30	Start laundry		Q.T.		Play with babies	Quiet play/Book in room/Chores	Sleep	Sleep
7:00	Babies/Ck chores	Breakfast prep	A.M. Chores		Play with babies		Mom dresses	
7:30		Breakfast and Bible time			A.M. Chores			
8:00	Preschool Bible/Nurse/Chk chores	Kitchen chores			Pick up/Play w/babies	Preschool Bible time/Play		Nurse/Play
8:30	B/S Scribe/Check Zak Bible study	Genesis Bible Study		Scribe Handwriting	Scribe Handwriting	Video		Play
9:00	Assignment/w/A	Ed game w/Sarah	With Mom	Legos w/Solomon	Ed game with Zak	Legos with Ben	Play in family room	
9:30	Assignment/w/Z	With Mom	Ed game/w Ben	Ed game w/Abi	Color w/Solomon	Color with Sarah		Sleep
10:00	Supervise/Nurse	Handwriting/Letters/Spelling			Letters	Designated toy play		Nurse
10:30								Play
11:00	Ben's reading	Writing lesson		Reading lesson	Reading lesson	A.M. Pick up toys		Play
11:30	Sarah's reading	Clean work area	Lunch prep	Clean work area	Reading lesson	Video		
12:00 p.m.				Lunch				
12:30	Put H&J down		Reading time	Kitchen chores				Play
1:00	Chk chores/Nurse			Fold laundry			Nap	Nurse/Nap
1:30		Reading time		Reading time		Nap/Book		
2:00	Mom nap	Review w/Mom	Free	Free				
2:30	Review with Zak		Review w/Mom	Free	Free	Playtime	Playtime	
3:00	Review with Abi							
3:30	Weaver/Nurse		Free	Weaver activity	Weaver activity			Nurse/Play
4:00	School prep			Free	Free			
4:30	Computer time							
5:00	Nurse			P.M. Cleanup	P.M. Cleanup			Nurse
5:30	Dinner prep			Video or Book/Dinner prep/T (Ben) TH (Solomon)				
6:00	Dinner			Dinner				
6:30	Nurse			Kitchen chores			Free	Nurse
7:00	Babies/Ck chores			Evening chores				
7:30				Free				Play
8:00				Bible time				
8:30	Put kids down			Bedtime				Play
9:00	Nurse			Sleep				
9:30	Free							Nurse/Sleep
10:00	Bedtime							

Ellen's Schedule

Time	Mom	Ryan (7)	Brandon (6)	William (4)	Austin (1)	Evan (1)
5:30 a.m.	Quiet time			Sleep	Sleep	Sleep
6:00	Exercise/Shower					
6:30	Computer					
7:00	Breakfast/Fix lunch	Rise/Room chores	Rise/Room chores	Sleep	Sleep	Sleep
7:30	Feed babies/Cleanup	Breakfast/Teeth/Chores	Breakfast/Teeth/Chores	Breakfast/Teeth	Breakfast/Teeth	Breakfast/Teeth
8:00	School with William	Spelling/Math	Play with twins	School with Mom	Play with Brandon	Play with Brandon
8:30	School with Brandon	Computer time	School with Mom	Free time	Crib/Books	Playpen/Toys
9:00	School with Ryan	School with Mom	Free time	Computer time	Free play	Free play
9:30	School with Brandon	Literature/Handwriting	School with Mom	Coloring	Playpen/Toys	Crib/Books
10:00	School with Ryan	School with Mom	Computer time	Play with twins	Play with William	Play with William
10:30	Read to older children	Scripture memory	Listen to Mom read	School with Mom	Nap	Nap
11:00	School with William	Scripture memory	Scripture memory	School with Mom	Nap	Nap
11:30		Music or Art	Music or Art		Nap	Nap
12:00 p.m.		Lunch	Lunch	Lunch	Nap	Nap
12:30		Family Bible time	Family Bible time	Family Bible time	Nap	Nap
1:00	Teaching babies	Free time	Free time	Rest	With Mom	With Mom
1:30	Rest	Rest	Rest	Rest	Nap	Nap
2:00	Project time		Play alone		Nap	Nap
2:30			Play alone		Nap	Nap
3:00	Cleaning/Chores		Chores		Play with Evan	
3:30	Ministry/Service		Play outside		Play with Austin	Play with Austin
4:00	Read to little children		Play outside		Listen to Mom read	Listen to Mom read
4:30	Supper prep	Play with twins	Free time	Scripture mem. w/Mom	Play with Ryan	Play with Ryan
5:00		Supper/Cleanup	Supper/Cleanup	Supper/Cleanup		
5:30						
6:00		Family events (AWANA, Church, Bible study, Hospitality, Visiting, Ballgames, Video/Game nights)				
7:00		Family events (AWANA, Church, Bible study, Hospitality, Visiting, Ballgames, Video/Game nights)				
7:30		Free time	Free time	Sleep	Bath/Teeth/Free time	Bath/Teeth/Free time
8:00	Baths and Cleanup	Bath/Teeth/Free	Bath/Teeth/Free	Sleep	Bath/Teeth/Free time	Bath/Teeth/Free time
8:30		Family devotions	Family devotions	Sleep	Sleep	Sleep
9:00	Cleaning/Chores			Sleep	Sleep	Sleep
9:30	Laundry			Sleep	Sleep	Sleep
10:00	Computer time			Sleep	Sleep	Sleep
10:30	Sleep			Sleep	Sleep	Sleep

Ellen's Alternate Schedule
(Used depending on husband's work schedule)

Time	Mom	Ryan (7)	Brandon (6)	William (4)	Austin (1)	Evan (1)
5:30 a.m.	Quiet time	Sleep	Sleep	Sleep	Sleep	Sleep
6:00	Exercise/Shower	Sleep	Sleep	Sleep	Sleep	Sleep
6:30	Computer	Sleep	Sleep	Sleep	Sleep	Sleep
7:00	Breakfast prep	Rise/Room chores	Rise/Room chores	Rise/Room chores	Sleep	Sleep
7:30	Feed babies/Cleanup	Breakfast/Teeth/Chores	Breakfast/Teeth/Chores	Breakfast/Teeth/Chores	Breakfast/Teeth	Breakfast/Teeth
8:00	Family devotions	Family devotions	Family devotions	Family devotions	Family devotions	Family devotions
8:30	Cleaning/Chores	Chores	Chores	Chores	Play with Evan	Play with Austin
9:00	Project time	Outside play	Outside play	Outside play	Play with Evan	Play with Austin
9:30	Read to little children	Outside play	Outside play	Outside play	Listen to Mom read	Listen to Mom read
10:00	Baths/Cleanup	Bath or Free	Bath or Free	Bath or Free	Bath time	Bath time
10:30		Bath or Free	Bath or Free	Bath or Free	Bath time	Bath time
11:00	School with William	Scripture memory	Scripture memory	School with Mom	Nap	Nap
11:30		Music or Art	Music or Art	School with Mom	Nap	Nap
12:00 p.m.	Lunch	Lunch	Lunch	Lunch	Lunch	Lunch
12:30	Family Bible time	Family Bible time	Family Bible time	Family Bible time	Family Bible time	Family Bible time
1:00	Teaching babies	Typing/Computer	Rest	Rest	With Mom	With Mom
1:30		Rest	Rest	Rest	With Mom	With Mom
2:00	Project time	Rest	Rest	Rest	Nap	Nap
2:30	School with Brandon	Math/Spelling/Writing	School with Mom	Free time	Nap	Nap
3:00	School with Ryan	School with Mom	With twins	Computer time	With Brandon	With Brandon
3:30	School with William	Science/Social studies	Computer time	School with Mom	Crib/Books	Playpen/Toys
4:00	School with Brandon	Free time	School with Mom	With twins	With William	With William
4:30	Supper prep	Play with twins	Free	Scripture mem. w/Mom	With Ryan	With Ryan
5:00	Supper/Cleanup	Supper/Cleanup	Supper/Cleanup	Supper/Cleanup	Supper/Cleanup	Supper/Cleanup
5:30		Supper/Cleanup	Supper/Cleanup	Supper/Cleanup	Supper/Cleanup	Supper/Cleanup
6:00	School with Ryan	School with Mom	Free	Free	Playpen/Toys	Crib/Books
6:30	Ministry		Play alone	Play alone	Free time	Free time
7:00		Family events/Pajamas/Teeth	Family events/Pajamas/Teeth	Family events/Pajamas/Teeth		
7:30		Family events/Pajamas/Teeth	Family events/Pajamas/Teeth	Family events/Pajamas/Teeth		
8:00		Family events/Pajamas/Teeth	Family events/Pajamas/Teeth	Family events/Pajamas/Teeth		
8:30	Mom reads	Listen to Mom read	Listen to Mom read	Listen to Mom read		
9:00	Cleaning/Chores	Sleep	Sleep	Sleep		
9:30	Laundry	Sleep	Sleep	Sleep		
10:00	Computer	Sleep	Sleep	Sleep		
10:30	Sleep	Sleep	Sleep	Sleep		

Kathleen's Schedule

Time	Mom	Quin (9)	Brenna (7)	Deirdre (5)	Grady (3)
6:00 a.m.	Grooming/Fix breakfast	Sleep			
6:30	Breakfast	Dress/Eat breakfast			
7:00	Dress Grady/Clean kitchen	Clean room/Brush teeth and hair			
7:30	Supervise chores	Chores			
8:00	Fix dinner		Chores		
8:30		Bible time			
9:00		Math		Play alone in room	
9:30		Math/Unit study		Play or Math	
10:00	School	M, T, TH/Language Arts/W/Handwriting		Play	
10:30			Mom reads aloud		
11:00		Unit study		Unit study or Play	
11:30					
12:00 p.m.		Dinner			
12:30	Supervise cleanup/Dishwasher		Kitchen cleanup		
1:00	Rest/Read		Rest/Read		
1:30					
2:00	Walk		Outside with Dad		
2:30	Current project				
3:00					
3:30	Quiet time		Rest/Read		
4:00	Read with Deirdre	Free	Play with Grady	Read with Mom	Play with Brenna
4:30	Play with Grady		Practice piano/Free	Free/Practice piano	Play with Mom
5:00			Cleanup/Laundry/Dishwasher		
5:30	Prepare supper		Free or Help Mom		
6:00			Eat supper		
6:30	Supervise kitchen cleanup		Kitchen cleanup		
7:00			Family time		
7:30					
8:00	Paper work	Read/Projects	Read/Projects		
8:30	Computer time		Sleep	Sleep	Sleep
9:00	Husband time or Read				
9:30					
10:00	Sleep				

*Fridays: Girls do extra chores and bake with Mom, Boys do extra chores with Dad, Art, Piano lessons
Saturday: 8:00 a.m. Breakfast followed by room cleanup and regular chores. Mom does business and paperwork, plans and prepares Sunday dinner
Sunday: 8 a.m. Breakfast, 8:30 a.m. Dress and tidy room, 9 a.m. Final preparations for services, Quick pick up, 9:30 a.m. Leave for services

Kathy's Schedule

Time	Mom	Doug (7)	Derek (5)	Kari (9 mo)
6:00 a.m.	Wake/Nurse Kari			Wake/Nurse
6:30	Devotions			Back to sleep
7:00	Breakfast	Sleep		
7:30	School prep/Start laundry			Sleep
8:00	Shower/Dress	Wake/Make bed		Wake
8:30		Breakfast/Dress/Teeth/Dishes		
9:00	Nurse/Phonics with Doug	Phonics with Mom	Free	Nurse
9:30	Phonics with Derek/Laundry in dryer	Play with Kari	Phonics with Mom	Play with Doug
10:00	Math with Doug	Math with Mom	Play with Kari	Play with Derek
10:30	Reading/Writing with Doug	Reading/Writing with Mom	Legos/Puzzles/Coloring/Laundry in	
11:00	M/Ironing; T/Mop; W/Fans, Dust; Th/Paper work	M/Dust, T/Van, W/Bathroom/Porch, Th/Vacuum	M/Vacuum, T/Window ledges, W/Tub/Glass door, Th/Mirror	Nap
11:30	Fold laundry	Piano/Bible memory	Bible memory/Computer	Wake up/With Mom
12:00 p.m.	Nurse/Lunch	Lunch		Nurse
12:30				
1:00	Phone calls/Dishes	Silent reading/Put laundry away	Look at books/Put laundry away	Playpen
1:30		Konos		
2:00				
2:30	Organization/Paper work/Computer	Seatwork/Computer	Handwriting	Nap
3:00		Play with Derek	Play with Doug	
3:30	Nurse Kari	Watch PBS		Up/Nurse
4:00	Play with Derek		Play with Mommy	Playpen
4:30	Free time	Free time	Free time	Play
5:00				
5:45	Dinner preparation		Cleanup for Daddy	
6:00		Bath (6:15)/Play with Kari	Bath (6:00)/Set table	Play with Doug
6:30			Dinner	
7:00			Family Bible time	
7:30	Cleanup		Daddy reads	
8:00	Kari bath		Bedtime	Bath
8:30	Nurse			Nurse
9:00	Catch up		Sleep	To bed
9:30	Relax			Sleep
10:00	Get ready for bed			
10:30	To bed			

Kim's Schedule

Time	Mom	Bekah (4)	Sam (2)	Bethany Grace (1)
5:00 a.m.	Sleep		Sleep	
5:30	Quiet time			
6:00	Shower/Dressed			
6:30	Chores			
7:00		Children up/Dressed/Breakfast/Wash faces/Brush teeth		
7:30				
8:00		Bible time/Nonconflict training time		
8:45	Time with Bekah	Time with Mommy	Room time	Playpen time
9:00				
9:30	Time with Sam	Room time	Time with Mommy	Assigned toy time
10:00	Time with Bethany		Assigned toy time	Time with Mommy
10:30	Read to all		Listen to Mommy read	
11:00		Outside time*		
11:30		Lunch		
12:00 p.m.				
12:30		Mommy reads to each individually on their beds before nap time		
1:00	Read to Bekah	Listen to Mommy read		
1:30	Chores			
2:00	Phone/Computer time	Nap	Nap	Nap
2:30	Scrapbooking/Chores			
3:00	Chores/Rest			
3:30	Dinner preparation		Up/Quiet time	
4:00			Snacks/Table time	
4:30	Supervise free play	Set table	Free play with all	Blanket time
5:00	Finish up dinner			
5:30			Book time	
6:00			Dinner	
6:30			Couch time	
7:00	Dinner cleanup		Play with Daddy, then family devotions	
7:30			Family devotions, then baths	
8:00	Free		Daddy reads before bed, then bed	
8:30	Time with Brooks		Sleep	
9:00	Bed			
9:30	Sleep			
10:00				

* Weather Permitting - If weather doesn't permit, art then exercise/play time.

M - Ballet, gone 2:30 to 4:00 p.m.

Kirstin's Schedule

Time	Mom	Grant (4)	Caleb (3)	Libby (10 mo)
6:00 a.m.	Shower/Dress	Sleep	Sleep	Sleep
6:30	Eat breakfast/Read Bible			Nurse/Free play
7:00	Nurse/Computer time			Free play
7:30	Computer time/Chores			
8:00	Breakfast for children	Breakfast		
8:30	Children dress/Brush teeth/Chores		Dress/Brush teeth	
9:00	Chores/Read to children	Video/Table time/Listen to Mom read		Free play
9:30				
10:00	Fold and put away laundry	Playtime with Caleb	Playtime with Grant	Nap
10:30	Chores			
11:00	Nurse/Chores	Free play	Free play/Help Mom with chores	Nurse/Playtime alone
11:30	Individual time with child		Playtime with Mom or Free play	
12:00 p.m.	Pick up toys/Prepare lunch	Pick up toys/Free play		Free play
12:30		Lunch		Highchair time
1:00	Clean kitchen/Chores	Free play	Free play	Free play
1:30	Chores			
1:45	Prepare children for naps	Prepare for nap		
2:00	Nurse/Prayer	Nap		Nurse/Nap
2:30	Rest			
3:00	Computer time	Free play	Nap	Nap
3:30	Chores	Help Mom with chores		
4:00	Nurse/Chores		Video	Nurse/Free play
4:30	Chores	Playtime alone		Free play/Playtime alone
5:00	Playtime with all children		Playtime with Mom and siblings	
5:30		Pick up toys		
5:45	Feed Libby		Free play	Eat solids
6:00	Prepare supper			Free play
6:30		Supper		
6:45				
7:15	Clean kitchen		Evening activities	
7:30	Evening activities	Evening activities		Evening activities
8:00	Evening activities/Nurse			Nurse
8:30	Prepare boys for bed	Prepare for bed		Bed
9:00	Hobby time	Sleep	Sleep	
9:30				
10:00	Computer time			Sleep
10:30				
11:00	Nurse/Bed			
11:30	Sleep			

Kristi's Schedule

Time	Steve	Kristi	Kati (7)	Josh (6)	Sarah (3)	Brady (2)
5:30 a.m.	Sleep	Prayer/Praise	Sleep	Sleep	Sleep	Sleep
6:00		Grooming/Make S lunch				
6:30	Grooming	Personal quiet time				
7:00	Quiet time with Kristi	Quiet time with Steve	Grooming/Room chores	Grooming/Room chores	Grooming/Room chores	Grooming/Room chores
7:30	Breakfast	Laundry/Alone time with Josh		Breakfast prep w/Mommy		
7:45	Depart for work					
8:00	Drive time	Breakfast	Breakfast	Chores	Breakfast	Breakfast
8:30	Personal quiet time	Chores	Laundry w/Mom/Chores	Breakfast cleanup	Laundry/Daily chores	Laundry/Daily chores
9:00		Phonics/Math with Josh	Read/Spell/Write	Phonics/Math w/Mom	Playtime with Brady	Playtime with Sarah
9:45				School Bible time	Playtime alone	Playtime alone
10:00	Work	Phonics/Math with Kati	Phonics/Math w/Mom	Read/Spell/Write (alone)		
10:45		Preschool w/Sarah, Bra.	Complete work	Complete work	Preschool with Mommy	Preschool with Mommy
11:00		Personal time (Sew, etc.)	Piano or Typing lesson	Education activity w/S,B	Education activity with Josh	Education activity with Josh
11:15				Playtime w/Sarah, Brady	Playtime with Josh	Playtime with Josh
11:30			Education activity w/S,B	Piano or Typing lesson	Education activity with Kati	Education activity with Kati
11:45			Playtime w/Sarah, Brady		Playtime with Kati	Playtime with Kati
12:00 p.m.		With Kati/Eat/Laundry	Lunch prep w/Mommy	Chores	Free time	Free time
12:30		Mail/With children	Laundry/Lunch cleanup		Lunch	Lunch
1:00		History/Science w/K, J	History/Science w/Mom	History/Science w/Mom	Playtime with Brady	Playtime with Sarah
1:45		Playtime w/Sarah, Brady	Individual work	Individual work	Playtime with Mommy	Playtime with Mommy
2:00		Computer/Free time	Quiet time	Quiet time	Nap	Nap
2:30			Rest/Silent reading	Rest/Silent reading		
3:00			Rest			
3:30						
4:00		Errands/Free/*B 1 x wk	Errands/Finish work/Free time	Errands/Finish work/Free time	Errands/Free time	Errands/* M 1 x wk
4:30		Errands/Free time				Errands/Free time
5:00	Depart from work	Errands/Free/*S 1 x wk	Errands/Free time	Errands/Free time	Errands/Free/*M 1 x wk	
5:30	Drive time	Dinner preparation with Sarah and Brady	Laundry or Free time	Laundry or Free time	Dinner prep with Mom	Dinner prep with Mom
5:45	Relax/Freshen					
6:00	Alone with children		Dinner	Dinner		
6:45		Cleanup dinner	Alone with Daddy	Alone with Daddy	Cleanup with Mommy	Cleanup with Mommy
7:00	Free time		Family devotions and Character training	Family devotions and Character training		
7:30	Bath/Bedtime for kids	Bath/Bedtime for kids	Story time with Sarah and Brady or Bath	Story time with Sarah and Brady or Bath	Bath/Story time with Kati or Josh	Bath/Story time with Kati or Josh
8:00	Time with Kristi	Time with Steve	Sleep	Sleep	Sleep	Sleep
9:30	Computer/Study time	Day end devotions				
10:00	Sleep	Sleep				
11:00	Sleep					

Lisa's Schedule

Time	Mommy	Abigail (6)	Josiah (6)	Samuel (4)	Jesse (2)	Matthias (5 mo)
4:30 a.m.	Nurse/Read Bible					Nurse
5:00	Milk goats	Sleep				
5:30	Wake and Help children	Wake/Dress/Room chores				Sleep
6:00		Morning family devotions				
6:30		Breakfast				
7:00	Nurse Matthias	Clean table	Sort laundry	Help Abigail	Help Josiah	Wake/Dress/Nurse
7:30	Pre-K with Jesse	Playtime with Matthias	Playtime with Samuel	Playtime Josiah	Pre-K with Mommy	Playtime with Abigail
8:00	Phonics with Josiah and Abigail	Phonics with Mommy		Playtime with Matthias	High chair time	Playtime with Samuel
8:30				Playtime with Jesse	Playtime with Samuel	Jumper time
9:00	Math/Phonics w/Samuel	Playtime with Jesse	Free time	Math/Phonics w/Mom	Playtime with Abigail	Nap
9:30		M,TH/Make soup	T/Sew with children	W/Art F/Cleaning		
10:00	Nurse Matthias	Playtime with Samuel	Playtime with Jesse	Playtime with Abigail	Playtime with Josiah	Nurse
10:30	Math w/Josiah, Abigail	Math with Mommy		Free time		Bouncy seat
11:00	Walk before lunch or Mommy and older children hang laundry if needed					
11:30	Lunch preparation			Outside		Jumper
12:00 p.m.		Lunch				Free
12:30		Story time				
1:00	Nurse Matthias	Independent time before nap				Nurse
1:30	Rest		Nap	Nap		Nap
2:00	Sew		Quiet book/Free			
2:30		Quiet book/Free				
3:00		Read aloud				
3:30		Fold laundry		Bouncy seat		Bouncy seat
4:00	Nurse Matthias	Outside				Nurse
4:30	Start dinner	Outside	Playtime with Matthias	Outside	Outside	Playtime with Josiah
5:00	Dinner prep/Milk goats	Set table/Help (rotate by weeks) or Free				Jumper
5:30		Dinner				Bouncy seat
6:00		Cleanup				Free
6:30		Evening family devotions				
7:00	Play with children/Bath		Play with children/Bath	Playtime with Mommy/Bath		Nurse
7:30	Practice piano			Playtime with Papa		
8:00	Nurse Matthias		Story/Bed			Nurse
8:30	Computer time	Sleep				
9:00	Catch up					
9:30	Bed					

Lorrie's Schedule

Time	Mom	John (11)	Levi (8)	Drew (6)	Dessaly (4)	Kiley (2)	Haley (Infant)
8:00 a.m.	Computer time	Make breakfast	Morning chores	Empty dishwasher	Gather laundry	Computer with Mom	Sleep
8:30	Walk	Eat breakfast					
9:00	Quiet time/Dress	Clean/Dress Kiley	Bkfst cleanup/Dress	Chores/Dress		Dress with John	Nurse
9:30	Chores	Saxon in LR	Math on computer	Time with Kiley	Play with Haley	Time with Drew	Time with Dessa
10:00	Preschool	Read to little ones	Play with Haley		Preschool		Time with Levi
10:30	Reading with Levi		Read with Mom		Story time		
11:00	BTS* with Levi	Math on computer	BTS* with Mom		BTS*		Sleep
11:30	BTS* with John	BTS* with Mom	Handwriting		Readywriter		
12:00 p.m.	Prepare lunch	Empty laundry				Lunch with Mom	Nurse
12:30		Eat/Five in a Row (School unit study)					With Mom
1:00	Time with Kiley	Time with Haley	Time with Dessa	Lunch cleanup	Time with Levi	Time with Mom	Time with John
1:30			Awana verses			Quiet time	Playtime
2:00		Creative pursuits/Free time					
2:30							
3:00							
3:30							
4:00							
4:30							
5:00	Prepare dinner			Room check			Playtime
5:30	Housework	Chores					Sleep
6:00		Dinner					
6:30	Time with Daddy	Dinner cleanup		Legos	Duplos		Nurse
7:00	Computer time	Time with Daddy			Time with Daddy		With Mom
7:30	Quilting					Time with Daddy	
8:00	Baths/Stories/Prayer				Baths/Stories/Prayer		Time with Daddy
8:30			Family devotions				
9:00		Read aloud				Bed	Nurse

*BTS stands for Building Thinking Skills

Pauline's Schedule

Time	Mom	Dustin (12)	Hannah (7)	Garrett (6)	Cynthia (3)	Sadie (2)	Timothy (4 mo)
5:30 a.m.	Nurse/Make lunch/brkfast for husband			Sleep			Nurse/Sleep
6:00	Quiet time						Sleep
6:30	Exercise						
7:00	Shower/Wake children			Room chores			Sleep
7:30	Chores/Make brkfst			Chores			
8:00	Eat/Cleanup			Eat breakfast			
8:30	Devotions/Nurse			Devotions			Nurse
9:00	Math with Dustin	Math with Mom	Play with Cynthia, S	Play with Tim	Play with Hannah		Play with Garrett
9:30	Preschool		Math		Preschool	Preschool	Walker
10:00	English with Dustin	English with Mom	Spelling/Writing		Assigned activity		
10:30	Phonics w/H, D	English	Phonics/Read	Read/Phonics	Computer with Sadie	Computer with Cyn.	Nap
11:00			Unit Study - Five in a Row				Nurse
11:30							Walker
12:00 p.m.	Make lunch	Drum practice	Reading		Help Mom		With Mom
12:30			Lunch			Nap	
1:00	Prep children for nap	Cleanup lunch	Computer	Time alone	Nap		Time alone
1:30			Voice of the Martyrs				
2:00	Rest	History	Nap	Nap			Nap
2:30	Laundry	Bible			Wake/Snack		
3:00	Free time	Science		Free play			
3:30	w/Dustin/Nurse	Game with Mom		Listen to Mom			Nurse
4:00	Read to children						
4:30	Dinner prep	Swim	Play with Tim	Play with C, S	Play with Garrett		Play with Hannah
5:00					Dinner prep		Walker
5:30	Dinner				Dinner		Nap
6:00				Dinner			
6:30	Nurse	Free time	Bath/Ready for bed	Computer	Look at books		Nurse
7:00	Computer time	Play w/C, S	Alone time	Bath/Ready for bed	Play with Dustin		With Dad or Mom
7:30	Bathe children	Shower/Bed prep	Read/Journal			Bath/Ready for bed	
8:00			Family worship				
8:30	Nurse	Bedtime or Stay up late with Dad and Mom (M/Dustin, T/Hannah, W/Garrett, TH/Cynthia, F/Sadie)					Nurse
9:00	Time with husband	Lights out					Sleep
9:30	Write	Sleep					
10:00	Bedtime						

Rebecca's Schedule

Time	Mom	Andrea (13)	Megan (11)
6:00 a.m.	Shower/AM prep	Sleep	Sleep
6:30	Bible/Prayer		
7:00	Meal prep/Cleanup		
7:30		Breakfast	Breakfast
8:00	Computer time	AM prep	Shower
8:30	School paperwork	Free	AM prep
9:00		Religion	
9:30	Math/Spelling/Grammar with Andrea	Math/Spelling/Grammar	Math/Spelling/Grammar
10:00	Math/Spelling/Grammar with Megan		
10:30	(45 minutes each)		
11:00	Meal prep/Cleanup	Reading	Reading
11:30		Lunch	
12:00 p.m.	Nap	Free	Free
12:30	Latin (4 times/wk)	Workbook (4 times/wk)	Latin (4 times/wk)
1:00		Science/History (4 times/wk)	
2:00	Art/Music	Art/Music/Typing (3 days a week)	Art/Music/Typing (3 days a week)
2:30	Check work, etc.		
3:00		Snack/Open/Free*	
3:30			
4:00			
4:30			
5:00		Weekly chores	
5:30		Daily chores	
6:00	Meal prep/Cleanup		Free
6:30		Dinner	
7:00	Time with girls	Time with Mom	Time with Mom
7:30	Free	Free	Free
8:00	Shower	Shower	
8:30	Tidy up/Tuck in	PM prep	PM prep
9:00	Mail/Planning	Read in bed	Read in bed
9:30	PM prep	Sleep	Sleep
10:00	Sleep		

*Open time (3-5 p.m.) rough schedule:
M - Mom (Drive her on her errands etc), T - Appointments (Dr, Ortho, Dentist, etc), W - Paperwork (Bills, Grocery List, Filing, etc), Th - Groceries, Errands, F - Cooking (the more labor intensive stuff): If we're home, the girls have free time.

Other notes: We also have one afternoon a week available to do homeschool group activities. Thursday we finish school at two so we have extra time to do grocery shopping/errands. Free time activities that the girls do - bike riding, reading, board/card games, computer, videos, skating, basketball, cooking, sewing, arts/crafts and some toys and puzzles. Laundry is washed/dried during school time. I usually start a load at nine and another right before/after lunch. When we have other activities like sports, club, church, etc. in the evening, the free time/time with me gets bumped. I have something about three evenings a month, and Megan does soccer one weeknight a week spring and fall.

Renée's Schedule

Time	Mom	Katie (7)	Hannah (4)	Will (3)	Ben (8 mo)
6:00 a.m.	Walk/Exercise	Sleep			
6:30	Quiet time				
7:00		Breakfast			
7:30	Shower/Dress		Free		With Mom
8:00	Morning chores/Help children get ready and Teach jobs		Dress/Brush teeth	Dress/Brush teeth	Dress/Brush teeth
8:30		Morning chores	Morning chores	Morning chores	Free
9:00	Reading/Phonics with Katie	Reading/Phonics with Mom	Play with Ben	Playtime alone	Play with Hannah
9:30	School with Hannah	Helping or Play with Ben	School with Mom	Play with Katie and Ben	Play with Will and Katie
10:00	Math with Katie	Math with Mom	Play with Will	Play with Hannah	Nap
10:30	Play/Preschool with Will/Ben	Helping or Play with Hannah	School or Play with Katie	Play/Preschool with Mom/Ben	Play/Preschool/Will and Mom
11:00	Bible with Katie	Bible with Mom			Play
11:30	Read w/Katie/Calendar/Diary	Reading with Mom/Free	Video or Playing with Will	Video or Playing with Hannah	Play
12:00 p.m.	Lunch prep	Helping or Play with Ben	Lunch	Lunch helper	Play with Katie
12:30			Cleanup		
1:00					
1:30	Prepare for naps	Quiet time	Quiet time	Prepare for nap	
2:00	Nap or Personal activities (phone/writing)			Nap	
2:30			Free	Free	
3:00		Afternoon chores			
3:30			Prepare for and Drive to soccer/Friday – Chores		
4:00			Soccer / Friday – Chores/Iron		
4:30			Free		
5:00	Dinner preparation	Dinner helper			
5:30				Free	
6:00			Dinner		
6:30					
7:00			Family free time		
7:30	Help with baths/Brush teeth		Bath/Brush teeth		
8:00			Family devotions		
8:30	Reading to Hannah/Will	Reading with Grandma or Dad	Reading with Mom	Reading with Mom	Listening
9:00	Time with Dale		Bedtime/Sleep		
9:30	Personal reading				
10:00	Bed				

Ricki's Schedule

Time	Mom	Amanda (13)	Morganne (11)	Matt (9)	Kate (7)	Olivia (6)	Zach (4)	Hope (2)	Andy (5 mo)
7:00 a.m.	Sleep	Dress/Bible	Dress/Bible	Sleep	Sleep	Sleep	Sleep	Sleep	Sleep
7:30	Nurse/Pray	Meal prep.	Dress Hope	Dress/Quiet time	Dress/Quiet time	Dress/Set table	Dress	Dress	Nurse
8:00	Eat/Walk			Breakfast	Breakfast	Breakfast	Breakfast	Breakfast	In swing
8:30	Walk	With Andy	Piano	Brkfst cleanup	Chores	Play with Hope	Clear table	Play with Olivia	Playtime
9:00	Shower/Dress	Piano	With Andy	Chores	w/Hope, Zach	Playtime	Play with Kate	Play with Kate	
9:30	Nurse/Read/H	Chores	Chores	Play w/Zach	Piano	Chores	Play with Matt	Read with Mom	Nurse
10:00				Family Bible	Family Bible	Family Bible	Family Bible	Family Bible	Nap
10:30				Family Bible	Family Bible	Family Bible	Family Bible	Family Bible	
11:00	Read/Play/Hope	English	English	Typing/Spelling	Science/History	Play w/Zach	Play w/Olivia	Read with Mom	With Mom
11:30	Preschool/Zach	Journal or Lunch prep	Journal or Lunch prep	Play with Hope	Typing/Spelling	Play w/Andy	Preschool	Play with Matt	With Olivia
12:00 p.m.		Lunch	Lunch	Lunch	Lunch	Lunch	Lunch	Lunch	Wake time
12:30	Nurse	Read to/Put Z,O for nap/Computer	Read to/Put Z,O for nap/Computer	Science/History	Lunch cleanup	Computer time	Clear table/Nap	Read w/girls	Nurse
1:00	School w/Kate	Science/History	Typing	Math	Math	Rest time	Nap/Rest	Nap	Nap
1:30	School w/Matt	Typing	Science/History	Math	Math	Workbook	Nap/Rest	Nap	Nap
2:00	School w/Olivia	Math	Math	English		Phonics w/Mm		Nap	Nap
2:30	School w/A,Mo	Math	Math	Journal		Math with help	Computer	Nap	Nap in swing
3:00	Chores	Chores	Chores	Chores	Chores	Writing/Typing	Chores	With Mom	Nurse
3:30	Chores	Chores	Chores	Chores	Chores	Chores	Play with Hope	Play with Zach	
4:00	Nurse			Free	Free				Nurse
4:30	Dinner prep.	Dinner prep or Play with little ones	Dinner prep or Play with little ones			Free			Playtime
5:00		Mom reads aloud	Mom reads aloud	Mom reads aloud	Mom reads aloud	Mom reads aloud	Mom reads aloud	Mom reads aloud	
5:30		Dinner	Dinner	Dinner	Dinner	Dinner	Dinner	Dinner	Nap in swing
6:00		Dinner	Dinner	Dinner	Dinner	Dinner	Dinner	Dinner	
6:30	Nurse	Alternate dinner cleanup/Bath	Free	Free	Free	Free	Clear table/Free	Free	Nurse
7:00	Read/Baths	Free	Free		Bath time		Bath and Read		Bath
7:30	Play w/Mom	Free	Free		Play with Mom		With Dad, girls, or Free	With Dad, girls, or Free	Wake
8:00	Devotion	Family devotions/Get ready for bed	Family devotions/Get ready for bed	Family devotions/Get ready for bed	Family devotions/Get ready for bed	Family devotions/Get ready for bed	Family devotions/Get ready for bed	Family devotions/Get ready for bed	Devotion/Nurse
8:30	Nurse								Nurse
9:00	Quiet time	Bedtime	Bedtime	Bedtime	Bedtime	Bedtime	Bedtime	Bedtime	

Sally's Schedule

Time	Mom	Jacob (11)	Mary (9)	Lucy (8)	Isaac (5)	Lois (4)	Rose (3)	Anna (1)	Ruth (3 mo)
5:30 a.m.	Devotion/Bath			Sleep				Sleep	Sleep
6:00	Breakfast	Devotions/Teeth/Breakfast/Clean room/Grooming			Devotions/Clean room	Devotions/Clean room			Eat/Clean/Mary
6:30	Walk	Chores	Chores	Potty Anna/	Breakfast/Teeth/Cleanup/Personal grooming/Anna potty with Lucy			potty with Lucy	With Lois
7:00	Preschool	Math	Math	Computer	Computer	Preschool	With Anna	With Rose	With Lucy
7:30	Preschool			Ruth/Kitchen			Preschool		With Mom
8:00	L./M,W,F M./T,TH	Play w/Isaac	Mom tutor or Seatwork	Mom tutor or Bear Math	Play with Jacob	Bear Math	Bear Math		Eat
8:30		Bible/Drawing				Computer	Play with Anna	Potty Mary, Play with Rose	Nap
9:00		Handwriting/Math drills/Spelling			Play with Rose	Computer	Play with Isaac	Play alone/fort	
9:30							Draw		
10:00		Latin/Greek/Subject of the day			On porch w/A.	With Rose	With Lois	With Isaac	
10:30		Subject of the day			At desk	With Anna	Alone in fort	Potty/With Lois	
11:00		Life lessons or Start lunch/Journal			Help w/lunch	Play with R/A	Lois	Lois	w/Lunch maker
11:30					Lunch				
12:00 p.m.					Drill			Play	Play
12:30	Time w/Jacob	Tutoring/Mom	Computer	Seat work		Chores		Potty w/L./Nap	Isaac
1:00	Misc. activities	Independent		With Ruth	With Lois	With Isaac	Computer		Lucy
1:30	Planning	Study			Free active play	Computer		Nap	Eat/Nap
2:00	Nap			Quiet time	Quiet time				Nap
2:30									
3:00		Projects						Potty/Jacob	Eat/Play
3:30				Projects				Projects	
4:00	Support group			Play with partner	Play with partner			Play	Play
4:30	Cooking			Free play	Free play				
5:00	Cooking/Read			Set table/Cleanup/Listen to reading					Eat/Nap
5:30				Dinner	Dinner				Nap
6:00									
6:30	Chores			Time with Dad (Dad picks one for activity with him)/Chores					Nap
7:00	Isaac/Anna		Chores	Mom/Chores	Mom/Chores	Chores	Chores	Potty/To bed/M	Eat/Play
7:30	Lois/Rose			Ready for bed	Ready for bed	Mom/Ready for bed	Mom/Ready for bed	Sleep	
8:00				Family worship		Sleep	Sleep		Play
8:30	Computer	Computer	Bed or Ruth	Bed or Ruth					
9:00	Read		Sleep						
9:30	Back ex./Lndry								Eat/To bed
10:00	Tom								
10:30	Sleep								Sleep
11:00									

Sally's Alternate Schedule
(Used when health needs dictate)

Time	Mom	Jacob (11)	Mary (9)	Lucy (8)	Isaac (5)	Lois (4)	Rose (3)	Anna (1)	Ruth (3 mo)
5:30 a.m.	Wake children Bath/Devotion	Sleep							
6:00	Dress/Breakfast	Personal checklist			Look at Bible / Clean room		Clean room	Potty/Lucy Breakfast/Teeth	Eat / Get clean/Mary
6:30	Walk		Drill songs / Chores	Drill songs / Help siblings	Drill songs	Drill songs			
7:00	Walk/Family worship				Cleanup/Family worship			With big girls / Family worship	
7:30	Math w/Lucy / Preschool	Independent school work	Start preschool / Seat work	Math / Seat work		Preschool			With Mom
8:00	Preschool		Seat work/Ruth						Eat w/Mary
8:30				Bible/Drawing					
9:00		Latin/Greek/Subject of the day			Play with Anna	Play with Rose	Play with Lois	Play with Isaac	Nap
9:30		Subject of day			Play with Rose	Play with Anna	Play with Isaac	Play with Lois	
10:00	Start lunch	Outdoor play or ten minute pick up and play in basement							Eat/Play
10:30	With Jacob	Tutor/Mom		Seat work	Watch Ruth	All girls play			With Isaac
11:00	With Mary	Seat work/room		Seat work	Computer		Set table/Listen to tapes		With Mom
11:30				Lunch			With family		With family
12:00 p.m.		Life Lessons/Cleanup/Journal							
12:30	Cleanup/Lndry				Free play	Computer	With family	Potty/Nap	Play
1:00									Eat/Nap
1:30		Projects						Nap	
2:00	Nap	Finish project	Computer	w/Little ones	w/Little ones	With Lucy	Nap		Nap
2:30		w/Little ones	w/Little ones	Computer	Computer	With Jacob		Potty	Eat/Play
3:00		Project	Project		Chores	With Mary			
3:30	Chores			Chores		Chores		Play	Play
4:00	Support group								
4:30	Cooking								
5:00	Cooking/Read out loud	Read with Isaac	With Lois	With Rose	With Jacob	With Mary	With Lucy	Cook!	Eat / Nap
5:30				Listen to reading/Clean/Set table					Nap
6:00				Dinner					
6:30				Family worship					Eat/Play
7:00	Isaac/Anna	Cleanup/Dad picks one child for activity with him			w/Mom or Dad	Cleanup/Dad's pick		w/Dad or Mom	Play
7:30	Lois/Rose	List/Math	Math	Ruth / List	Computer	Ready for bed/With Mom		Sleep	Play
8:00		Math					Sleep		
8:30	Misc. activities	Computer							
9:00					Sleep				
9:30	Bedtime	Sleep							
10:00									

Shannon's Schedule

Time	Mom	Bryana (5)	Bethany (3)	Caleb (2)
5:00 a.m.	Quiet time		Sleep	
5:30	Quiet time/Shower		Sleep	
6:00	Computer		Sleep	
6:30	Cook		Sleep	
7:00		Breakfast		
7:30	Chores		Video	
8:00	Assist children		Chores	
8:30	Toddler time	Video		Toddler time
9:00	Preschool	Play with Caleb	Preschool	Play with Bryana
9:30		Kindergarten	Play with Caleb	Play with Bethany
10:00			Alone time	Alone time
10:30		Family school		
11:00		History/Science		
11:30	Free	Free	Kitchen helper	Free
12:00 p.m.		Lunch		
12:30	Chores	Silent reading		
1:00	Laundry/Iron	Read-alouds		
1:30			Nap	Nap
2:00	Sew/Study/Scrapbook/Household Management	Nap		
2:30				
3:00				
3:30		Teatime		
4:00		Art/Music		
4:30	Cook	Kitchen helper		Free
5:00		Chores		
5:30		Dinner		
6:00	Cleanup			
6:30	Walk/Exercise	Daddy time		
7:00	Bathe children	Devotions		
7:30		Bath		
8:00		Good-nights		
8:30	Free		Sleep	
9:00			Sleep	
9:30	Alone with hubby		Sleep	
10:00	Bedtime!		Sleep	

Sheila's Schedule

Time	Mom	Rob (8)	Blake (5)	Sierra (3)	Michael (1)	Christian (1)
7:00 a.m.	Wake/Time with the Lord	Sleep		Sleep	Sleep	
7:30	Lord					
8:00	Exercise prep	Wake/Clean room				
8:30	Exercise	Play and Learn				
9:00	Nurse/Shower/Dress	Time with babies		Wake	Nurse	
9:30			Breakfast			
10:00			Cleanup			
10:30			Family devotional			
11:00			Chores		Bible video in play pen	
11:30						
12:00 p.m.			Lunch			
12:30	Cleanup/Nurse		Cleanup		Nurse	
1:00			Family story time		Nap	
1:30						
2:00	Help children with educational pursuits/	Afternoon choices: Errands with Mom/Alone time with Mom (Rob, Blake, and Sierra each have one hour per week with Mom)/Science project/Art project/Tennis practice/Bug catching/Creative play/Field trips/Visiting				
2:30	Phone calls/Mailings/					
3:00	Other activities					
3:30						
4:00	Nap/Rest or Read	Quiet alone time			Nap	
4:30						
5:00			Dinner preparation			
5:30			Dinner			
6:00		Cleanup			Play	
6:30		Tae Kwon Do/Library/or Family charity				
7:00						
7:30		Evening snack				
8:00		Evening pick up				
8:30		Bedtime preparation				
9:00		Evening devotional				
9:30	Nurse/Bob's meal prep	Bedtime			Nurse/Bedtime	
10:00	Time with Bob			Sleep		
10:30	Computer					
11:00	Book writing					
11:30	Home business					
12:00 a.m.	Development					
12:30	Bed!					

Sheri's Schedule

Time	Mom	Michael (10)	David (6)	Andrew (4)	Joshua (3)	Tirzah (infant)
5:30 a.m.	Devotion/Prayer			Sleep		
6:00	Shower/Dress					
6:30	Wake children/Nurse	Wake up!!! Dress/Make beds				Nurse
7:00		Breakfast/Brush teeth				Play
7:30						
8:00		Morning chores				
8:30	Preschool w/Andy, Josh	Phonics w/David	Phonics on computer	Preschool with Mom		Nap
9:00	Math with Mike	Math with Mom	Writing	Play with Josh	Play with Andrew	
9:30	Math with David	Writing	Math with Mom	Quiet center time		
10:00	Nurse Tirzah	Read to Andrew	Play with Josh	Story with Mike	Play with David	Nurse
10:30				Bible		
11:00				Lunch		
11:30						
12:00 p.m.	Ready for quiet time	Misc. school work	Quiet time			Play
12:30	Mom & Tirzah time	Computer time			Nap	Time with Mom
1:00	Nurse Tirzah	Silent reading	Computer time	Quiet time or Nap		Nurse
1:30	History with boys	History				
2:00	Science or Art with boys	Science or Art				Nap
2:30			Afternoon chores			
3:00			Exercise time with children			
3:30			Supervised outdoor play			
4:00	Nurse Tirzah			Free		Nurse
4:30	Dinner prep		Free or Awana work or Play with Tirzah		Play with a brother	
5:00			Dinner/Cleanup			
5:30						
6:00	Computer time	Free		Bath time with Dad	Bedtime	Play or Nap
6:30	Nurse				Sleep	Nurse
7:00			Story time with Dad			
7:30	Family time (Monday/Awana; Tuesday/Science experiments with Dad; Wed. & Thurs./no Dad until 8:00 p.m.; Friday/Family night)					
8:00	Lil' guys to bed	Free	Free	Bedtime		Play
8:30	Nurse/Morning prep*	Bedtime	Bedtime		Sleep	Nurse
9:00	Dale's time		Sleep			Bedtime
9:30	Ready for bed			Sleep		

*Morning prep includes setting out our clothes, setting the breakfast table, etc.

First Thursday of the month is shopping day; first Friday and Saturday of the month is for "Once a Month Cooking."

Sherri's Schedule

Time	Mom	Bobby (3)	Daniel (2)	Stephen (6 mo)
5:00 a.m.	Nurse	Sleep		Nurse
5:30	Quiet time			Nap
6:00	Shower/Dress			
6:30	Chores	Dress/Brush teeth/Make bed (Daddy helps)		Dress (by Daddy)
7:00		Breakfast		
7:30	Nurse	Free		Nurse
8:00	M - Clean upstairs	M/W/TH/F - Help Mom/Free		With Mom/brothers
8:30	T - Grocery store	T - Grocery store		
9:00	W - Clean downstairs	F - MOPS (1st of month)		Nap
	TH - Clean bathrooms			
	F - Free or MOPS			
9:30		Snack		
10:00		Preschool		
10:30	Nurse	Play together in living room		Nurse
11:00	Time alone with boys or	Play alone in room	Time with Mommy	Play on floor in living room
11:30	MOPS (1st Friday of month)	Time with Mommy	Play alone in room	
12:00 p.m.		Lunch		
12:30	Rest			Nap
1:00	Computer time	Nap/Rest		
1:30				
2:00	Nurse			Nurse
2:30	Early dinner prep/Fold laundry	Play together upstairs/Help Mommy		Play alone in crib
3:00				Play on floor in living room
3:30		Snack		
4:00		Walk/Exercise		
4:30	Feed Stephen	Free		Eat
5:00	Dinner prep	Dinner helper or Free		Play on floor in living room
5:30		Dinner		Sit in high chair
6:00	Cleanup/Bread	Play with Daddy		
6:30	Nurse	Bath/Bible story/Bed (by Daddy)		Bath (by Daddy)/Nurse
7:00	Rob's time	Sleep		
7:30	Personal time - sew, scrapbook, read			
8:00				
8:30	Prep for bed/Bible with Rob			
9:00	Sleep			
9:30				

Sherry's Schedule

Time	Mom	John (5)	James (4)	Emily (2)	Anna (7 mo)
6:00 a.m.	Prayer time/Housework	Sleep			Sleep
6:30	Shower/Hair				
7:00	Get dressed/Help children with hair	Make bed/Get dressed/Hair			Sleep
7:30	Breakfast	Breakfast/Clear table			Eat
8:15	Start laundry/Chore training	Gather/Sort laundry/Chores			Floor play
8:30	Read to Emily	Computer time with James	Computer time with John	Time with Mom	
8:45	Phonics or Math with James	Play with Emily	School with Mom	Play with John	Playpen time
9:05		Music time			
9:15	Laundry/Chores		Help Mom		
9:30	Phonics/Writing with John	School with Mom	Play with Emily	Play with James	
10:00	Paperwork/Calls, etc.		Room time		Nap
10:30	Monday/Extra cleaning - Tuesday/Ministry work - Wednesday/Errands - Thursday/Outdoor activity - Friday/Free time				
11:00					
11:30	Lunch prep/Eat lunch	With Sis or Help with lunch	Help Mom	M/W w/John; Tu/Th w/James	Eat
12:15 p.m.	Clean kitchen		Free play		Floor play
12:45			B4FIAR		
1:15	Catnap	Rest time	Rest time	Nap	Nap
1:30	Catch up paperwork, calls, etc.				
2:15	Math with John	Math with Mom			
2:30	Finish math with John	Finish math with Mom		Free play	
3:15	Get snacks ready	Play with Emily	Play with Anna	Play with John	Play with James
3:30	Dinner prep			Snack time	
3:45	Dinner prep/Housework		Free play/Outside if nice		Play by Mom
4:00		FIAR		Computer time	Play by Emily
4:30	Activity with all children		Pick up house		Exersaucer
5:00	Reading/Character training/Review memory verses/Games (Mom choose)				Floor play
5:30	Set table and Eat dinner				Eat
6:00	Clean kitchen		Clear table		Floor play
6:15	Time with Rob		Free play		
6:45	Laundry		Play with Dad		Catnap
7:00			Brush teeth/Baths/Get pajamas on		
7:45	Cuddle with Anna		Bible time/Prayers		Bottle/With Mom
8:00	Children to bed		Bed		

Tami's Schedule

Time	Mom	Mark (Jr. High)	Troy (High school)
6:00 a.m.	Up/Bed made/Dog out/Coffee	Sleep	Sleep
6:20	Quiet time		
7:00	Ready for walk	Up/Shower/breakfast	Shower/Breakfast/Quiet time/Bible
7:15	Walk		
8:00	Shower/Breakfast	Math	Math
8:45	School with Troy	Seat work (~ 20 min. history, science, English, spelling or writing)	School with Mom – Grade/Discuss
9:30			With Mom – Sentence Analysis
10:00	Chores	Chores	Chores
10:30	School with Mark	With Mom – Bible/Through subjects	Science – Biology or Chemistry
11:15			History – World or Economics or Government
12:00 p.m.	Lunch (20 min rest)	Lunch	Lunch
1:30	School with Mark	1:30-2:30 With Mom/Through subjects	English/Vocabulary
2:15	Read	2:30 With Mom/Mom reads book	Piano practice
3:00	Mail/Paperwork/Phone calls/Start supper	Free	Free
4:30	Transport to practices and lessons/Errands	Practices	Practice piano/Piano lesson
6:30	Finish supper/Eat/Cleanup/Any evening activities	Whatever needs to be done – Dishes, Walk dog, Evening activities, etc.	Whatever needs to be done – Dishes, Walk dog, Evening activities, etc.

Tami's Schedule

Time	Mom	Mark (Jr. High)
6:00 a.m.	Up/Bed made/Dog out/Coffee	Sleep
6:20	Quiet time/Study for Bible study I lead	
7:30	Breakfast/Shower	Up/Shower/Breakfast
8:00	Work with Mark and Projects	Math
8:45		English
9:30	Exercise workout with Mom – stretch, weights, walk, jog, tennis accuracy	Exercise workout with Mom – stretch, weights, walk, jog, tennis accuracy
11:00	School with Mom	History with Mom
11:45		Spelling with Mom
12:15 p.m.	Lunch	Lunch
1:15	Biology with Mark	Biology with Mom
2:00	Projects	Art
2:30	Dressed and Transport to tennis	Change clothes/Transport – tennis
3:00	Life activities/House cleaning/Laundry/Grocery shopping/Errands/Paperwork/Phone calls/Supper/Eat/Cleanup/Any evening activities such as choir, Wed. night church, Army social events	Tennis – 3:00-5:00 – as late as 8:00 some days
8:00	Bible with Mark	Bible with Mom
8:30	Reading with Mark	Reading with Mom

Tanya's Schedule

Time	Mom	Whitney (13)	Andrew (5)	Schuyler (3)
6:00 a.m.	Wake/Shower/Dress/Make bed	Sleep	Sleep	Sleep
6:30	Bible/Prayer	Rise/Dress/A.M. Chores		
7:00	Unload dishwasher/Start laundry/Fix Schuyler's hair	Make bed/Prepare breakfast/Set table	Wake/Dress/A.M. Chores	Wake/Dress/A.M. Chores
		Breakfast/Teeth (Whitney helps Schuyler)		
7:30	Breakfast/Cleanup			
8:00	Preschool with Schuyler	Grammar	Math	Preschool with Mommy
8:30	School with Whitney Math/Literature/Grammar	School with Mom Math/Literature/Grammar	Spelling/Writing	Preschool workbooks / Book time
9:00			Piano	Outdoors
9:30	School with Andrew Math/Phonics/A.M. Reading	Activity with Schuyler	School with Mommy	Activity with Whitney
10:00		Science (M/W/F) or History (T/Th)	Math/Phonics/A.M. Reading	Room time
10:30		Bible school		
11:00	Spanish with Andrew	Math	Spanish with Mommy	Table time (art)
11:30	Grade papers/Prepare lunch	Math/Spelling	Letters & Sounds/Language 1	Math manipulatives/Lunch helper
12:00 p.m.		Lunch/Cleanup		
12:30	Andrew P.M. Reading/Vacuum LR	Logic	P.M. Reading/Computer	Go potty/Get blanket/Get ready for nap
1:00	Nap or Rest	Literature	Science (M/W/F) or History (T/Th)	Nap
1:30		Rest or Silent reading		
2:00	Projects	Writing	Room time	
2:30	Play with Andrew and Schuyler	Piano	Playtime with Mom	
3:00				
3:30	Time with Whitney	Time with Mom	Outdoors	Outdoors
4:00	Fold laundry	Spanish		
4:30	Cleaning/Chores		P.M. Chores	
5:00	Dinner preparations	Time with Andrew and Schuyler	Playtime with Whitney or Dinner helper (T/Th)	Playtime with Whitney or Dinner helper (M)
5:30		Free	Play outdoors or Video	Play outdoors or Video
6:00		Dinner		
6:30	E-mail/Supervise cleanup		Dinner cleanup	
7:00		Free	Free/Family devotion at 7:45	
7:30				
8:00	Bathe Andrew and Schuyler	Computer	Bath/Teeth/Ready for bed	Bath/Teeth/Ready for bed
8:30	Read stories	Bath/Ready for bed	Bedtime stories/Sleep 8:45	Bedtime stories/Sleep 8:45
9:00	Walk with Andy	Free		Sleep
9:30	Ready for bed/Computer			
10:00	Computer or Read	Sleep		
10:30	With Andy			
11:00	Sleep			

Tracy L's Schedule

Time	Mommy	Courtney (6)	Joshua (4)	Jacob (2)	Jessica (Infant)
6:00 a.m.	Wake up/Make beds/Room chores/Get dressed/Brush teeth and hair				
6:30	Nurse baby	Spelling	Finish room chores		Nurse
7:00	Dress/Personal grooming	Reading	Computer time	Playtime with Jessica	Playtime with Jacob
7:30	Cook breakfast/Courtney	Scripture memory, AWANA	Set table for breakfast		Playtime in playpen
8:00		Breakfast/Morning chores			
8:30	2nd grade work/Courtney	One-on-one tutoring/Mom	Play with younger ones	Play with Joshua and Jessica	Play with Joshua and Jacob
9:00	Lawn care/Pet care/Outside		Outside play		
9:30	Nurse baby/Read to children		Listen to Mom read		
10:00	Phonics with Joshua	Handwriting	Phonics with Mom	Playtime alone at table	Nap
10:30	M – Cleaning/T – Courtney W – Josh/TH – Jacob F – Jessica		Play quietly in rooms		
11:00	Preschool/Josh/Jacob/Jessica	Before lunch chores	K5 with Mom and little ones	Preschool with Mom	
11:30	Exercise	Math with Josh	Math with Courtney	Art at table	Play on floor
12:00 p.m.	Lunch/Prepare for naps/Nurse		Lunch/Cleanup/Before nap chore		Lunch and playtime
12:30	Computer time	Playtime	Nap	Nap	Playtime with Courtney
1:00	Cleaning/Organizing	Science			
1:30	Nurse/Devotion	Quiet activities			Nurse
2:00	Quiet time				
2:30	Rest	Computer math or Science	Workbook/Quiet activities	Playtime alone	
3:00	M/W-Sewing, T-Support group, TH-Finance, F-School planning and records		Arthur	Nap	Nap
3:30	Straighten house/Start dinner	Math	Play with Jacob	Play with Josh	
4:00	Nurse/AWANA with Josh	Social Studies	AWANA/Singing	Book time	Nurse
4:30			Baths and Playtime		
5:00					
5:30	Dinner preparation		Before Dad arrives chores		Playtime alone in playpen
6:00			Playtime and Dinner helpers		Playtime
6:30			Dinner and Cleanup		Dinner
7:00					Playtime
7:30	Nurse/Evening devotion		Ready for bed/Devotion		Nurse
8:00			Sleep		
8:30	Paul's time				
9:00	Reading and Writing				
9:30	My time (shower, nails, etc.)				
10:00	Sleep				

Tracy W's Schedule

Time	Mom	Tag (7)	Keene (6)	Blaze (4)	Gage (3)	Raimy (1)	Rab (2 mo)
5:00 a.m.	Nurse						Nurse
5:30	Bible study	Sleep					Sleep
6:00	Make bread/CSwork						
6:30	Dress/Get ready						
7:00	Dress Raimy / Breakfast prep w/T	Dress/Make bed/ Breakfast helper	Dress/Make bed/Look at books			Dress/Play in boys' room with books	Sleep
7:30	Breakfast/Cleanup	Breakfast/Unload dishwasher every other month			Breakfast		
8:00	Training time	Training time/Monday only – sort laundry			Preschool with Mom	Free/with family	
8:30	Preschool w/B, G	Phonics workbooks	Play w/Raimy in LR			Play w/Keene in LR	
9:00	Nurse/Dress Rab/ With T, K	Italics	Explode the Code / Italics	Play with Raimy in toy room	Computer time	Play with Blaze in toy room	Dress / Nurse
9:30	Math with T/K	Spelling Power / Math with Mom		Computer time	Play alone		
10:00	Reading with Keene	Play with Gage	Reading with Mom	Play alone	Play with Tag	Nap	Hold or in bouncy
10:30		Song time and Memory verse/P.E. outside					
11:00	P.E./Lunch prep	P.E./Computer time	P.E./Lunch helper	P.E/Play with Gage	P.E./Play with Blaze	P.E./Play in play pen	Nap in swing
11:30	Lunch prep	Computer time	Lunch helper	w/Gage/Lunch/Free	w/Blaze/Lunch/Free	Play in play pen/Lunch/Free	
12:00 p.m.	Lunch/Cleanup	Lunch/Free	Lunch/Free				Nurse
12:30	Story time/Tag reads	Read aloud/Listen to Hist., Science curr.	Listen to Tag/Hist., Science curriculum	Listen to Tag and Mom read		Nap	Bouncy
1:00		Rest or play w/Rab	Rest				Nap or with Tag
1:30	Charter school work	Play alone	Play alone	Nap	Nap		Nap
2:00		Play w/Blaze if up	Play alone	Play w/Tag			
2:30	Make phone calls	Play w/Keene, Blaze	Play w/Tag, Blaze	Play w/Tag, Keene			
3:00			Small snack/Gage helper				
3:30	Draw Squad w/T, K	Draw Squad w/Mom		Free	Play outside		
4:00	Nurse						Nurse
4:30	Bathe ½ of children	Baths (Partners are Tag/Blaze, Keene/Gage/Raimy) or Computer or Look at books in living room					
5:00	Dinner prep w/Blaze	Play w/R outside	Computer time	Dinner helper	Play outside	Play w/Tag outside	Play
5:30	Tidy house	Listen to book on tape or music in living room/Lie on floor or sit on couch to see book					
6:00			Dinner				
6:30	Cleanup/Prepare		Cleanup toys inside and out			Free	Play
7:00	Walk to mailbox	Walk to mailbox with Mom (one child only) or Play with Dad				Play with Dad	Play
7:30	Nurse/Listen to story	Listen to Dad read story		Color in toy room within earshot of story		Sleep	Nurse
8:00	Chat w/hubby	Dad does teeth and bedtime/Mom says goodnights					Sleep
8:30	Computer/Free/Shwr			Sleep			
9:30	Get ready for bed						
10:00	Sleep	Sleep					

Maxwell's Chore List
Daily Chores

Mom	Nathan (21)	Christopher (16)	Sarah (16)	Joseph (9)	John (7)	Anna (5)
Cleanup breakfast	Dinner cleanup	Bring laundry upstairs	Make breakfast	Bedroom maintenance	Bedroom maintenance	Bedroom maintenance
Dress Mary	Unload dishwasher	Lunch cleanup	Toothpaste on little ones toothbrushes	Empty kitchen trash	Breakfast helper	Wipe down all the bathroom sinks
Wash/Fold/Put away laundry		Dinner cleanup	Make lunch	Clear and wash table Sweep after all meals	Mail out	Lunch helper
Make dinner			Dinner cleanup	Play room pick up at bedtime		
Mary ready for bed						

Weekly Chores

Mom	Nathan (21)	Christopher (19)	Sarah (16)	Joseph (9)	John (7)	Anna (5)
Vacuum upstairs	Clean Dad and Mom's bathroom	Clean downstairs bathroom	Clean main bathroom	Vacuum stairs	Empty pencil sharpener	Dinner helper/ Wednesday
Dust upstairs	Dust ceiling fans	Oil dining room table	Windex computer screens	Clean van		Dust dining room chairs
Ironing	Clean front of dishwasher	Clean top of frig and stove hood	Dust window ledges and vents	Straighten garage		
Sheets	Clean sliding patio doors and front storm door	Mow our yard and Grandad's	Clean silverware drawer	Dinner helper/Monday	Dinner helper/Tuesday	
School planning	Vacuum downstairs every third week			Vacuum front of house (Wednesday)	Vacuum front of house (Monday)	
School record keeping	Cut and bag bread every other week		Make bread	Fold and put away clothes (Monday)	Fold and put away clothes (Monday)	
	Weed eat yards		Empty trash/Thursday	Vacuum stairs	Dust dresser	

Monthly Cleaning/Extra Chores

	Nathan (21)	Christopher (19)	Sarah (16)
Week One	Vacuum living room furniture	Damp wipe floorboards in living room, dining room, front entryway, and all halls	Dust living room, hall and front entry pictures.
Week Two	Mop kitchen floor, mop bathroom floor	Clean washer/dryer area. Wipe floorboards in downstairs bedrooms	Damp wipe floorboards in bathrooms and bedrooms upstairs
Week Three	None	Damp wipe light covers and spot clean marks on walls	None
Week Four	Wash and dry dining room light fixtures	Vacuum and wipe under kitchen sink, Clean all the mirrors you do not clean every week, Sweep and clean garage step.	Dust crib slats, 409 if necessary.

Debbie's Children's Chore Chart

Name	Early Morning Chores	Every Morning Chores	Kitchen Chores	Evening Chores
Zak (Age 9)	M/Clean hall bathroom T/Vacuum stairway, downstairs W/Trash TH/Vacuum upstairs F/Vacuum rugs in garage	Make bed Clean room Dress Sweep hall bathroom Feed dog	Clear off table (Train Solomon) Clean table and benches Sweep kitchen and laundry area Put away clean glass dishes Check garbage and recyclables	
Abi (Age 8)	M/Organize Tupperware/Books T/Check and organize pots and pans, replenish vegetables W/Clean downstairs bathroom TH/Clean upstairs bathroom F/Tupperware and books	Make bed Clean room Dress	Wash dishes Clean sink area, put sponges and brushes away neatly Clean all counters and the top of the stove Wipe off the sink, empty water	P.J.s for self and younger sisters Help with baths on Tues/Sat.
Ben (Age 6)	Daily/Collect laundry, sort, bring largest load to laundry room M/Wash upstairs walls, doors, and knobs W/Help Zak empty trash F/Wash downstairs walls, doors, and knobs	Room chores/Dress/Feed dog/Sweep garage steps **After Lunch Chores** Fold laundry/Put in piles for each family member/Put clean clothes in proper person's room and put your clothes and Solomon's away	Put away food Throw away garbage on counters Check, dry, and put away clean dishes (help Sarah to learn this). Check to see children's dishes and silverware are neatly put away (help Sarah learn this).	P.J. and put away clothes, bath time on Tues/Sat
Sarah (Age 5)		Make bed/Clean room/Dress Play with babies until breakfast	Put away clean childrens' dishes and silverware/Get your pick up bucket and check all floors/Check bathroom counters and put things away	P.J.s, teeth, baths on Tues/Sat.
Solomon John (Age 4)		Dress/Room cleanup		P.J.s, teeth, baths on Tues/Sat.

Tracy's Children's Chore and Art Charts

Courtney (Age 6)	Joshua (Age 4)	Jacob (Age 2)
Feed cat	Feed fish	Empty trash
Clean glass through house	Dust his room/living room	Clear table
Dust furniture	Unload dryer	Take dirty laundry from bathroom to laundry room
Unload dishwasher	Bring newspaper in house	Take water to cat
Sort laundry	Straighten bathrooms	Water plants
Put away laundry	Put away laundry	**11:30 Art Schedule** Mon/Coloring on white paper
Organize Tupperware/Pots and pans	Wash table, chairs, and highchair after meals	Tues/Finger paints
Vacuum		Wed/Coloring in coloring book
Sweep kitchen/front porch		Thurs/Water colors/tempera paints
Check mail		Fri/Cut out, color, and paste activity

Sample Activity Worksheets

Activity Worksheet for Daddy

Rise, Personal grooming, Prepare for work	30 minutes
Devotions with Kristi	30 minutes
Breakfast	15 minutes
Drive time	45 minutes
Arrive @ work, Personal quiet time	30 minutes
Work	8 hours
Drive time	45 minutes
Freshen up and Relax	15 minutes
Dinner	45 minutes
Alone time with Kati {F, Su}, with Josh {M, Sa}, with Sarah and Brady {W}	15 minutes
Family devotions and Character training	30 minutes
Free time	30 minutes
Alone time with Kristi {M, W, F, Sa, Su}	1 ½ hours
Computer time/Study time	1 ½ hours
Sleep	7 ½ hours

Activity Worksheet for Mommy

Rise, Prayer and Praise time	30 minutes
Personal grooming, Prepare Steve's lunch	30 minutes
Personal Devotions	30 minutes
Devotions with Steve	30 minutes
Breakfast, Alone with Josh, Start laundry	30 minutes
Chores	1 hour
Math and Phonics with Josh	45 minutes
Family school Bible time	15 minutes
Math and Phonics with Kati	45 minutes
Preschool with Sarah and Brady	15 minutes
Personal time (Writing, Reading, Sewing)	1 hour
Lunch preparation, Alone with Kati, Eat	30 minutes
Mail and Sit with children	30 minutes
History and Science with Kati and Josh	45 minutes
Playtime with Sarah and Brady	15 minutes
Computer time, Sewing, etc.	1 hour
Rest	1 hour
Run errands, Free time	1 ½ hours
Dinner prep and Cook	30 minutes
Dinner	45 minutes
Dinner cleanup	15 minutes
Family devotions and Character training	30 minutes
Bathe children and Put them to bed	30 minutes
Alone time with Steve {M, W, F, Sa, Su}	1 ½ hours
Day ending devotions, Prayer and Praise	30 minutes
Sleep	7 ½ hours

Activity Worksheet for Kati (Age 7, Grade 2)

Rise, Personal grooming, Room chores	30 minutes
Breakfast	30 minutes
Laundry and Chores	30 minutes
Individual work (Reading, Spelling, Handwriting)	45 minutes
Family school Bible time	15 minutes
Phonics and Math with Mommy	45 minutes
Finish up individual work	15 minutes
Piano or Typing lessons	30 minutes
Educational activity with Sarah and Brady/Playtime with Sarah and Brady	30 minutes
Lunch preparation, Alone time with Mommy, Eat	30 minutes
Lunch cleanup and Laundry	30 minutes
History and Science with Mommy and Josh	45 minutes
Individual History and Science	15 minutes
Quiet time	30 minutes
Silent Reading and Rest	1 ½ hours
Run errands with Mommy or Finish individual work or Free time	1 ½ hours
Laundry or Free Time	30 minutes
Dinner	45 minutes
Daddy time {F, Su}, Shower time {M, T, Th, Sa}	15 minutes
Family devotions and Character training	30 minutes
Quiet time and Prayer with Sarah and Brady {M, W, Sa}, Shower {F, Su}	30 minutes
Sleep	11 ½ hours

Activity Worksheet for Josh (Age 6, Grade 2)

Rise, Personal grooming, Room chores	30 minutes
Breakfast Preparation, Alone with Mommy, Eat	30 minutes
Chores	30 minutes
Breakfast cleanup	30 minutes
Phonics and Math with Mommy	45 minutes
Family school Bible time	15 minutes
Individual work (Reading, Spelling, Handwriting)	60 minutes
Educational activity with Sarah and Brady/Playtime with Sarah and Brady	30 minutes
Piano or Typing lessons	30 minutes
Daily Chores	30 minutes
Lunch	30 minutes
History and Science with Mommy and Josh	45 minutes
Individual History and Science	15 minutes
Quiet time	30 minutes
Silent Reading and Rest	1 ½ hours
Run errands with Mommy or Finish individual work or Free time	1 ½ hours
Laundry or Free Time	30 minutes
Dinner	45 minutes
Daddy time {M, Sa}, Shower time {T, Th, Su}	15 minutes
Family devotions and Character training	30 minutes
Quiet time and Prayer with Sarah and Brady {T, Th, F}, Shower {M, Sa}	30 minutes
Sleep	11 hours

Activity Worksheet for Sarah (Age 3)

Rise, Personal grooming, Room chores	30 minutes
Breakfast	30 minutes
Laundry and Chores	30 minutes
Playtime with Brady	45 minutes
Family school Bible time	15 minutes
Playtime alone	45 minutes
Preschool with Mommy and Brady	15 minutes
Educational activity with Josh/Playtime with Josh	30 minutes
Educational activity with Kati/Playtime with Kati	30 minutes
Free time	30 minutes
Lunch	30 minutes
Playtime with Brady	45 minutes
Playtime with Mommy and Brady	15 minutes
Nap	2 hours
Run errands w/Mommy or Free playtime {at least once per week w/Mommy for 30 minutes}	1 ½ hours
Help Mommy prepare dinner	30 minutes
Dinner	45 minutes
Help Mommy cleanup dinner	15 minutes
Family devotions and Character training	30 minutes
Bath, Quiet time and Prayer w/Kati {M, W, Sa}, w/Josh {T, Th, F}	30 minutes
Sleep	11 ½ hours

Activity Worksheet for Brady (Age 2)

Rise, Personal grooming, Room chores	30 minutes
Breakfast	30 minutes
Laundry and Chores	30 minutes
Playtime with Sarah	30 minutes
Family school Bible time	45 minutes
Playtime alone	15 minutes
Preschool with Mommy and Sarah	45 minutes
Educational activity with Josh	15 minutes
Playtime with Josh	15 minutes
Educational activity with Kati	15 minutes
Playtime with Kati	15 minutes
Free time	30 minutes
Lunch	30 minutes
Playtime with Sarah	45 minutes
Playtime with Mommy and Sarah	15 minutes
Nap	2 hours
Run errands w/Mommy or Free playtime {at least once per week w/Mommy for 30 minutes}	1 ½ hours
Help Mommy prepare dinner	30 minutes
Dinner	45 minutes
Help Mommy cleanup dinner	15 minutes
Family devotions and Character training	30 minutes
Bath, Quiet time and Prayer w/Kati {M, W, Sa}, w/Josh {T, Th, F}	30 minutes
Sleep	11 ½ hours

Mary's Nursing and Sleeping Schedule

Time	Birth to 3 Months	Time	4 Months to 10 Months	Time	10 Months to 13 Months
6:00 a.m.	Nurse/Back to sleep	5:30 a.m.	Nurse/Sleep	8:00 a.m.	Wake up/Breakfast
9:00	Nurse/Awake	8:00	Up/Play	9:15	Nurse
10:15	Nap	9:15	Nurse/Play	10:30	Nap
12:00 p.m.	Nurse/Awake	10:30	Nap	11:30	Wake up
1:15	Nap	11:30	Wake up/Play	12:15 p.m.	Lunch
4:15	Nurse/Awake	12:45 p.m.	Nurse/Play	12:45	Nurse
5:30	Nap	1:30	Nap	1:30	Nap
7:30	Nurse/Awake	4:15	Nurse/Play	4:30	Nurse
9:00	Nurse/Sleep	6:15	Nap	6:30	Dinner
Morning nap dropped at 13 months.		7:15	Nurse/Play	8:30	Nurse/Sleep
Mary weaned at 18 months.		9:00	Nurse/Sleep		

Resources

Accent Publications, P.O. Box 36640, Colorado Springs, CO 80936-6640. Preschool Sunday School Curriculum.

Hadidan, Allen and Connie; and Will and Lindy Wilson. *Creative Family Times: Practical Activities for Building Character in Your Preschooler*. Moody Press, 1989.

Pearl, Michael and Debi. *To Train Up a Child*. Michael and Debi Pearl, 1010 Pearl Road, Pleasantville, Tenn. 37147, 1994.

Tripp, Tedd. *Shepherding a Child's Heart*. Shepherd Press, P.O. Box 24, Wapwallopen, PA 18660, 1995.

Website, Homeschool Scheduling, http://www.titus2.com/d-schedule.htm

Additional Resources

 Managers of Their Homes (this book). To order additional copies, please visit www.Titus2.com or call (913) 772-0392.

 Just Around the Corner, Encouragement and Challenge for Homeschooling Dads and Moms by Steven and Teri Maxwell. Information on page 176.

 Preparing Sons to Provide for a Single-Income Family by Steven Maxwell. Information on page 177.

 Homeschooling with a Meek and Quiet Spirit by Teri Maxwell. Information on page 178.

Titus2.com

Titus2.com, a website by Steve and Teri Maxwell, is designed to challenge, encourage, and strengthen homeschooling parents. There are several message boards as well as free articles.

Every month, Steve and Teri each write an article of challenge and encouragement for home-school parents. To receive each month's Dad's and Mom's Corners via e-mail, visit www.Titus2.com and sign the guest book.

MOTHBoard (Managers of Their Homes Board)–An Internet message board designed and intended to be a support for moms who are using *Managers of Their Homes* (MOTH) as a tool for their daily homeschool scheduling. Only encouraging messages (no flames; no bad language) are approved on the board–creating a "safe haven" for moms! Topics include: chores, scheduling snow days, scheduling craft time, schedules and teenagers, nursing schedules, and so on. To visit the message board, go to: www.Titus2.com/mothboard

MOMSBoard–An Internet message board/forum for the discussion of topics relating to Titus, Chapter 2. The purpose of MOMSBoard is to allow you to share your questions and ideas with other moms in a positive, "safe" atmosphere (no flames; no bad language). Topics include: submission, modesty, pregnancy, child training, homeschooling, and more. To visit the message board, go to: www.Titus2.com/momsboard

Just Around the Corner

Encouragement and Challenge for
Homeschooling Dads and Moms

By Steven and Teri Maxwell

Just Around the Corner is a compilation of Steve and Teri Maxwell's monthly Dad's and Mom's Corners. These articles were originally written to encourage and support their local homeschool group. However, they have been so well received that they are now requested via e-mail every month by thousands of homeschool families.

The Maxwell's have also been asked to put the Corners together into this convenient-to-read book format. You will find the Mom's Corners grouped together in the front of the book and the Dad's Corners in the back. The Corners are all indexed so that you can read the ones relating to a specific topic you are interested in, if you so choose.

Because most of these articles deal with family life in general, many Christian non-homeschool families find them useful as well. Topics addressed in *Just Around the Corner* include: anger, depression, child training, and husbands loving their wives.

Steve's writing will challenge dads in their role as the spiritual head of the family. Teri's writing addresses many aspects of daily life that often frustrate or discourage a mom.

With three of the Maxwell children now being adults, Steve and Teri write from the perspective of having seen the truth of God's Word put into practice. At the same time, they are still in the trenches homeschooling five children. You will have a candid vantage point as you see them fail, succeed, laugh, and cry while they endeavor to serve the Lord Jesus Christ.

Now you can enjoy the support and insights found in this unique, indexed collection containing over five years' worth of Dad's and Mom's Corners.

For information visit: www.Titus2.com

Or call: (913) 772-0392

Preparing Sons
to Provide for a Single-Income Family
By Steven Maxwell

In today's world of two-income families, preparing a son to provide for a single-income family seems an overwhelming task. Christian parents will find it helpful to have a purpose and plan as they raise sons who will one day be responsible for supporting a family.

Steve Maxwell presents the groundwork for preparing your son to be a wage-earning adult. He gives practical suggestions and direction to parents for working with their sons from preschool age all the way through to adulthood. You will be challenged to evaluate your own life and the example you are setting for your son.

As the father of eight children, three of them now wage-earning adults, Steve has gained valuable experience he openly shares with other parents. Learn these principles from a dad whose 24-year-old homeschooled son has purchased a home debt free and whose second son is financially able to do the same. Steve explains how it is possible for parents, with a willing commitment, to properly prepare their sons to provide for a single-income family.

"You are dealing with topics that no one I know of has dealt with as thoroughly and practically as you have." Dr. S. M. Davis

"Preparing Sons was a big blessing to my husband. All you ladies should get a copy for your husband and every church library needs one." Shelly

"Brothers, I highly recommend the book for those of you who have not read it. I really appreciate all the obvious prayer, effort, and experience that went into making this book. The Lord is using it for His Glory in our family." Les

For information visit: www.PreparingSons.com and www.Titus2.com

Or call: (913) 772-0392

Homeschooling with a Meek and Quiet Spirit

By Teri Maxwell

Homeschooling moms are a wonderful group of women! There isn't a more determined, dedicated set of women in the entire world! These ladies have chosen an unpopular, difficult path that comes with little outside encouragement. Yet, they have set their faces on obedience to the Lord and what they know is best for their children—no matter what it costs them personally!

Even so, there are issues homeschooling brings up that are very common to most who homeschool. These common issues speak of what happens inside a heart when mom becomes responsible for her children's education, when they are home with her all day every day, and when she adds several hours' worth of homeschooling into a full schedule as a wife, mother, homemaker, and Christian.

A desire of a homeschooling mother's heart is to have a meek and quiet spirit instead of the discouragement, fear, and anger she often experiences. She can cope with the myriad of daily difficulties and decisions that a homeschooling lifestyle brings with it, as long as she is having the right responses to them. Let her be fearful, worried, anxious, frustrated, irritated, or angry, and this mom realizes she is undermining all she wants to accomplish by homeschooling.

Because Teri Maxwell has walked the homeschooling path for many years, she knows firsthand the struggle for a meek and quiet spirit. The memories from her early homeschooling years of often being worried and angry rather than having a meek and quiet spirit are unpleasant. Her prayer is that as she shares the work the Lord has done in her heart, through homeschooling, you would be encouraged that He can do the same for you. She also desires that you could learn from the lessons He has taught her so that you would begin to have a meek and quiet spirit long before she did.

Will your journey toward a meek and quiet spirit be completed upon finding the perfect spelling curriculum or deciding which chores your child should be doing? Or does the answer lie on a different path? In these pages, Teri offers practical insights into gaining a meek and quiet spirit that any mom can apply to her individual circumstances. She transparently shares the struggles God has brought her through and what He has shown her during these many homeschooling years.

In *Homeschooling with a Meek and Quiet Spirit*, you will discover the heart issues that will gently lead you to a meek and quiet spirit. Come along and join Teri as you seek the Lord to homeschool with a meek and quiet spirit!

For information visit: www.Titus2.com

Or call: (913) 772-0392

Scheduling Kit Order Form

The easiest way to order is via credit card by calling (913) 772-0392 during business hours (9-5), CST. Please note: in order to buy additional scheduling kits for your own personal use you must have registered your book with us - see the back page of this book for more information.

- - - - - ✂ -

ORDERING INFORMATION:

___ SCHEDULING KITS ($5)

SUBTOTAL:

SHIPPING AND HANDLING ($3 EACH):

SALES TAX (KS RESIDENTS ONLY, ADD 7.3%, INCLUDING S&H):

ORDER TOTAL:

MAILING INFORMATION:

NAME
(FIRST) (LAST)

ADDRESS

CITY

STATE   ZIP

TELEPHONE   NUMBER OF CHILDREN

PAYMENT INFORMATION:

MAKE CHECKS PAYABLE TO "MANAGERS OF THEIR HOMES" (OR MOTH), OR:

CREDIT CARD NUMBER: _____

EXPIRES: _____

SIGNATURE: _____

MAIL YOUR ORDER TO:

Managers of Their Homes
2416 South 15th Street
Leavenworth, KS 66048-4110

☎ (913) 772-0392

ORDERING INFORMATION:

___ SCHEDULING KITS ($5)

SUBTOTAL:

SHIPPING AND HANDLING ($3 EACH):

SALES TAX (KS RESIDENTS ONLY, ADD 7.3%, INCLUDING S&H):

ORDER TOTAL:

MAILING INFORMATION:

NAME
(FIRST) (LAST)

ADDRESS

CITY

STATE   ZIP

TELEPHONE   NUMBER OF CHILDREN

PAYMENT INFORMATION:

MAKE CHECKS PAYABLE TO "MANAGERS OF THEIR HOMES" (OR MOTH), OR:

CREDIT CARD NUMBER: _____

EXPIRES: _____

SIGNATURE: _____

MAIL YOUR ORDER TO:

Managers of Their Homes
2416 South 15th Street
Leavenworth, KS 66048-4110

☎ (913) 772-0392

Prices subject to change without notice.   July, 2001

Registration information is
on the back side of this page.

ADDITIONAL REGISTRATION COMMENTS

Register Your Book Today!

Why should you register your copy of *Managers of Their Homes*? Because when you mail your completed registration form, you:

- ◆ Have permission to copy the Scheduling Kit for your own personal use.
- ◆ May purchase additional Scheduling Kits for your personal use, should you request it.
- ◆ Will be made aware of other information or products should we feel the Lord leading us in that direction in the future.
  Note: We do NOT sell or allow anyone else to use our database. It remains completely confidential.

We believe the background information provided in *Managers of Their Homes*, along with the sample schedules in the Appendix, are key to producing a workable schedule. Therefore, we could not offer the kits separately from the book to others. That is one reason why we tried to offer the book and kit at a very affordable price.

May the grace of our Lord Jesus Christ be with you all,

Steve and Teri (www.Titus2.com)

INSTRUCTIONS:

1 FILL IN THE LOWER PORTION OF THIS FORM
2 MAIL THE LOWER PORTION TO THE ADDRESS LISTED AT THE BOTTOM OF THE PAGE

FOR YOUR RECORDS

DATE REGISTERED: _____

✂ -

REGISTRATION INFORMATION:

NAME _____
    (FIRST)   (LAST)

ADDRESS _____

CITY _____

STATE _____ ZIP _____

TELEPHONE _____

E-MAIL _____

THIS IS MY FIRST ATTEMPT AT SCHEDULING ❑ YES ❑ NO

THE BOOK WAS ❑ VERY HELPFUL ❑ MODERATELY HELPFUL ❑ NOT USEFUL

❑ YES! I have e-mail and would be interested in receiving a monthly e-mail of encouragement and challenge written by Steve and Teri Maxwell, authors of *Managers of Their Homes*! (Note: if you check the box, please make sure your e-mail address is on the proper line above. You may discontinue receiving the monthly messages at any time for any reason.)

COMMENTS:

COMMENTS _____
_____
_____
_____
_____
_____
_____
_____
_____
_____
_____
_____
_____
_____
_____
_____
_____
_____

MAIL THIS FORM TO:

Managers of Their Homes Registration
2416 South 15th Street
Leavenworth, KS 66048-4110

(PLEASE USE THE BACK OF THIS FORM FOR ADDITIONAL COMMENTS!)